Advance Praise for

BE NOBODY

• • • • • • •

"When we strive to be somebody, we are actually striving to be
somebody else. This somebody else is the root of all our problems.
The key to awakening is being who you already are. But as Lama
Marut dares to tell us in this delightfully written and wise book,
this authentic somebody is nobody at all. Reading this book is easy,
and understanding it is liberating. I invite you to do both."

—Rabbi Rami Shapiro, author of
Perennial Wisdom for the Spiritually Independent

"In his refreshing and compelling new book, *Be Nobody*, Lama
Marut gives us a road map to living life in the realm of an Everyday
Joe in order to accomplish great happiness and connectedness and
to begin to offer the very best we can access. He gives us a truly
clear and vivid understanding of the present-day dilemma of the
drive toward 'I' and the fact that this drive is leading to depression,
isolation, and diseased thinking. And then he outlines a way that
leads to joy by showing us how to practice a new thought pattern
that encourages focus on anything but self. This is an amazingly
powerful piece of work from a truly unique and dynamic nobody."

—Mary McDonnell, actress

"Lama Marut's *Be Nobody* fiercely examines our preoccupation with the 'I,' revealing how living on the 'Me Plan' can never satisfy the hungry ego. The antidote he offers is truly liberating, not only for oneself but for all sentient beings."

—Michael Bernard Beckwith,
author of *Life Visioning*

"Writing with great sensitivity to the stress we all feel, Lama Marut helps us see that we strive to be valued by trying endlessly to be more and more special. We aim to be somebody, but only find tension and loneliness as we never reach the bar. What good is getting star billing if you never feel like a star? Laying out a clear spiritual alternative, he dares us to become nobody: a state of complete authenticity, where we are present to our lives and joyfully connected to all. This is no mystical pipe dream; the ideas in this book point to something every one of us can do. All of us want to be happy. We owe it to ourselves to become nobody. Put this transformative book by your bed, and read it again and again."

—Lindsay Crouse,
Academy Award–nominated actress

"*Be Nobody* is a great spiritual guide for people of all faiths. Lama Marut's description of our bondage to our egos is both entertaining and sobering. After providing an incisive diagnosis of the human condition, he not only offers an understanding of how to leave suffering behind, but also provides practical and achievable steps for doing so. I am recommending this book to all my friends and parishioners."

—**Rev. Dr. Brian Baker**, dean of Trinity Cathedral, Sacramento, CA

BE NOBODY

BE NOBODY

LAMA MARUT

ATRIA PAPERBACK
New York London Toronto Sydney New Delhi

BEYOND WORDS
Hillsboro, Oregon

ATRIA PAPERBACK
A Division of Simon & Schuster, Inc.
1230 Avenue of the Americas
New York, NY 10020

BEYOND WORDS
20827 N.W. Cornell Road, Suite 500
Hillsboro, Oregon 97124-9808
503-531-8700 / 503-531-8773 fax
www.beyondword.com

Managing editor: Lindsay S. Brown
Editors: Henry Covey, Emily Han
Copyeditor: Sheila Ashdown
Proofreader: Linda M. Meyer
Design: Devon Smith
Composition: William H. Brunson Typography Services

First Atria Paperback/Beyond Words trade paperback edition June 2014

For information about special discounts for bulk purchases, please contact Simon & Schuster Special Sales at 1-866-506-1949 or business@simonandschuster.com.

The Simon & Schuster Speakers Bureau can bring authors to your live event. For more information or to book an event, contact the Simon & Schuster Speakers Bureau at 1-866-248-3049 or visit our website at www.simonspeakers.com.

Manufactured in the United States of America

10 9 8 7 6 5 4 3 2 1

Library of Congress Cataloging-in-Publication Data

Smith, Brian K.
     Be nobody / by Lama Marut.—First Atria Paperback/Beyond Words trade paperback edition.
          pages   cm
     Includes bibliographical references.
     1. Self.   2. Spiritual life—Religious aspects.   I. Title.
     BL65.S38M35 2014
     204'.4—dc23

                                                                    2013048132

ISBN 978-1-58270-454-8
ISBN 978-1-4767-3804-8 (ebook)

The corporate mission of Beyond Words Publishing, Inc.: *Inspire to Integrity*

The moment you want to be somebody,
you are no longer free.

—Jiddu Krishnamurti

CONTENTS

CONTENTS

This book is dedicated to Cindy Lee, true companion, partner, muse, and the best friend I could have ever hoped for.

Preface:
Don't Give Me That
Old-Time Religion!

Traditions are group efforts to keep
the unexpected from happening.

Barbara Tober

A gospel song I was taught in church as a kid advises us not to be all newfangled when it comes to our spiritual life. Instead of getting caught up in the modern world and its trappings, we should just stick with "that old-time religion":

> *Give me that old-time religion*
> *Give me that old-time religion*
> *Give me that old-time religion*
> *It's good enough for me*

Well, it wasn't good enough for me as an adolescent, and it's not good enough for me now either. A religion that isn't relevant to the current conditions under which we live is by definition *irrelevant*, isn't it?

My own spiritual life has been shaped by a variety of influences, and I suspect that this is the case for many of us. I was brought up a

Christian (my father and grandfather were ordained Baptist ministers), was baptized and steeped in that tradition through many years of religious instruction (including formal graduate study in a divinity school), and to this day have a deep and abiding connection to the Christian faith.

In addition, for over thirty years of my life I was employed in the academic study of comparative religion with an emphasis on Hinduism, visiting India many times for my research. In the most extended of those sojourns, I made a deep connection to a learned and devout Hindu teacher who helped me not only with my Sanskrit but also with how to live a life guided by spiritual principles. My personal religious sensibilities have been profoundly enhanced by this teacher and by my acquaintance with Hindu Sanskrit classical texts that I have had the opportunity to teach to students in both academic and spiritual contexts over the past three decades. As will be evident to readers of this book, I have integrated the wisdom found in Hindu scriptures like the Upanishads, the Yoga Sutra, the Vijnana Bhairava Tantra, and the Bhagavad Gita into my overall understanding of the spiritual life.

And in 1998, I began an intensive study and serious practice of Tibetan Buddhism, eventually taking ordination as a Buddhist monk and teaching the philosophy and training offered in that tradition. I have had a lifelong attraction to the Buddhist tradition and its emphasis on compassionate and mindful living as well as its mind-expanding teachings on the true nature of reality. And upon deeper study I discovered to my delight that in Buddhist texts there are oft-repeated directives encouraging the student to think for him- or herself; to not blindly accept on faith anything that one hasn't tested in practice; and to remain intellectually and spiritually open to what is useful and beneficial no matter where one encounters it. It seems to me that it is a Buddhist dogma to not be overly attached to any particular dogma. If I have correctly understood what is meant by the term "Buddhist," I am proud to identify myself as one.

So the question of what or who I am when it comes to religion is not entirely clear—even, or especially, to me. Am I a Christian, a Hindu, or a Buddhist? Is it important or even necessary to pick just one? How could I just erase years of experience with any one of these three main influences on my personal spiritual life?

Many readers are probably at least as religiously complicated as I am. So many of us nowadays are religious hybrids, blended composites and combinations of a number of religious and philosophical traditions—spiritual mongrels, if you will. Even those of us who closely relate to one or another of the world's religions have been exposed to and influenced by other religions in ways that are unprecedented in world history.

In the days of yore, most people lived in closed societies and were more excusably parochial, provincial, and unaware of the whole range of religious and cultural alternatives. Our world is a much bigger and more diverse place. We live in a global community of instantaneous communication and the World Wide Web; we reside in nation-states that are increasingly multicultural and religiously heterogeneous. The containers in which we once kept ourselves are now leaking all over the place.

We know way more about each other than ever before, and none of us is left unaffected by the mutual influencing and syncretistic blending that's occurring on all kinds of levels. There are significant ramifications of such intermingling when it comes to a spiritual life that isn't futilely trying to stay cloaked in "that old-time religion."

These days, claiming a religious identification (or refraining from doing so) is an option, not just an unalterable accident of birth. While we may have been born and brought up as one thing or another (or without any religious training at all), we now exercise more choice than ever before about our personal beliefs, identities, and spirituality.

Fully 44 percent of Americans currently say they have a religious affiliation different from the one they were born into.[1] No matter which religion our parents or guardians identified with, we spiritual crossbreeds now easily slip out of one category and into another.

And in addition to all of us spiritual mongrels, there are increasing numbers who disavow any religious affiliation whatsoever. This trend toward religious nonidentification is growing. One recent study has predicted that organized religion is an endangered species—probably "set for extinction"—in no less than nine of the world's developed nations: Australia, Austria, Canada, the Czech Republic, Finland, Ireland, the Netherlands, New Zealand, and Switzerland.[2] Another poll indicates that nearly two-thirds of those living in Great Britain no longer regard themselves as religious.[3]

Even in the United States, a country that is statistically much less disenchanted with institutionalized religion than most of Europe and other parts of the developed world, thirty-three million Americans now claim no formal religious association. According to a recent survey conducted by the Pew Forum on Religion and Public Life, the "nones" ("none of the above," the religiously nonaffiliated) are the fastest growing group in America—increasing by 25 percent in just the past five years—and they're the only demographic that is expanding in every state. And the numbers are largest among younger people. According to the poll, 30 percent of the "older millennials," born between 1981 and 1989, are counted among the "nones"; among the "younger millennials"—those born between 1990 and 1994—34 percent are religiously unaffiliated.[4]

Nonaffiliation with any particular religion does not necessarily mean a disinterest in living a spiritually oriented life. Sixty-eight percent of the "nones" in the United States say they believe in God, while 37 percent describe themselves as "spiritual" but not "religious." One in five said that they pray every day.[5] In Canada, according to a Forum Research poll, two-thirds of the population claim to be "spiritual" while only one-half say they are "religious." But a quarter of those who say they adhere to "no religion" still profess a belief in God.[6]

In addition to the religiously affiliated, the spiritual mongrels who have been shaped by several traditions, and the "nones" who prefer to remain religiously unidentified but spiritually alive, there is another category of those trying to live the good life in today's changed world. We can call them the "undos."[*]

"Undos" are those of us who are trying to break free from the confines of religious labeling without jettisoning the helpful teachings and methods found in those traditions. Being an "undo" is not quite the same as being a "none." Divesting oneself of a particular religious designation presumes that you have had one to begin with—that one has been trained in one or another of the world's spiritual traditions. To be an "undo," a person must first have been a Hindu (or a Buddhist, Christian, Jew, Muslim, Sikh, or whatever). But having steeped him- or herself in this or that tradition, the "undo" chooses to drop the shell of religious identification in order to try just to be a good human being rather than an upstanding, card-carrying member of any one particular faith.

Whatever the label—affiliated, mongrel, none, or "undo"— growing numbers of people are seeking a meaningful existence outside the confines of the traditional religious identities associated with "that old-time religion." In light of such trends, the Dalai Lama recently declared (on his Twitter stream, no less!) that he is "increasingly convinced that the time has come to find a way of thinking about spirituality and ethics beyond religion altogether."[7] In his recent book *Beyond Religion: Ethics for a Whole World*, the Dalai

Lama outlines a program for how to live the good life that presumes "religion alone is no longer adequate" for the task:

> One reason for this is that many people in the world no longer follow any particular religion. Another reason is that, as the peoples of the world become ever more closely interconnected in an age of globalization and in multicultural societies, ethics based on any one religion would only appeal to some of us; it would not be meaningful for all. . . . What we need today is an approach to ethics which makes no recourse to religion and can be equally acceptable to those with faith and those without: a secular ethics.[8]

Living an ethical life—a life of selflessness rather than unbridled egoism, of integration and interconnection rather than alienation and myopic narcissism—is not just for those who choose to follow one or another of the established religions. It is the key to true happiness for any individual, and the foundation for creating a better world. For "when you have 'isms,'" as Lama Surya Das once said to me, "you have schisms."

Too often, however, the identification with one or another of the institutionalized religions has become just another excuse to rehearse the need to *be somebody* in the ego's never-ending appetite for self-aggrandizement. When, in truth, the founders of the different religions of humankind become founders only retroactively. They weren't teaching "isms," they were only conveying their understanding of life, of *what is*.

And if there's one thing we know about the great spiritual exemplars of history, it's that they were humble. We don't admire and canonize people who pose as self-important and superior. There is no "Saint Barry the Arrogant" or "Saint Tricia the Pompous." Our paragons of the past, as well as the present, are those who seem truly willing to *be nobody*, to be the servants, not the masters, of others.

The point is not to be a Buddhist but to learn how to become a Buddha; not just to identify with the label "Christian" but to live a Christlike life; not simply to join a religion as a way to strengthen one's sense of self but to actually live a good life, a life characterized by egoless concern for others.

"I am not a Hindu, nor a Muslim am I!" declared the fifteenth-century Indian mystic Kabir. "I am this body, a play of five elements; a drama of the spirit, dancing with joy and sorrow."[9] Saint Paul similarly asserted in Galatians, "There is neither Jew nor Greek, slave nor free, male nor female, for you are all one in Christ Jesus."[10] The Buddha, it is said, "did not teach any religion at all."† The practice of any spiritual path—whether or not it is designated as such by one or another of the usual trademarks—should lead not toward the elevation of the ego but rather to the self-negation and destruction of vanity that's entailed in *being nobody*.

What? Be nobody? I've spent my whole life trying not to be just a nobody!

Before you throw this book off the nearest bridge, let's be clear about our terms. First off, there is a difference between the egoistic "somebody self" who regards itself as worthless—a nothing, a complete zilch—and *being nobody*. The latter does not refer to our sense of personal, individual identity that can and should be improved—especially if it is insistent on its worthlessness. Somebody who *thinks* they're a nobody is self-consciously defining themselves as such, whereas somebody who has *become* nobody is unselfconsciously absorbed in something much greater.

"Nobody," as we use the term here, refers to our deepest nature, our "true self," which is ever-present and in no need of improvement. It is our highest source of joy and strength, the eternal reservoir of peace and contentment to which we repair in order to silence the persistent demands and complaints of the insatiable ego.

Letting go of our preoccupation with being important and significant will not be easy. Laboring at being somebody for so long digs deep ruts of habit, and some ingrained part of us will surely resist the required "ego-ectomy." But there's a great relief in dropping the ego's restrictive inhibitions and demands for affirmation and magnification. We know this instinctually, and we crave such relief. Our deepest need is to identify not with something small and particular but with that which is greater, universal, and transcendent.

With the rise and vapidity of social networking and "reality" television, the veneration of the ego, celebrity, and instant fame, and the closed-minded arrogance of religious fundamentalism and fanaticism, the questions revolving around the nexus of spirituality and identity have never been more pressing, even as the quest for authenticity and genuine happiness remains perennial.

We all have the capability to be completely self-possessed and truly happy rather than neurotically self-obsessed and continuously discontented. We all have the potential to be the ocean and not just a wave, the clear blue sky and not merely a cloud passing through, the silence and not some particular name or label.

So before you burn this book or toss it in the can—*This is complete rubbish! Nonsense! I really am somebody, and the meaning of life is to be more of a somebody, not less!*—give that "somebody self" a bit of a rest and see if there isn't something to all this. If we lay aside our knee-jerk resistance, we'll soon realize that the happiness and self-satisfaction we all seek cannot be found through perpetually attempting to supersize our insatiable egos.

They say that nobody's perfect.
So why not be nobody?

Notes:

* My use of the term "undo" is inspired by Swami Satchidananda, who writes the following in his book *Beyond Words*: "People often ask me, 'What religion are you? You talk about the Bible, Koran, Torah. Are you a Hindu?' I say, 'I am not a Catholic, a Buddhist, or a Hindu, but an Undo. My religion is Undoism. We have done enough damage. We have to stop doing any more and simply undo the damage we have already done.'" (Yogaville, CA: Integral Yoga Publications, 1977), 85.

† In chapter 13 of the world's oldest printed book, the *Diamond Cutter Sutra*, the Buddha asks one of his disciples, Subhuti, this provocative question: "What do you think, Subhuti? Has the Buddha taught any religion at all?" We imagine that good old Subhuti might very well have suspected this was some sort of joke, maybe a trick question. (*What the hell, man? Why are you asking me this? What else have you been doing for all these years here in northern India except for teaching us religion? You weren't instructing us in better agricultural methods or how to yodel, now were you?*) Instead, Subhuti gives the right answer: "No, Lord. The Buddha has not taught any religion at all." In the passage cited here, the word I've rendered as "religion" is *dharma*—admittedly not exact, but probably as close to our concept of "religion" as one gets in the Sanskrit texts. A very similar assertion is found in Nagarjuna's *Root Verses on the Middle Way*: "Peace is the pacification of all perception and all conceptualization. No religion (*dharma*) whatsoever was ever taught by the Buddha." (24–25).

Introduction:
Living in the iEra

Humility does not mean thinking less of yourself
than of other people,
nor does it mean having a low opinion of your own gifts.
It means freedom from thinking about yourself at all.
—William Temple

We're all desperately trying to be somebody. No one wants to be a loser, a small fry, a big zero, a washout, a nonentity. Nobody, it seems, wants to be just a nobody.

We're all en masse, and in pretty much the same ways, struggling to be unique individuals. This obsessive quest for distinctive identity drives us all equally, for we all believe that happiness and fulfillment will come through distinguishing ourselves, through being "special." Our contemporary culture of consumerism, materialism, narcissism, and the worship of fame encourages the idea that we will be happy only when we become exceptional.

But maybe we've got it wrong—exactly wrong.

Maybe our deepest and most authentic happiness will be found only when we finally lay down this heavy burden of trying to be a somebody, of perpetual ego-enhancement and compulsive self-consciousness. Perhaps it is precisely in a state of egolessness, in an utter lack of self-preoccupation, that we will actually become nobody and thereby access something much larger, much more amorphous and less exclusive.

Maybe true fulfillment in life requires an emptying, not a filling.

FROM THE "ME DECADE" TO THE "IERA"

Selfishness and self-indulgence have always been with us. For thousands of years, the sacred texts of the world's great religious traditions have warned us of the danger of inordinate preoccupation with ourselves, just as they have also provided the most potent tools we have for overcoming it.

But arguably, over the past few decades, at least in the so-called developed nations, we've seen a dramatic rise in—and a cultural validation of—an all-too-human tendency toward self-indulgence. Now more than ever before, we seem to be increasingly preoccupied with "me"—so much so that it seems no exaggeration to describe the whole zeitgeist as an obsession with the self. This excessive self-concern, now pervading virtually every aspect of our lives, is an example—perhaps even the most salient example—of a real "First World problem."

More than thirty-five years ago, journalist Tom Wolfe dubbed the seventies the "Me Decade."[1] The social and political concerns and upheaval of the sixties had given way to a culture of individual self-centeredness. And in 1979—at the tail end of this decade of self-preoccupation—Christopher Lasch published *The Culture of Narcissism*, a scathing critique of "the culture of competitive individualism, which in its decadence has carried the logic of individualism to the extreme of a war of all against all, the pursuit of happiness to the dead end of a narcissistic preoccupation with the self." Lasch's book remains one of the most accurate portraits of the world we still inhabit.[2]

Lasch argues that every age produces a typical personality structure that accords with that particular society's characteristic patterns. "Every society reproduces its culture—its norms, its underlying assumptions, its modes of organizing experience—in the form of personality."[3] And the personality definitive of our time and culture, Lasch identified as "narcissistic":

> Narcissism appears realistically to represent the best way of coping with the tensions and anxieties of modern life, and the prevailing social conditions therefore tend to bring out narcissistic traits that are present, in varying degrees, in everyone.[4]

Such traits revolve around an all-encompassing fixation on the self:

* The insatiable greed, extravagance, sense of entitlement, and demand for immediate gratification that are the hallmarks of rampant consumerism
* The end of the work ethic and its transformation into an ethic of leisure and hedonism*
* The short-sighted exploitation of resources, personal and shared, without regard for future consequences or posterity
* The total dependence on others for validation of one's self-esteem
* The cult of celebrity and our vicarious fascination with the glamorous "lives of the rich and famous"
* The "culture of spectacle" and entertainment that has infected just about everything, from politics to sports to religion

These defining trends, already recognizable in the late 1970s, have been magnified and multiplied in the years since. The culture of narcissism has mutated and grown in all kinds of ways.[5] Among its many other expressions, it now saturates every aspect of popular culture.

We watch television shows and YouTube videos that revolve around the ennoblement of ordinary people into the suddenly famous: *American Idol*, *The Voice*, and the whole array of so-called reality shows on television; or viral YouTube footage that places a previously unknown talent into instant stardom (think Justin Bieber).[6] We bob our heads to the lyrics of popular songs, many of which revolve around how totally awesome the surrogate singer is, not to mention the products he or she wears, drives, and consumes. We read magazines endowed with such revealing titles as *Self* (as if we need to be coaxed into thinking about ourselves even more than we already do!).

The narcissistic worldview informs the way we view politics as a popularity contest or "race." It transforms news into another "show" to entertain us. Journalism today often centers far more on the journalist than it does on the subject matter of the report.

And, of course, many advertisers shamelessly exploit our narcissism when creating our desire for cool new products: iPhones, iPads, iPods—all the "i" gadgets pitched to the "I" and its insatiable hunger for attention.

It is also predominantly the neediness of the self, and not really an interest in others, that is reflected in our present addiction to nonstop communication. There are now 3.14 billion email accounts worldwide, from which we transmit millions of emails each day. We call each other all the time; we send each other nearly 200,000 text messages *every second* from the over six billion mobile phone subscriptions worldwide; and half a billion of us worldwide have Twitter accounts.[7]

All of this emailing, calling, messaging, and tweeting is not so much to "reach out and touch somebody," as a phone company slogan once had it. It is mostly about reaching out so that others will acknowledge and affirm us.

And then there's the exponential increase in usage of the social networks, Facebook being the behemoth of them all, with well over one billion participants, or nearly 20 percent of all the earth's inhabitants.[8] With Facebook, it's all about the thumbs-up "likes," isn't it?

> *Do you like what I just said? Do you like this photo of my cat?*

And beneath it all, the real question:

> *Do you like me?*

Social networks are amazing communication tools that can be (and occasionally are) employed for very beneficial purposes. Unfortunately, most often the postings are of the narcissistic order, some more blatant than others. It's sad, but it's also typical of our self-possessed times, staring at our monitors, that we peg our self-worth on how many Facebook friends give us a thumbs-up, with our Instagram hearts throbbing for more notches on the proverbial post. Like Narcissus, we are enamored of our own reflections in the (now digitized) mirror. When will we realize that we'll never get enough thumbs-up to satisfy the ego, no matter how many photos we share, no matter how many witticisms and observations on life we contribute to the Web's global conversation?

Facebook doesn't have a "don't like" option, and that's definitely not an oversight. It's only the "likes" that any of us is really interested in. But it's disingenuous to think that the "somebody self" will ever feel like "somebody enough" by resorting to methods like this.[9]

• • •

Yes, the "Me Decade" has stretched out into what I call the "iEra," an epoch not just dominated by the glut of information but also by the magnification of the "I" who is situated at the nexus of this flurry of communication. But while we have been encouraged to maintain perpetual self-absorption and are inundated with "iProducts" and "iMedia," the "iEra" can never wholly satisfy the "I" it ceaselessly entices. We remain unhappy and dissatisfied, now more than ever before.

In light of this unprecedented exaltation of the ego and its insatiable need to be acknowledged, fulfilled, pampered, and "liked," it's worth reminding ourselves: There is not a single authentic spiritual tradition that enjoins us to be *more* self-preoccupied, *more* full of ourselves, or *more* narcissistic than we already are. When it comes to achieving happiness in life, obsession with the self has traditionally been identified as the problem, not the solution.

As C. S. Lewis wrote way back in 1952, "Men have differed as regards what people you ought to be unselfish to—whether it was only your own family, or your fellow countrymen, or every one. But they have always agreed that you ought not to put yourself first. Selfishness has never been admired."[10]

Until now, perhaps—and much to our detriment.

PROSPERITY, NARCISSISM, AND PANDEMIC DEPRESSION

Is it just coincidental that, with the narcissism and self-obsession so enshrined in our society, we're simultaneously witnessing an equally breathtaking increase in the rate of mental illness?

Take depression as just one example. Depression is a debilitating disease—I know! I was hospitalized with a clinical case of depression when I was in my early thirties. I was a complete mess, incapacitated by the inner voice that repeatedly told me I was worthless and that there was nothing I could do to change that. And even run-of-the-mill self-esteem problems, as most everyone can attest, are no picnic in the park.

The statistics tracking our current condition are alarming: The US Department of Health estimates that over twenty million Americans currently suffer from depression. Another source claims that 15.7 percent of the population is depressed.[11] Prescriptions for anti-depressants have skyrocketed, rising 400 percent over the past twenty years, with more than one out of ten Americans over the age of twelve now taking these medications.[12] In many places, depression has now become one of the leading causes of absenteeism from work.

It is not an exaggeration to say that depression has become pandemic. The World Health Organization has predicted that by 2020 it will be the second most fatal illness, trumped only by heart disease.[13] Perhaps most shockingly, depression is increasing at astounding rates among young people. In the last thirty years, the United States has seen a 1,000 percent increase in the disease among adolescents.[14]

And it's not accidental that the precipitous rise in depression has occurred concurrently with two other modern trends, which themselves are interrelated: the dramatic increase in material prosperity in the developed nations, and the parallel obsession with the self, which consumerism encourages, aggravates, and excites.

• • •

The rates of depression—as well as associated ailments like anxiety and stress, and mental illnesses such as bipolar disorder—have risen precisely in those places where material prosperity has also substantially increased. In little more than a generation, we have gone from a society in which expensive consumer goods, once only available to the elite, are now readily purchasable by the masses: cars (now regularly equipped with cameras, computers, and talking GPS), televisions (now, like the movies, in realistic high-definition or 3-D), telephones (they've gotten so "smart"!), and computers (formerly only possessions of the government and large research universities, now standard issue, in constantly updated better, faster, and more compact versions). And leisure activities formerly reserved for the mega-rich—including exotic holidays now made possible by nearly universal access to air travel—are currently enjoyed by most of us commoners.

You can't afford to be depressed if you're just trying to stay alive. Depression is itself a kind of luxury good, available only to those for whom the material necessities of life are a given. It may not only be one of the *entitlements* of the economically privileged but also one of the *entailments*.

In the post–World War II era, we were promised happiness through acquiring and consuming, and for sixty-plus years now we've dutifully been acquiring and consuming. We all got cashed up and started amassing all kinds of stuff. We began buying ovens and refrigerators even before they became self-cleaning and self-defrosting. We've obediently purchased pretty much everything they've brought into the marketplace, from transistor radios (remember those?) to iPods; from clunky black-and-white televisions to the sleek fifty-two-inch plasma flat-screens; from pocket calculators to handheld supercomputers.

Maybe by now it has dawned on us that we've gotten everything they promised us and much, much more. And isn't it just as obvious that desires are being created and implanted in order to get us to buy more?

Yeah, so you already have the big black iPod, but now we've come up with this white itsy-bitsy model! Last year's car? It may still run fine, but it's so outdated!

Either we got everything and are still not satisfied, or we had our expectations raised so high that we feel it's our right to have everything and then, when we don't get something, we feel cheated. In either case, since we've placed all our hopes for happiness on self-fulfillment through consumerism, when it doesn't bring us what we expected, well, then there's a big crash.

Once we have staked our claim on owning everything, we are left with not much of anything when it comes to inner peace and contentment.

IT'S NOT SELF-HELP IF IT'S ALL ABOUT YOU

It seems quite likely that many of us feel so bad not only because we are encouraged, at every turn, to remain dissatisfied (so we will buy more) but also because of an insistence that we continually brood about how we're feeling. We're all constantly keeping our fingers on our own pulse:

Am I OK? Are my needs being met? Am I recognized and appreciated enough? Am I somebody enough yet?

This obsession with the self emanates not only from egocentrism but also from deep insecurity. There's a dark side to the culture of narcissism—in fact, maybe there's *only* a dark side. According to the ancient texts, as we shall see in chapter 2, one of the karmic causes of depression is an overweening interest in oneself at the expense of thinking of others. In a time and place where "it's all about me"—

where the promotion of the first-person pronoun demands a "me first" attitude—it's no wonder that we're plunging into depression in unparalleled numbers.

The self, as we'll see below, is both our best friend and our worst enemy. And it's only the "best friend self" that can save us from our own self-destructive tendencies; it's only by improving ourselves that we'll feel better about ourselves.

Trivializing the pain and suffering that is associated with the mental afflictions brought on by the "somebody-self" mentality is neither compassionate nor fair. But neither is offering panaceas that don't get at the real root of the problem or, worse, aggravate it by promoting as the cure that which is in fact the cause. After all, there are effective and ineffective methods of self-improvement and self-help.

It's not self-help if it's all about you. It's not genuinely self-serving to live only in the service of the ego instead of in the service of others. It's only through cultivating real humility and an unselfish spirit, and not through indulging in yet more self-absorption, that a healthy and deeply felt self-esteem can emerge.

It's important that we not mistake humility for self-abasement or confuse depression with self-forgetfulness. An individual with low self-esteem who feels like a "real nobody" is not actually *being nobody* as we'll be using the phrase in this book. Rather he or she is *somebody posing as a nobody*—and that's a very different thing.

There's a kind of perverse pride in the "somebody self" who feels special and exceptional in feeling so bad. And if we imagine that we can help ourselves through more, and not less, self-centeredness—and that includes obsessing about how lousy we feel all the time—our efforts to improve our self-image will inevitably backfire.

As stated in the preface, there is a difference between the egoistic "somebody self" who regards itself as worthless—a nothing, a complete zilch—and *being nobody*. Our limited, personalized, and individual self—which may regard itself with healthy self-esteem or unhealthy self-debasement—is distinct from the unlimited, shared, and universal "nobody self." Identifying with the latter is quite different from identifying with something contemptible. "Nobody" refers to our ever-present "true self," our greatest source of joy and strength, the eternal reservoir of peace and contentment to which we repair in order to silence the persistent demands and complaints of the insatiable ego.

Consider this: We all know that it is in those moments when we completely lose ourselves—engrossed in a good book or movie, engaged in an all-consuming task or hobby, or immersed in our child's or lover's gaze—that we are truly happy. These experiences point to something extremely important: *Our greatest joy comes when we vacate ourselves and give ourselves over to something or someone else.* It is when we manage to "stand outside of ourselves" (*exstasis*) that we experience *ecstasy*.

True and deeply felt self-esteem comes not through the exhausting quest for more and more ego inflation. It comes only when the ego and its endless demands are quieted and quenched, when the lower self is emptied and the fullness and plentitude of the Higher Self arise.

It is only when we stop narrating the play-by-play of our lives and actually start living in an unmediated and direct way that we become really present and fully engaged. It is only when that little voice inside our head finally shuts up that we become wholly assimilated with what's actually happening, and become truly happy.

It is important to have a good, healthy sense of self-worth, and the point of being nobody is certainly not to become servile, a doormat on which others can trample. But thinking that we will feel fulfilled only if we become *more special than others* leads to an increase, not a diminishing, of anxiety and dissatisfaction.

Wanting to be somebody unique—or somehow "more unique than others"—is actually quite common: there's nothing special about wanting to be special. But it is this very drive for radical individuality and superiority that keeps us feeling isolated and alone. In the end, the willingness to let go and *be nobody* is what's really extraordinary, and it is the only means for real connection with others and communion with what is real.

• • •

As the successor to *A Spiritual Renegade's Guide to the Good Life* (Beyond Words, 2012), *Be Nobody* takes the quest for real happiness into new territory. As with its predecessor, this book draws upon the universal truths of the world's venerable religious and philosophical traditions and distills them into an accessible, practical handbook for finding happiness and fulfillment in our modern, everyday lives. The principles may be ancient, but the presentation is up-to-the-minute.

It is a spiritual truism that only by loosening our grip on the lower, egoistic self will we discover our real potential. *Be Nobody* maps out this journey from egoism, selfishness, and the obsession with individual identity to the spaciousness and freedom of abiding in one's true and authentic nature. Such a goal—living one's life fully and happily in the here and now—is not just for the spiritual elite or the mystic but is achievable by anyone ("religious," "spiritual," "secular humanist," or "none of the above") who understands and implements the right ideas and practices.

The desirability of such self-transcendence has been recognized for millennia by the world's spiritual traditions. The mystics have all encountered this blessed state, and acquiring a deep familiarity with it on a permanent basis seems to be what is meant by the Eastern terms *satori*, *samadhi*, *nirvana*, *moksha*, *mukti*, and so on.

In Christianity, too, one finds the concept of *kenosis* (from the Greek word for emptiness)—the "self-emptying" of one's own ego in order to become entirely receptive to the divine will. As the great theologian of the last century, C. S. Lewis, writes in *Mere Christianity*,

> The terrible thing, the almost impossible thing, is to hand over your whole self—all your wishes and precautions—to Christ. But it is far easier than what we are all trying to do instead. For what we are trying to do is to remain what we call "ourselves"...[15]

The goal of a spiritual life is to bring true happiness to the practitioner. To that end, the purpose of spiritual cultivation is not to learn to become *better than* others, but rather to become *better for* them. The religious traditions, as opposed to the modern secular sensibility of narcissism, consumerism, and greed, have always recognized that the inflation of the egoistic self is not the solution; rather, it is the problem.

Be Nobody unfolds in four sections:

In part 1, "Desperately Seeking Somebody," we review one of the main sources of stress and anxiety in our lives: the interminable search for personal identity in what are only temporary and ever-shifting roles. We are forever trying to find some stable self in the guises we assume: "*I am* a father/mother/son/daughter/friend/lawyer/doctor/teacher/surfer/blogger/Christian/Buddhist/secular humanist," and so on. Whether these roles are chosen by us or given to us to play, when we wholly identify with one or another of this cast of characters, we lose touch with our deeper, changeless nature. And when we take excessive pride in one or another of these individual or group identities, we not only separate ourselves from those who are not like us, we also imagine we're superior to them—and by doing so, set ourselves up for a big fall.

Part 2, "Making a Better Somebody Out of Nobody," begins with a "Where's Waldo?" search for the self we are so sure we have—a quest that leaves us clutching at straws and chasing shadows. We are not who we think we are, but by the same token we are nothing other than who we think we are. And this realization is the key to true self-improvement: the development of a better self-conception. Here we learn how karma really works to upgrade the "somebody self" into a happier, more self-satisfied model. And we also learn that it is by changing our sense of who we are that we change the world around us.

Part 3 is entitled "Losing the 'Somebody Self,'" and in this section we explore the joy we feel when we drop our inner narratives and self-conscious facades and truly experience life as it is. We are happiest when we lose ourselves—in empathetic love and compassion for others and in really "getting into the zone" when we are fully engaged in an activity with *mindful unselfconsciousness*. It is in these moments of self-transcendence that we find the real heart and soul of what it means to be alive.

We conclude with a return to the pressing question of self-identity in part 4, "Everybody Is Nobody." Who or what is this "nobody self" that lies at the base of our being and that all of us somebodies universally share? And how can we live in a way that integrates more of our true nature into our daily lives? Posing less as a "special somebody" and being more of just an "Ordinary Joe" infuses our individual existence with more humility, more of a sense of connection to the world and the people in it, and much more true and abiding contentment and joy.

Each chapter ends with an "Action Plan" exercise to help put this all into practice and further incorporate what we've talked about into our daily lives. It's one thing to read about how to live a happier, more fulfilling, more satisfying life. It's another to actually start doing it. It doesn't take much to make a significant change. But it does require at least some modification of our old patterns of thought and action— old habits that, if we're honest with ourselves, have not really worked out the way we'd hoped.

Collected at the end of the book in a section called "Dropping into Your True Nature," you'll find very simple and brief meditations you can do whenever you have a free minute or two in the day. They are samplings from 112 such meditations found in a rather astonishing eighth- or ninth-century AD Indian text called the Vijnana Bhairava Tantra, "Methods for Attaining the Consciousness of the Divine." The really remarkable thing about the techniques prescribed in this text is how mundane they seem. According to this ancient scripture, dropping into our true nature and communing with our Higher Self is way easier than we might think!

• • •

Liberation from the anxiety of always feeling that you have to be "somebody" is found only in true selflessness and freedom from the ego's restrictions, where solace is found in relaxing into life rather than trying endlessly to micromanage it for one's own selfish ends. The following pages offer instruction for attaining such liberation from the lower self without having to seclude oneself in a monastery or retire to a cave in the Himalayas. This book is meant to challenge you to incite the biggest revolution of all: the overthrow of the self-centeredness and self-consciousness that are the root causes of our dissatisfaction, and the embrace of our true potential and source of our real happiness.

Happiness is ours for the taking, but it cannot be achieved without doing the hard work of letting go of old habits of thinking and acting and plunging into the new and untried.

Notes:

* This trait of the "culture of narcissism" has been coupled with, rather than superseded by, a "cult of busyness" that we'll discuss in chapter 7.

I'm nobody! Who are you?
Are you nobody, too?
Then there's a pair of us—don't tell!
They'd banish us—you know!

How dreary to be somebody!
How public like a frog
To tell one's name the livelong day
To an admiring bog!

—Emily Dickinson

PART I

DESPERATELY SEEKING SOMEBODY

1

Sticking Our Faces into Carnival Cutouts

It is possible to move through the drama of our lives without believing so earnestly in the character that we play. That we take ourselves so seriously, that we are so absurdly important in our own minds, is a problem for us.

—Pema Chödrön

It's a funny thing how we adults so rarely stop to ponder the big questions in life: What's the meaning of it all? Is there a God? Why do bad things happen to good people, and vice versa? And just where did I put my car keys?

Young people in their teens and early twenties, as they are entering into adulthood, tend to pose and chew on these queries quite a bit. But apart from professional philosophers and those in the throes of a midlife crisis, we grown-ups get too busy with our families, professions, and ongoing responsibilities to stop and reflect much on these really important puzzles (except maybe for the location of the car keys).

And of all the great mysteries, there's one that surely must count as the most pressing, persistent, and perplexing:

Who am I?

"Know thyself," said Socrates, succinctly summing up the biggest of all life's challenges. Sounds good . . . and sounds a lot easier than it turns out to be.

Although we spend the preponderance of each day, every day, preoccupied with and enamored of the self, we nevertheless are perpetually confused and uncertain as to who we are so fascinated by. "What we are looking for," observed Saint Francis, "is what is looking."[1] But when we try to catch hold of this elusive self, it seems to evaporate into thin air.

Knowing oneself seems to be an itch we can't quite scratch. And just like any unreachable itch, it's really driving us crazy.

While there are lots of conundrums in life, genuine and deep self-knowledge is perhaps the biggest mystery of all—as well as our biggest obsession. We instinctually feel that we must be *somebody*, but we can't quite put our finger on who that somebody might be. We are aware that we are aware, but we're a bit clueless as to exactly who it is that is aware.

Or, as Alan Watts has cleverly put it in limerick form,

> *There once was a man who said, though*
> *It seems that I know that I know,*
> *What I'd like to see,*
> *Is the I that knows me,*
> *When I know that I know that I know.*[2]

Perhaps because locating the true self—here depicted as the self that "knows that I know that I know"—has proven to be so difficult, we gravitate to forged imitations of the real article in the hope that they might suffice. Because self-discovery turns out to be so perplexing, we attempt instead a self-fabrication. We create a character for ourselves and then elevate it—temporarily, at least—to the status of genuine identity.

Like boardwalk tourists poking our faces in the two-dimensional carnival cutouts depicting the muscle man and bathing beauty, we are forever trying to find some authentic self in the multitudinous, temporary, and ever-changing roles we assume in life. We clutch at straws, claiming to actually *be somebody* to avoid the free fall that we fear is entailed in being nobody.

We find ourselves in relationships with others and then glom on to such guises as our true identity ("*I am* a father/mother/son/ daughter/friend/lover/husband/wife," and so on). Or we identify with our jobs and professions ("*I am* a carpenter/lawyer/doctor/ teacher," and so on). Or we earn degrees, certificates, and titles, and present them as our true identity ("*I am* a licensed mechanic/certi- fied yoga instructor/PhD").

We have our hobbies and leisure pursuits ("*I am* a surfer/ camper/blogger/roller blader/stamp collector") and our racial, reli- gious, economic, and national personae ("*I am* white/middle class/ Christian/American"). We create online avatars or Facebook identi- ties in the hope that a virtual persona will suffice for our self-image. We even, in a true act of desperation, identify ourselves with our past traumas ("*I am* a recovering survivor of alcoholism/drug addiction/ childhood abuse/divorce") or current feelings ("*I am* angry/happy/ jealous/depressed").

We try to find ourselves through these *identifications*, a word that derives from the Latin term "to make the same." We make a role "the same" as the player of the role, or constitute the experiencer as "the same" as the experience the experiencer experiences.*

But who is the "I" that we at different times assert is one or another (or the sum total of all) of these guises? Who's the person that takes on all these personae? Who is it that's sticking his or her head into each of these two-dimensional cutouts?

"All the world's a stage," Shakespeare said, "and all the men and women merely players. They have their exits and their entrances, and one man in his time plays many parts."[3] These various roles are sometimes chosen and sometimes given to us to enact, but when we wholly identify with one player or another in this revolving cast of characters—doing our best to keep up with the necessarily frequent costume changes—we set ourselves up for confusion, dissatisfaction, and frustration. We are confused about which one of the multiple roles truly identifies us; we are dissatisfied by the attempt to make any one of these parts truly fulfill us; and we are frustrated by the limitations inherent in each and every one of these personae.

Bewildering when you actually think about it, right? All these different versions of "me"!

A character played by Lily Tomlin in her one-woman show, *The Search for Signs of Intelligent Life in the Universe*, voices what may be a common sentiment: "All my life, I've always wanted to be somebody, but I see now I should have been more specific."[4]

Mistaking the authentic self for what are just multiple, transient, and conditional guises—creating at best a fractured and confused sense of identity—we are diverted from the quest to uncover our deeper, changeless nature. We identify with what has been called the "lower self"—the ego, persona, personality, or "self-image"—instead of communing with the real McCoy, what has been variously termed the higher or authentic self, the soul, the spirit, our true nature or being. "We have a hunger for something like authenticity, but are easily satisfied by an ersatz facsimile," as Miles Orvell puts it.[5]

The self, it seems, is in an ongoing identity crisis. We're spending our lives in a series of caricatures, impersonating somebody or another, substituting one persona after another for a real person.

When it comes to self-realization, we've been settling for a bunch of wooden nickels. And trying to find our authentic self in such a weak currency has not, and will not, pay off.

THE COMMON WISH TO BE SPECIAL

If there's one thing we're pretty sure of when it comes to our perception of ourselves, it's that we are unique. We all, each and every one of us, want to think of ourselves as truly individual, as one of a kind. Most of us, and in much the same kind of way, think of ourselves as special—and wish to be *even more special*, for it is in our hoped-for extraordinariness that we believe we will find true fulfillment and happiness.

In an age when depression has reached epidemic proportions in our so-called developed nations, it is important to foster a healthy sense of self-esteem in order to combat the spiraling trend toward self-abasement. We need to find ways to help reverse this trend—for our own good and for the good of others who are also susceptible to this tendency, for the true causes and cures of this modern ailment are not the ones usually on offer in many therapeutic and "self-help" circles.

Now, lest you think I'm telling you that you're *not* special, please know that I'm not saying that at all. You are indeed special, distinct, and one of a kind, and you should honor that. Fostering a good, healthy sense of self-acceptance is an essential basis for a happy life. And this process must begin early. Parents need to instill in their children a sense of self-worth. You've probably seen the meme—a picture of a small child with the caption "God made me, and God doesn't make junk!" Every child deserves to believe that they are not "junk."

Mr. Rogers—surely one of our modern saints, who positively influenced a whole generation in America—repeatedly told young viewers of his television show that they were his friends and he liked them just the way they are. The whole salubrious message was encapsulated in a song entitled "You Are Special."

> *You're special to me . . .*
> *You are the only one like you.*[6]

This beneficial promotion of self-affirmation, "You are special," is also crucially important to convey to those who are, for one reason or another, cut off from some or all the ways a person's worth is measured in our society—those without much money, whose profession (or lack thereof) is not afforded much status, or who are otherwise unable to draw upon the usual social props for their sense of self-worth.

When I was a boy, my father occasionally took me on weekend trips from our home in St. Paul, Minnesota, to Chicago—the big, big city for all us Midwesterners. We'd go to the Shedd Aquarium, the Museum of Science and Industry, Maxwell Street Market, and other places of urban wonder. And my dad, being a second-generation Baptist minister, would also bring me on Saturday mornings to a large auditorium for the weekly service conducted by a young and exceptionally dynamic pastor, the Reverend Jesse Jackson.

The organization was called Operation Breadbasket, an offshoot of the Southern Christian Leadership Conference, formed to help foster economic development among disadvantaged people like those living on the South Side of Chicago. And the highlight of the weekly service was when the charismatic Reverend Jackson would get behind the pulpit and do his thing, call-and-response style:

> *Rev. Jackson: Say, I am!*
> *Crowd: I am!*

Rev. Jackson: Somebody!
Crowd: Somebody!
Rev. Jackson: I may be poor.
Crowd: I may be poor.
Rev. Jackson: But I am . . .
Crowd: But I am . . . .
Rev. Jackson: Somebody!
Crowd: Somebody!
Rev. Jackson: I may be young.
Crowd: I may be young.
Rev. Jackson: But I am . . .
Crowd: But I am . . .
Rev. Jackson: Somebody!
Crowd: Somebody!
Rev. Jackson: I may be on welfare.
Crowd: I may be on welfare.
Rev. Jackson: But I am . . .
Crowd: But I am . . .
Rev. Jackson: Somebody!
Crowd: Somebody!

And on the chant went, reaching greater and greater pitches of enthusiasm:

I may be small, but I am somebody!
I may make a mistake, but I am somebody!
My clothes are different, my face is different, my hair is
*   different, but I am somebody!*
I am black, brown, white. I speak a different language.
But I must be respected, protected, never rejected!
I am God's child!

I am somebody!
I AM SOMEBODY![7]

And, of course, we all are indeed somebody, and we should all be a self-respecting somebody. Each of us has our own personality, shaped by our distinctive genetic makeup, personal history, life choices, and so on—what the Eastern traditions would regard as the fruition of our individual karma. Accepting the cards you've been dealt is the condition of possibility for playing them well in the game of life.

We truly are, each and every one of us, special and unique like a snowflake, and we all should accept who we are with dignity and a certain sense of self-assurance and pride.

YOU: YOUR BEST FRIEND AND WORST ENEMY

The kind of healthy self-respect Mr. Rogers and Jesse Jackson encourage is unquestionably a positive thing. But feeling comfortable with one's individuality is really just the starting point for more advanced forms of self-discovery. Like possessing enough food, proper shelter, and leisure time, having a strong positive sense about one's distinctive individuality is a prerequisite for deeper spiritual pursuits.

The spiritual quest begins, one might say, where many of the traditional therapeutic processes leave off. Mental health therapy in its myriad forms—from the rigors of psychoanalysis to the most user-friendly self-help book—has, at bottom, the same function. The fundamental purpose of the therapeutic approach is *to make us feel better about ourselves*—to make us feel that we're all somebody special.

And that's great . . . as far as it goes.

But the spiritual approach, as opposed to the merely therapeutic, should regard a strong, positive sense of one's distinctive individual identity as the starting point, not the end result. "One should raise up the self by oneself, and not degrade oneself," as it says in the great Hindu classic, the Bhagavad Gita. But the text goes on to note, "For the self is its own best friend and its own worst enemy."[8]

Building a good, healthy ego is a necessary step in the task of true self-realization, but it is not sufficient in and of itself. The affirmation of the lower, personalized, and individual self is not, according to the religious traditions, true self-knowledge. In the deeper search for one's irreducible core, identifying with and clinging to the ego is in fact the obstacle. The best friend turns into the worst enemy.

We must, as the saying goes, lose the self to find it. We must get beyond the ego—the "special somebody" self—if we are to discover our deeper, more genuine, and more universal identity. In such a quest, feeling special and unique repositions itself as the problem, not the solution.

The journey to true self-knowledge is like climbing a ladder. One must start on the lower, foundational rungs. But to move higher, we must also be willing to ascend, leaving the lower rungs behind. Once we've established a proper sense of self-worth, individuality, and specialness, we are ready to take the next steps.

We must, in a word, have a good, healthy ego in order to proceed with the ego-ectomy necessary to discover our real nature.

"When there is no 'I,' there is liberation," as it says in another ancient Sanskrit text of the Hindu tradition. "And when there is an 'I,' there is bondage."[9] And this truth is repeated in countless ways in the scriptures and classics of other world religions:

✦ "Since all the disasters, sufferings, and fears in the world come about from the grasping to a self, then how is this grasping beneficial to me? Without abandoning the self, suffering cannot be abandoned, just as without avoiding fire one cannot avoid being burned" (Shantideva, Buddhism).[10]

✿ "Above all the grace and the gifts that Christ gives to his beloved is that of overcoming self" (Francis of Assisi, Christianity).[11]

✿ "He who attends to his greater self becomes a great man, and he who attends to his smaller self becomes a small man" (Mencius, Confucianism).[12]

✿ "There is an irreducible opposition between the deep transcendent self that awakens only in contemplation and the superficial, external self that we commonly identify with the first person singular. We must remember that this superficial 'I' is not our real self. It is our 'individuality' and our 'empirical self,' but it is not truly the hidden and mysterious person in whom we subsist before the eyes of God. The 'I' that works in the world, thinks about itself, observes its own reactions, and talks about itself is not the true 'I' that has been united to God in Christ" (Thomas Merton, Christianity).[13]

✿ "Owing to ignorance of the rope, the rope appears to be a snake; owing to ignorance of the Self, the transient state arises of the individualized, limited, phenomenal aspect of the Self" (Shankara, Hinduism).[14]

While our unique individuality serves as a starting point, it cannot function as the end-all of the quest to "know thyself." To move beyond our fascination and attachment to our particularity, we must gain an appreciation for what we share with all the other somebodies out there.

NEVER SOMEBODY ENOUGH

The need to feel special is not in and of itself special. We all want to portray ourselves—to ourselves and to others—as being in one way or another *extraordinary*. If we don't feel this foundational sense of specialness at all, it is indeed important to find ways to increase our sense of self-worth—and there are plenty of resources available in the therapeutic establishment to facilitate that. And throughout this book, we'll be discussing some surefire methods for increasing self-esteem.

But what we also may start to suspect is that, at a certain point— after shoring up the foundation of a necessary and beneficial sense of self-worth—the interminable pursuit of *being somebody* can become a heavy load to carry.

If, for example, we believe that our "specialness" derives from what we have achieved rather than from *who we really are*, we will be forever striving to be important enough, famous enough, rich enough, loved enough, accomplished enough.

The eminent psychiatrist Thomas Szasz noted, "People often say that this or that person has not yet found himself. But the self," Szasz argued, "is not something one finds, it is something one creates."[15] And it is true that most of us peg some important part of our identity to our accomplishments in whatever arenas of life we deem important. But if we overvalue the idea that self-worth is tied to a *created specialness*, most of us will never feel we have produced a special enough self.

If we fully buy into an accomplishment-based understanding of selfhood, we'll be perpetually trying, and endlessly failing, to be *somebody enough*.

When we wholly identify with one or another of the roles we play in the ongoing drama that is life, we may begin to suspect that no matter how successful we are—no matter how many promotions we win, how much money we accumulate, how much praise we receive— it will never be sufficient. If this is the gauge of self-approval, the bar will always be moving higher; there will always be more hoops to jump through and more rivers to cross, with no end in sight.

We often glorify and idealize those who seem to *really be somebody*: the rock star, the Olympic athlete, the A-list actor, the mega-rich or supremely famous. But even off-the-charts superstars like Madonna can never quite measure up when it comes to this kind of achievement-based understanding of the self. As she candidly confessed in an interview, no matter how successful she became, she never quite felt that she was "somebody enough":

> My drive in life comes from a fear of being mediocre. That is always pushing me. I push past one spell of it and discover myself as a special human being but then I feel I am still mediocre and unin-teresting unless I do something else. Because even though I have become Somebody, I still have to prove that Somebody. My strug-gle has never ended and I guess it never will.[16]

Madonna fears "being mediocre"—that is, not being "Madonna enough." Similarly, the great hockey player Wayne Gretzky has complained that "The hardest part of being Wayne Gretzky is that I get compared to Wayne Gretzky." Cary Grant also reportedly once declared, "Everyone wants to be Cary Grant. Even I wish to be Cary Grant."[†]

These testimonials should give us a clue about pinning our hopes for identity and self-satisfaction on achievement alone. If Madonna can't be Madonna enough; if Wayne Gretzky can never quite live up to being Wayne Gretzky; and if even (the real) Cary Grant wanted someday to be (the ideal) Cary Grant, well, what hope is there for us less-than-superstars?

The ideal of a "special self" one wishes to construct through accomplishment tends always to outstrip the reality, leaving one feeling incomplete, inadequate, and continually running to try to catch up. The fear of *not* being so special after all—*the anxiety of being ordinary*—haunts and follows even those among us who seem to have reached the very apex of our chosen endeavors, and it is endemic among those of us who, by and large, are actually pretty ordinary when it comes to our abilities and our achievements.[17]

While Socrates encouraged us to "know thyself," others have pointed out that self-knowledge is sometimes bad news! If the worth of the self we're trying to know and identify with is judged by performance-based criteria, we will usually find ourselves perpetually coming up short. We will encounter a self that is forever not special enough, a somebody who is not big enough.

Although even the most ordinary of us apparently would rather not think of ourselves as such, the burden of being special is perhaps a much heavier weight to bear.

Too Special for Our Own Good

And then there's the other side of the coin. If we're not suffering from neurotic apprehension that we're not *special enough*, we're puffed up with the narcissistic arrogance of thinking we're somehow more special than others. The desperate need to be special easily morphs into a competitive quest to feel superior in one way or another. Fearing that we'll be seen as nobody and urgently trying to be somebody, we get too big for our britches. We become too special for our own good.

As Pema Chödrön notes in the epigraph to this chapter, it's a mistake to overestimate the role and ignore who is really playing that role. It is a given that we are all unique individuals, but attaching to and elevating our uniqueness is not the recipe either for true happiness or for more comprehensive self-knowledge.

It's somewhat ironic that, driven by the belief that we'll be happy only by being distinctive, separate, and unique, we end up collectively pursuing this Holy Grail of redemptive individuality in very similar ways. The reader might recall a scene in that Monty Python movie, *Life of Brian*, in which a mob pursues Brian, the supposed messiah, and surrounds his home. The reluctant savior appears at the window and implores the assembled masses to stop being sheep and to think for themselves. Brian shouts to them, "You're all individuals," and the crowd, en masse, answers, "We're all individuals."

But then one lonely little voice at the back says, "I'm not."

And he's the one who got it right. It is truly an act of independence and freedom to recognize that we're all alike and that nobody is really more somebody than anyone else. The one who realizes he's no more special than others is the truly special one.

WE'RE ALL IN THE SAME BOAT: THE GREAT EQUALITY

The emphasis on being special—embracing our uniqueness and individuality as if true self-fulfillment were to be found in *being somebody* or, even worse, being *more of a somebody* than others—can blind us to the essential ways that we are fundamentally alike, and can serve to divide rather than bring us together in our shared humanity.

Clinging to the particular and the individual precludes opening ourselves up to the general and universal. It is only by laying down the burden of individuality that we can begin to embrace our larger Self, the true core of our being that we share with all others. It is getting in touch with this universal part of ourselves that brings us joy, in large part because it relieves us of the strain of having to be somebody in particular by plugging us into what we have in common with others.

As opposed to the modern, secular emphasis on individuality (which can so easily turn into narcissistic self-absorption and prideful superciliousness), the world's spiritual traditions emphasize our commonalities and kinship. Rather than focusing on what sets us apart, the spiritual traditions highlight what binds us together.

We can begin to receive intimations of a deeper sense of who we are—an identity that transcends the anxiety of being somebody—by recognizing that underlying our superficial differences is a great equality that links us with all others.

The Dalai Lama likes to emphasize that although we are indeed unique individuals, there are two basic desires we all share as living beings:

> In our quest for happiness and the avoidance of suffering, we are all fundamentally the same, and therefore equal. . . . Despite all our individual characteristics, no matter what education we may have or what social rank we may have inherited, and irrespective of what we may have achieved in our lives, we all seek to find happiness and to avoid suffering during this short life of ours.[18]

Put simply, we all want to be happy and avoid pain, and we are all exactly alike in that we have these two fundamental wishes. And this, by the way, we share with all sentient life. It matters not if you're a squirrel or a CEO, an insect or the president of the United States. Every living being just wants to attain happiness and evade suffering.

But we are also equal in that we are not very savvy about how to obtain these goals. While we all want to avoid it, suffering is endemic to life. And while we all desire true happiness, few of us are very good at actually achieving it.

• • •

All religions are premised on the recognition that, in the absence of spiritual training, life will just repeatedly kick our helpless asses.

Acknowledging this fact of life is the sine qua non for getting serious about finding an alternative to perpetual victimhood.

If life just flowed merrily on for us, there would be no need for self-cultivation. We could just relax and enjoy ourselves, like Adam and Eve in the Garden of Eden. But, as the myth in Genesis tells us, we are not in a paradisiacal garden anymore (in case you hadn't noticed). We're in a deep, dark, dangerous forest and need guidance to find our way out.

This acknowledgment of our collective predicament was emphatically encapsulated in the first words that came out of the mouth of the Buddha after he achieved his Awakening: "*Y'all are suffering*," he declared (loosely translated). From the point of view of a truly self-realized being, all of us, equally, are in deep doo-doo.

This is the first of the four so-called Worthy Truths in Buddhism, and the starting point for any serious attempt at a spiritual life designed to bring an alternative.[‡] "Houston, we have a problem," as the astronauts said when they realized their spaceship wasn't working anymore. Our spaceships aren't working. We all have a problem. Our lives are shot through with difficulties, stress, dissatisfaction, and the like.

Suffering, in a word.

Oh, Buddhists, they're so negative! What do you mean "Life is suffering"? Cheer up, already! Maybe you guys should get out more—enjoy a movie or a nice dinner, or go dancing or something!

Of course, the Buddha didn't mean that life for everyone is an unremitting series of tragedies—although, for some of our fellow human beings living on this very same planet, daily life is indeed a relentless set of challenges. Billions go hungry every day; billions do not have proper shelter, clothing, water, and medical care, while nearly equal numbers do not have basic political freedoms, educational opportunities, or even the ability to read. Billions also suffer from deep-seated psychological and emotional problems that make their daily life a living hell.

And all of us, no matter how privileged and sheltered we are from the more extreme forms of misery, are subject to misfortune. The things and people in our lives, even our own health and welfare—all of it is precarious.

In fact, we can accurately consider ourselves to be perpetually in one of two possible situations: *we are either in the midst of a disaster or between them.* These are, for all of us equally, the only two options in this life.

When we're in the middle of a disaster, the truth that life involves suffering is not debatable. We've all been there, and many of us are there right now. It's when tragedy hits that the scales of denial fall from our eyes.

When it comes to traumatic experiences, everyone has their own tales to tell. One of mine occurred early on in my adult life. My first marriage, to my high school girlfriend, took place at the tender age of eighteen. Within a year it was over. These were the days before "no fault" divorces, so, in addition to the pain of having my wife leave me, I had to endure the further torment of having my friends testify in court about what a bad husband I had been. (This was not untrue, but nevertheless it hurt to hear it publicly declared by my own friends.) By age nineteen, the hopes and expectations I had had about what an adult life would look like had been cruelly crushed. I was completely devastated and spun into a deep depression.

When we're in the middle of a disaster, the fact of suffering is viscerally felt and intellectually obvious. It is, at such times, painfully indisputable, and we don't need to be convinced then that life is suffering. But there are two things we do need to try to remember in those difficult but potentially eye-opening circumstances.

The first is that suffering isn't just random bad luck; rather, encountering misfortune is inevitably part of living life. We all lose loved ones. We all get sick, get old, and die. Or, as the Buddha summed it up, we don't get what we want, we do get what we don't want, and we don't get to keep forever the things and people we love.

It's not some strange anomaly when tragedy befalls us. Suffering is in the very nature of our lives. We are slapped in the face with this truth when we're in the middle of the disaster, but when we're in between disasters it's important to remember that the next one (*when* it comes, not *if*) will greet us in the same manner as the last one.

The second thing to remember—and this one is even harder than the first—is that, when the suffering nature of life whacks you upside the head, *it's not just you.* As we have seen, we all want to feel special, and when we experience catastrophes we embrace those negative experiences also as something that distinguishes, or even defines, us. *This is so unfair*—we often think at such times—*I have been singled out for this misfortune.*

When it comes our time to undergo difficulties, we all feel like poor Job in the Bible, who, shaking his fist toward the sky, demands to plead his case to the one who has unjustly rained such torment down on him.

Why me? Why me?

There's a story told in the Buddhist scriptures about a woman who has just lost her only child. She goes to the Buddha and pleads with him to restore her son to her. Surprisingly, the Buddha agrees— but under one condition. "Go to every home in the village," he instructs the grieving mother, "and bring me a mustard seed from the household that hasn't had a tragedy like yours." The poor woman starts knocking on doors and, well, you can guess the outcome. Let's just say she didn't bring back any mustard seeds to the Buddha.

Suffering doesn't make you special any more than the need to feel special makes you special. We have all been there, and we'll all be there again. Anyone who has been alive more than a few years has already taken huge hits, as any therapist, counselor, or clergyman who regularly listens to people's stories can attest. Everyone has tales of woe; we are all the walking wounded. When I hear about what people—ordinary people, everyday people, just like you and me— have gone through, I'm often amazed that any of us can even get out of bed and carry on.

No one is getting through life unscathed. We're all in the same boat, and when it comes to our susceptibility to suffering, that boat is the *Titanic*. And while the experience of disaster is ubiquitous, there are no objective criteria for measuring whose suffering is worse. There's no scale of suffering, such that yours is a 6.8 while someone else only scores 4.2.

While we might feel our own trials to be greater than others, it is necessary to realize that *suffering is subjective*. What one person finds unbearable another might skate through, and what someone might find trivial is another's unmitigated nightmare.

There's a story about a young girl who had just begun college. She had been admitted to the same school both her mother and grand-mother had attended. Both mom and grandma had also been active members in one of the school's most popular sororities; indeed, membership in that sorority had sort of defined their whole lives. Even as alumnae, this girl's maternal kinfolk continued to financially support the sorority, regularly attend the annual reunions, and so on. Most importantly for the story, they instilled in the young lady how crucially important it would be for her to also be inducted into the society of Alpha Delta Awesome, or whatever it was.

Guess what happened? She didn't get in. Having heard about how great Alpha Delta Awesome was her whole life, and knowing full well the expectations her mother and grandmother had of her carrying on this family tradition, she was utterly devastated by the rejection.

So a bit of a thought experiment here: Was the suffering that this young lady experienced as a result of being rebuffed by some damned sorority comparable to what many of us would regard as a much more serious disappointment? Is it possible, or could it even be likely, that *from her point of view* the trauma was felt as deeply as, say, another might feel having a career tank, or having something precious get stolen or lost, or even having a major health problem or being in the midst of a divorce?

Realizing that suffering is both subjectively experienced and universally encountered—no one is having an easy life here!—is a crucial step toward breaking out of the loneliness of individuality and recognizing what we share with all others. Personal suffering need not simply further and solidify our sense of distinctiveness, but can open us up to a compassionate empathy that enlarges our sense of self.

· · ·

No one wants to suffer. All of us try to avoid it the best we can. And conversely, we all want to be happy and enjoy life, and this is the second way in which we are all exactly alike.

The desire for happiness (and for avoidance of pain) is fundamental to our nature as living beings. It drives us all day long, and it lies behind all of our life choices. As psychologist Mihaly Csikszentmihalyi puts it, "While happiness itself is sought for its own sake, every other goal—health, beauty, money, or power—is valued only because we expect that it will make us happy."[19]

Although everything we do throughout the day—throughout our whole lives—is done with the hope that it will bring us more happiness (and less pain), many of us may perceive happiness as something that occurs accidentally, once in a while, through causes unknown and unknowable.

The very etymology of the word *happiness* contains within it the idea that it is, so to speak, *hap*hazard. We feel *hap*less when it comes to obtaining real happiness; we have a sense that, when it seems that things are going right, it's all just a matter of *hap*penstance. It might appear that happiness, like its opposite (a four-letter word for excrement, as one sees on bumper stickers), just *hap*pens.

Happiness doesn't just happen; it is caused, like everything else. And there is a universally affirmed method taught in the spiritual traditions to achieve true and lasting happiness. That method involves less, not more, self-centeredness; it entails relinquishing the individual's insatiable demands and losing oneself in something larger.

While we sometimes think of happiness as a randomly occurring phenomenon, we even more often associate true happiness with the pleasuring of the ego—"making *myself* happy" through trying to find joy in what we label "self-fulfillment," "self-satisfaction," or any other of the myriad concepts that have "self" as the first component ("self-respect," "self-indulgence," "self-importance," and so on). Although, as we've seen, it is essential to have self-esteem to be strong enough to move things to the next level, we must transcend egoism if we are to find both our true identity—what unites us with all others—and the real and authentic source of joy.

Compulsively trying to be somebody, we keep ourselves imprisoned by our own egotistical addiction to being more, better, and higher.

True happiness doesn't involve fulfilling the ego's needs for high status, the love and admiration of others, a beautiful body, or a trophy wife or arm-candy husband. True happiness, in other words, will not be an attribute of the lower, smaller, individual self. It is only when we access our higher, universal, true identity that we experience the profound and unshakeable euphoria we all seek.

The purpose of life is to find an alternative to ubiquitous suffering; the whole point is to find the lifeboat and get off the freakin' *Titanic*. And that's another way in which we are all the same: we all have the capability of discovering the lifeboat that's been there all along.

We all, equally, have this capacity for deep-rooted happiness, because we all, equally, have a spirit, universal in nature, at our core. This is the great and fundamental equality, assumed in all the world's spiritual traditions. In Christianity, we are taught that we all—sinner and saint alike—are capable of redemption and salvation. And similarly in Judaism, we are all regarded as equal before God. In Islam, the Qur'an declares that "All peoples are a single nation,"[20] while in the Hindu tradition it is presupposed that we all have the potential to break through the illusion of individuality and realize the true nature we share in common.

And in Buddhism, each and every living being is said to have what is called "Buddha nature," the inborn potential to realize one's Higher Self.

Everyone has this Buddha nature, and nobody has more of it than anyone else. When it comes to our true identity—our deepest and happiest sense of self—we are not hierarchically ordered individuals with different types and degrees of specialness. Rather, we're perfectly, 100 percent equal and alike.

According to the Buddhist texts, recognizing this capability to achieve our highest destiny—a potential we all have, each and every one of us—is the true remedy for the depression and low self-esteem that many of us suffer as a result of our identification with a lower, individual self:[21]

> Never be discouraged and think,
> "How could someone like me become Awakened?"
> The Buddha, who speaks the truth,
> Has said these true words about this:
>
> "Even those who were flies, gnats, bees, and worms
> Obtained the highest enlightenment, so hard to obtain,
> Because of their perseverance."[22]

Because we are not really just the "somebody"—the particular, discrete, and separate individual—that we believe ourselves to be, we can reach the highest happiness. But it will require effort and perseverance to discover who we really are. It will especially demand a willingness to undergo the kind of de- and re-identification entailed in the ego-ectomy we spoke of earlier.

We must die to be born again. We must be prepared to let go of the caterpillar to which we are so attached if we are to soar free as the butterfly we are truly meant to be.

TWO BIRDS SITTING ON THE SAME TREE

Our capital "S" Self, our Buddha nature, our soul—whatever name one wishes to give it—is definitely not the individual ego. There is a part of each and every one of us that has never been born and will never die—an eternal, uncreated, and universal Self that is not "somebody" and has never been "anybody," but is both "nobody" and "everybody." And it is this part of us, labeled the "wise one" in the following verse from the ancient Indian Upanishads, that is truly extraordinary.

The wise one has never been born and never dies. It has not come from anywhere, nor has it become anyone. It is unborn, unchanging, eternal, and primordial. It is not killed when the body is killed.[23]

Our real specialness lies not in our uniqueness but in what we share with all others. It is who we really are, and it is who we really want to be. It is what makes it possible to overcome our sense of separation and aloneness and feel a part of a larger whole.

We long for it and take our greatest joy when we reconnect with it. According to Hindu scriptures, the little voice inside—the mouthpiece of the ego—quiets down, and the atomistic, unhappy self is enveloped into something much greater: "Conceits such as 'This is who I am' or 'I am not this' are destroyed for the practitioner who has become silent, knowing that everything is encompassed within the true Self."[24]

Real self-knowledge requires us to drop the identification with the changing cast of personae that prevent us from knowing the real nature of the face that's peeking from behind those assorted carnival cutouts.

There is, in each one of us, a tension between our identification with a lower, individual self (we all want to be "somebody") and the yearning for union with the true Self. We are at war with ourselves; we are a house divided; we are existentially schizophrenic.

And what is at stake in this internal struggle is our true happiness, our sense of fulfillment, and the end to the feelings of desperation, inadequacy, and victimization. One of the older Upanishads provides this metaphor:

Two birds, inseparable friends, perch on the same tree. One of them eats a tasty fig while the other looks on without eating. Sitting on that same tree, the lower, deluded self is overwhelmed by the belief that he is a powerless victim and he despairs. When he sees the other, the beloved Master, and realizes that all greatness is his, then his despair vanishes.[25]

It is our own embrace of the personal, smaller, individual self—the bird that always needs another tasty fig to feel like a better somebody—that perpetuates our suffering and discontentment. And it is by knowing our true and universal self—the bird that is always satisfied and never feels the compulsion to be more or better—that we can end it.

And we will know this true self not *as ourselves* but in the blissful relief of *not having to be ourselves*, of finding the peaceful and ever-satisfied "beloved Master" within.

• • •

In the following pages of this book, we will survey the different battlegrounds where war is being waged between the "two birds perched on the same tree"—the ego or "somebody self" and the authentic "nobody self." It is an inner conflict between our anxious striving to *be somebody* and our deepest feelings of contentment or "at-one-ment" that occur when we get back in touch with the stillness and the feeling of interconnectivity made possible only by *being nobody*.

Action Plan: Generating Compassion for the Suffering of Others

Take five or ten minutes each day to stop and reflect on the problems others are currently facing. Begin by thinking about your relatives and friends and the difficulties they are wrestling with in their lives. Generate what should be a natural sense of compassion for their suffering and make a plan for something you could do to help relieve at least some of their pain.

Then have a look at the news of the day and reflect on what it must be like to be one of the millions of people who are currently in the midst of a major disaster. Try to overcome the tendency to let such news reports pass through the consciousness without touching the heart. These are people just like you, with the same desire to be happy and avoid pain, and they are currently experiencing a terrible catastrophe.

Resolve not to use current events as just another form of entertainment; rather, use them as a daily opportunity to generate empathy and a sense of connection to the suffering of others.

Notes:

* Cf. Eckhart Tolle's observation in *A New Earth: Awakening to Your Life's Purpose*: "One of the most basic mind structures through which the ego comes into existence is identification. The word 'identification' is derived from the Latin word *idem*, meaning 'same,' and *facere*, which means 'to make.' So when I identify with something, I 'make it the same.' The same as what? The same as I. I endow it with a sense of self, and so it becomes part of my 'identity'" (New York: Penguin Books, 2005), 35.

† For these and other such examples—including the groupie who said of every rock star she'd slept with, "He's great, but he's no Mick Jagger," until she finally did bed Mick Jagger. She then reported, "Great, but no Mick Jagger"—see Wendy Doniger's *The Woman Who Pretended to Be Who She Was: Myths of Self-Imitation* (New York: Oxford University Press, 2004).

‡ The other three "truths" are (1) that suffering is caused (and not by anyone or anything other than ourselves), (2) that there is an alternative to suffering, and (3) that there is a method for attaining the true happiness that is our birthright.

2
What Goes Up Must Come Down

Proud people breed sad sorrows for themselves.
—Emily Brontë

PRIDE AND PREJUDICE

A healthy sense of self is the necessary foundation for further spiritual progress. We're all unique individuals—everyone truly is a special snowflake—and we should all honor our own singular gifts and achievements.

But when self-affirmation tips over into self-importance and vanity—when that little "somebody self" birdie starts chirping a bit too loudly and arrogantly—it becomes another part of the problem rather than a step on the way to the solution.

Pride is a major weapon in the ego's arsenal; it is closely associated with the compulsion to *be somebody*. Taking overweening pride in some particular and temporary personal characteristic or adventitious circumstance in order to feel superior to other people—to be *more special than others*—is a fool's game. It seizes on something we think makes us truly special (one personal trait among many—beauty, youth, strength, intelligence, talent, or how much money one has, what one owns, or one's professional status or religious affiliation) and absurdly elevates it above all other possibilities in order to make ourselves *supremely* special.

And if we set too much store by such fleeting and ephemeral phenomena, when they change or we lose them, we become devastated. Instead of taking pride in being somebody oh-so-exceptional, we crash hard, as this inflated sense of the special self is punctured and contracts.

Pride is universally identified in the world's religions as one of the biggest dangers for a spiritual practitioner; it often makes it onto the short list of vices. And what's most relevant at this juncture is that pride is the lifeblood of the "somebody self's" interest in feeling superior to others. As C. S. Lewis notes,

> Now what you want to get clear is that Pride is *essentially* competitive—is competitive by its very nature—while the other vices are competitive only, so to speak, by accident. Pride gets no pleasure out of having something, only out of having more of it than the next man.[1]

Excessively impressed with and attached to our sense of uniqueness and individuality, we distinguish ourselves from those over whom we tower. And with pride inevitably comes its twin sister: envy. We become jealous of and estranged from those who are *even more special* than we are (richer, smarter, better looking, more gifted or accomplished).

Feeling *too special* alienates us from others—from both those we suspect are above us and those we place below us. Our yearning to be somebody not only implicates us in the fear that we'll never be *somebody enough*; it also requires others to be *less of a somebody* than we are. With pride comes not only envy but prejudice.

It is not by further isolating and separating ourselves from others that we will find the genuine happiness we seek. True happiness will not come from feeling better than others any more than it will spring forth from envy and resentment toward those we feel are our betters. True happiness comes only through realizing what connects us to one another—the unity that lies beneath superficial differences.

Taking disproportionate pride in our individuality, we become enmeshed in judgment over those we deem inferior, thus further detaching ourselves from our fellow human beings. And most ironically, this attempt to feel better by ranking ourselves above others backfires and produces the exact opposite effect. For as we shall see in this chapter, it is pride that the spiritual traditions have identified as the main cause of low self-esteem.

What goes up must come down. When we take pride in whatever we latch onto in order to pose as someone superior to others, the result is that we become somebody who thinks of themselves as just a worthless nobody.

TRYING TO BE SOMEBODY BY ASSOCIATION

One of the many ways we attempt to define and distinguish ourselves—while also paradoxically trying to overcome the isolation and disconnection we abhor—is through identification with a group. We fabricate at least a part of our personal sense of identity by subsuming ourselves within a collectivity.

We describe and designate ourselves, at least to some degree, by hitching our personal wagons to some communal star:

"*I am* an American, Australian, Japanese, German"—identifying ourselves with our native or adopted nation.

"*I am* white, black, Asian, indigenous"—identifying ourselves with one of the (remarkably few, given human diversity and millennia of interbreeding) racial groupings.

"*I am* poor, working class, middle class, upper middle class, or (more rarely and immodestly) stinking rich"—identifying ourselves with our economic status.

"*I am* a Democrat, Republican, progressive, democratic socialist, Green Party member"—identifying ourselves with our chosen political party.

We all have a strong desire to belong to something greater, to meld our unique little individual snowflake into a larger snowball.

When it comes to the dynamics behind group affiliation, we once more butt up against the internal civil war between the compulsive drive to *be somebody* and the craving for the release and freedom that comes from *being nobody*.

On the one hand, it seems that our desire to join a community is inspired by an innate drive to transcend the loneliness and isolation of singularity. And as such, it is certainly a positive thing. The impulse to connect with others, to identify with a group, seems to be a variant of the urge we all have to drop the obsession with individualism and lose ourselves in something greater. Our interest in associating our discrete, isolated lower selves with a nation, a race, an economic class, or a political party is, from this point of view, motivated by a kind of secular expression of our spiritual longing to drop being ourselves and *be nobody* through connection to a larger whole.

As we know from personal experience, it is exactly in those times when we discard the burden of self-consciousness and the striving to be somebody that we feel a sense of relief, spaciousness, and fulfillment. And so it is that we can lose ourselves in a group, gaining a sense of belonging and camaraderie, which is all well and good . . . up to a point.

If we exaggerate the defining importance of any one of these group identities and take pride in our communal sense of self, we're asking for trouble. For each of them is a mere role we play (or have been given to play) in the game of life, and each is quite different from our essential and higher Self. If we focus monomaniacally on any one of these social personalities—elevating it to a supreme position, and then submerging the lower individual self into this collective identity—we have the complete formula for fanaticism and for a new kind of alienation from others.

Individual identification through the collecting and blending of various communal identities can at best only partly, and never essentially, define any of us. For an individual's connections with a set of groups is only a small component of what comprises that person. Each of us is much more (or, you might say, ultimately much less!) than the groups with which we are associated.

We are not wholly defined by being card-carrying members of one club or another, and when it comes to our true nature, our wallets are altogether empty of such nonessential credentials.

Our attempts to forge some kind of special individual identity through our memberships in larger social groupings are all just more carnival cutouts into which we stick our particular faces. In the great internal war that we discussed at the end of the last chapter, it seems as though identification through association is most often aligned with the "be somebody" side of things rather than the "be nobody" faction.

What over-identifying with one or another of our collective guises inevitably entails is not only being included in some group but also *not* being included in others. Groups are defined negatively as well as positively: If I'm an Australian, it means I'm not a New Zealander; if I'm a Democrat, I'm certainly not a Republican.

For while the ego is immersed in and defined by the group, the group is in turn usually defined by who is excluded. And when we constitute membership in one or another of these collectivities as exclusive, separating out an "us" from a "them," we obscure or even deny the deep commonalities we share with all other living beings.

We seek to overcome the pangs of loneliness and isolation and gain a sense of community in such group identifications. But if we overestimate them and give them overweening dominance in how we think of ourselves, we re-create the conditions for estrangement from and animosity toward others. Submersion of one's distinct individuality into a group identity can end up being just a repositioning of the will to be somebody.

And too often, being somebody requires that we not be somebody else, and once again we find ourselves alienated from others.

TOO HEAVENLY MINDED AND NO EARTHLY GOOD

It is especially ironic that religious identities have so often functioned to separate human beings into oppositional factions. As with our association with other groupings, identifying with and taking pride in one or another of the religious traditions—"*I am* a Buddhist, Christian, Hindu, Muslim," or whatever—endows us with a sense both of belonging and of distinctiveness. But insofar as our connection to one or another of the organized and institutionalized religious "isms" is understood to preclude rather than enable our sense of a shared humanity, it has at least the same divisive, if not lethal, potential as national or political identities.

Living in an age when boundaries of all sorts are breaking down, traditional markers of religious identity are increasingly anachronistic. What really matters is not the particular group one adheres to, but rather the universally promoted spiritual message, which is one of tolerance, love, and respect for others, no matter what tribe they are a part of.

There was once a group of young Westerners who were visiting India back in the sixties, in the early days of the Tibetan exodus from Chinese persecution and the establishment of refugee communities in places like Dharamsala. The Dalai Lama at that time was not the famous international figure and Nobel Prize recipient he is today, and according to this anecdote the motley crew of European and American hippies walked right up to His Holiness's house and banged on his door.

And the Dalai Lama, as the story goes, came to the door and said, "Hello. What can I do for you?" and joined the Westerners on the verandah for a bit of a chat.

The discussion, as one might guess, turned to the topic of religion. One of the Westerners was quite adamantly antireligious and got into his host's face about it: "How can you in good conscience act as leader of a world religion? Religion has caused nothing but trouble throughout human history—it's been nothing but a source of violence, dissention, and animosity! How can you justify yourself?"

The Dalai Lama purportedly said this: "Religion is really not about vertically dividing ourselves into separate compartments like Hindu, Buddhist, Muslim, Jew, Christian, Taoist, and the rest. Rather, it's better to draw the line horizontally. Those who practice religion, regardless of label, are pretty much all alike. And those who don't practice religion, whether formally affiliated or not, are also pretty much alike."

So what unites all the real practitioners of religion, regardless of which (if any) of the world's faiths they adhere to? Surely the core message of any authentic spiritual path is the cultivation of a universal love, leading to a sense of unity among all people, irrespective of differences in culture, race, economic standing, political belief . . . or formal religious affiliation (or the lack thereof). Those who are practicing religion (and this includes those who disavow formal association with any particular religion) are practicing being more expansive and inclusive in their love, compassion, empathy, and sense of interconnectedness with others. And those who aren't practicing the true intent of religion are in the business of creating more, not less, divisiveness and ill will among people—often very loudly!

Religion, it has been said, is like a swimming pool. *All the noise is coming from the shallow end.*

Back in my academic days, I once had the opportunity to join a group of students who were having lunch with one of the eminent scholars of comparative religion at the time, Wilfred Cantwell Smith. At some point in the conversation, Professor Smith was asked whether he was a Christian. The answer was quite memorable: "I can't really say. You'll have to ask those who know me—my family and friends."

To be a real Christian (or Buddhist, Hindu, Jew, Taoist, and so on) means that you try to live like one. And surely that must include living a life guided by the universally extolled religious principles of kindness and love (not animosity and hatred) for others, and the cultivation of harmony and fraternity with (and not estrangement from and enmity toward) others.

If we want to claim *to be* a Buddhist, Christian, Muslim, Hindu, Taoist, and so on, we should try to act like one. And this will not involve trying to *be somebody* by means of exclusive religious branding, but rather will necessitate cultivating the willingness to *be nobody* through the practice of humility, universal brother- and sisterhood, and the abandonment of egoistical self-regard—even, or especially, when enveloped in a religious guise.

If we're too obsessed with our religious identity, we can lose sight of our responsibilities to our fellow human beings. We become so "heavenly minded" that we're "no earthly good," as the Johnny Cash song would have it:

> You're shinin' your light, and shine it you should
> But you're so heavenly minded you're no earthly good.[2]

Overweening pride of all sorts has disastrous consequences. If someone brags about standing, they surely will fall, as the Man in Black so aptly notes in the song. But there's no pride like spiritual pride. Taking undue self-satisfaction in our religious affiliation or, even worse, in our supposedly exceptional spiritual realizations, blinds us to the very thing a genuine path is supposed to lead to—the end of the clinging to the little, egoistic self, and the realization of our true universal nature and interconnection with all others. If we're too heavenly minded and proud, we're no earthly good at all.

JUDGE NOT, LEST YE BECOME A JUDGMENTAL PRIG

It is easy to forget that learning to *be nobody* is both the ultimate goal of any authentic spiritual path and the royal road to true happiness. The very institution that throughout history has been responsible for transmitting this redemptive message has also repeatedly been usurped in order to subvert and invert the good news. Pride in one's religion has too often been used to shun those with beliefs that differ from one's own—to judge and condemn outsiders in order to extol and congratulate the insiders.

It is, of course, not just religious people who are proud and judgmental. This is yet another way in which we are alike—we all have the tendency to be forever placing ourselves above and judging others. But it's sad to say that, when it comes to being judgmental and feeling superior, so-called religious people often seem to excel.

We do not become better and happier people by elevating ourselves over others or through judging. *Au contraire.* Judging destroys our wisdom, our forbearance, and our love and compassion, and leaves us just feeling smug and isolated.

Here's how it goes, if you're like me: We encounter a complex, constantly changing person or transitory situation, and then we freeze-frame the picture and impose some immutable characteristic on our snapshot: "He *is* a bad person; she *is* a liar." Passing judgments like this—and we all tend to do it, don't we?—denies a basic fact of life: everything and everybody is impermanent and in a perpetual state of flux and change.

We know how complex we are—each one of us is an incredibly intricate mass of experiences, proclivities, memories, opinions, influences, and feelings. We're so complex, it's hard to know who we really are! But when we encounter one another, we seem to forget that others are at least as complicated. When such meetings occur, it's like one tiny edge of the huge balloon that is "me" touches a minute portion of the massive balloon that is "you." And on such paltry, fragmentary evidence, I make my determination: "He is such an irritating person! She is so conceited!"

"Judging," observes author William Young, always "requires that you think yourself superior over the one you judge."[3] And it is always in the service of ego-enhancement, for as Eckhart Tolle points out,

There is nothing that strengthens the ego more than being right. Being right is identification with a mental position—a perspective, an opinion, a judgment, a story. For you to be right, of course, you need someone else to be wrong, and so the ego loves to make wrong in order to be right.[4]

Judging is, therefore, both deeply implicated in ignorance and precludes any sort of deep sense of kinship between ourselves and others. Instead of bringing us closer, the tendency to judge tears us apart. Rather than helping us appreciate our commonalities (including our common tendency to be judgmental!), judging imposes a rank order where (in our imaginations, at least) we're on top and others cower guiltily below.

As Mother Teresa said, "If you judge people, you have no time to love them."[5] And as Jesus advised long before, "Judge not, that you be not judged." What goes around will come around: "For with what judgment you judge, you will be judged; and with the measure you use, it will be measured back to you."[6] We know how unfair and hurtful it feels to have others judge us to be essentially this or that—wrong, bad, ugly, stupid, and so on. And yet, as usual, we create the causes for more of this by doing it to others.

•   •   •

Now, let's be clear. To refrain from judging does not mean that we no longer are allowed to make distinctions among things. In Buddhism, the ability to discriminate is counted as one of the five physical and mental parts, or "aggregates" (*samskaras*), that make up our very being.* We cannot help but discriminate; it is innate to our nature, and without it everything would be one big indistinguishable blob.

But there is a difference between judgment and what we might call "discernment." To discern means simply to recognize things as distinct from one another (from the Latin *discernere*, *dis-* meaning "apart" and *cernere* meaning "to separate"). And with its connotations of being able to recognize or comprehend something ("He discerned a pattern in his behavior"), it is not bound up in ignorance (as with judgment) but rather it is the essence of wisdom.

While judgment inhibits learning, discernment is the very soul of it. It functions to distinguish, among other things, what works to bring happiness and what doesn't. Discernment involves identifying what is good for ourselves and others and what is not; what will be useful in our quest to live the good life, alone and in company, and what will only bring more pain.

Discernment is discrimination minus the self-righteousness and egoism that accompany judgment. It is fundamentally egalitarian rather than hierarchical—what I correctly discern to be beneficial for myself will also be good for you. Hurting others, selfishness, self-cherishing, and, yes, judging are not conducive to happiness, either for me or for anyone else. Loving-kindness, compassion, equanimity, and wise discernment bring happiness to anyone who cultivates them.

Discernment helps us honor Jesus's advice to take care that there be no hypocrisy fouling our evaluations:

> And why do you look at the speck in your brother's eye, but do not consider the plank in your own eye? Or how can you say to your brother, "Let me remove the speck from your eye"; and look, a plank is in your own eye? Hypocrite! First remove the plank from your own eye, and then you will see clearly to remove the speck from your brother's eye.[7]

There's a difference between different modes of differentiating. It's not discrimination that's the problem here. But we often exercise the discriminating capacity in a judgmental modality, a way of differentiating that is conducive neither to our own happiness nor to the betterment of our relations with others. This very same ability to discriminate can be used to appreciate the distinctive and unique beauty and goodness in every particular thing and being. We all are indeed special somebodies . . . equally special in our own way.

One way to foster a healthy exercise of discrimination is to note that in every person there are good attributes as well as bad; in every situation, no matter how difficult and challenging, there are positive aspects and things to learn. Every cloud has a silver lining; every "problem" can also be seen as an opportunity; every person possesses at least some admirable and loveable traits if we look for them.

We perversely are so drawn to the negative side of things that we systematically ignore the positives that are always present—in ourselves, in another person, in a situation, and in groups (national, ethnic, social, economic, or religious) other than our own.

It's like when we get a small sore, cut, or scratch. The whole rest of the body is fine, but instead of thinking about all the bits that are OK, all the parts that are working well, we become obsessed with this one little scab and we keep picking at it. We fixate on the dark cloud instead of the silver lining.

Since we all innately have the ability to differentiate, why not exercise that power to choose that which will bring more happiness to ourselves and others instead of less, and that which will bring us together rather than separate us?

BIG FISH IN A SMALL POND

Whether we pride ourselves on our individual status, possessions, or accomplishments, or on our association with a national, ethnic, or religious group, when such vanity serves to prop up our sense of importance, it sets us up to fall.

Egotistical pride is universally regarded as an obstacle to true spiritual progress, and therefore to true happiness. In the Tibetan

Buddhist tradition, pride made it onto the list of the top five or six of the "mental afflictions" that militate against our sense of well-being and contentment. The whole of the religion known as Islam takes its name from the Arabic term for overcoming one's pride and practicing submission (*islam*) to God's will. And in Catholicism, pride is listed among the "seven deadly sins"—and, indeed, is often regarded as the worst of them. C. S. Lewis calls it "the essential vice, the utmost evil":

> According to Christian teachers, the essential vice, the utmost evil, is Pride. Unchastity, anger, greed, drunkenness, and all that, are mere fleabites in comparison: it was through Pride that the devil became the devil; Pride leads to every other vice; it is the complete anti-God state of mind.[8]

Pride is a vice not so much because it is "bad" but because it is self-destructive. From a karmic point of view, as we shall see below, pride is one of the principal causes of depression and low self-esteem. What is elevated too high will fall very low; what rises up into the stratosphere comes crashing down into the depths.

Pride sets itself up to lose, in both the short run and the long run. In the short run, pride can only sustain its illusion of superiority by remaining a big fish in a small pond.

In my own case, I have taken pride in my intelligence since I was in elementary school. I remember feeling quite pleased back then to think that I was the smartest kid in my class. This may or may not have been true—relative "smartness" is slippery to measure, and memory definitely plays its tricks—but in any case there were only twenty or thirty others to whom I could compare myself.

Convincing myself that I was "the smartest" was less sustainable in high school—especially since I nearly flunked eleventh grade due to truancy!—and even harder to maintain in college (there was that course in logic that I just barely passed, and plenty of other ego deflators and reality checks along the way). But it really wasn't until I got to graduate school that this particular illusion was completely blown out of the water. The truth finally penetrated through all the levels of self-deception that sustained my pride. It became indubitable that there were plenty of people way smarter than me—for there they were, lots of them, teeming around me at the university every single day.

And then, of course, a new mental affliction arose: envy. But that's a different story.

The point is just that pride in anything (intelligence, wealth, technical skill, physical beauty or strength or flexibility, or even in one's supposed spiritual attainments) can only be maintained in willful isolation from those who would challenge it.

While depression and problems associated with low self-esteem are on the rise, it is not contradictory to observe that it is actually the narcissistic *overestimation* of the self that lies at the heart of this beast. One modern expert has baldly stated, "There doesn't seem to be a great deal of really low self-esteem. The average person already thinks that he or she is above average."[9] This double-faced Janus—simultaneously insecure and arrogant, self-abasing and self-absorbed—is consistent with the neurosis that arises with the self-preoccupation definitive of our culture.

So here's one helpful hint for solving the problem of pride: If you're liable to take inordinate self-regard due to your intellect, go to Harvard or the University of Chicago and hobnob with some hardcore eggheads. If you are vain about your good looks, stop hanging around with people you feel are obviously uglier and enter a beauty contest! If you think you're so amazing because of your money, quit socializing with those who have less and chill with really rich people!

If you think you're cool because of the flexibility you demonstrate when at your local yoga studio, go to an international yoga conference and check out the real competition.

Get the fish out of the small pond and into the ocean!

Pride takes a lot of work to maintain and prolong—not only in light of the constant real-life challenges to its inflated sensibility but also because of the impermanent and changing nature of the things we take pride in. The financial position or professional status, the popularity and fame, the cleverness or brainpower, and (especially!) the appearance and abilities of the physical body are unreliable. That's why pride and insecurity are actually two peas in a pod.

THE KARMIC CAUSES OF DEPRESSION

But it's the long run—the karmic consequences of pride—that we're especially concerned with here. So let's cut to the chase, shall we?

> Led by pride into the lower realms, they are even in this human life deprived of joy. They will be servants who feed on others' leftovers—stupid, ugly, and weak. Stuck up with pride and miserable, they will be despised by everyone.[10]

As we unpack this verse from the Buddhist classic *Guide to the Bodhisattva's Way of Life*, we see that, first of all, the karmic principle of "What goes around comes around" is here reformulated as "What goes up must come down." The high shall be made low; the first shall be last. The proud will sink in the afterlife into "lower realms," and even in this life will feel inferior, like "servants" of others. Those who take pride in their intellect will see themselves as stupid; those whose arrogance centers on their good looks will regard themselves as ugly; and those vain about their strength will feel weak.[11] Having been too proud, one perceives oneself as inadequate intellectually and physically and, in general, will feel unloved by others ("despised by everyone").

The proud, according to the laws of karma, will become the depressed.

But what's really interesting and insightful about this passage is that it also states that the proud will remain proud, even after they have been brought low: "*Stuck up with pride* and miserable," the text says, pointing not only to the idea that karma tends to replicate itself (one of the effects of pride being a future propensity to continue to feel pride), but also to the fact that *one can be proud even while simultaneously feeling miserable, inadequate, and unloved.*

Or perhaps it's like this: it is possible to be *proud of* feeling miserable, inadequate, and unloved.

• • •

Medical science has not identified any single cause of depression. A whole array of factors, external and internal, is said to be capable of triggering it in any given individual. External causes might include family conflict, interpersonal conflict, bereavement, job loss, major life changes, and drug or alcohol abuse. (Sounds like a description of life itself, doesn't it?) Internal causes seem a bit more vague: previous negative experiences (e.g., a history of depression), "personality" (e.g., a tendency toward perfectionism), medical illness, and "family disposition" (i.e., bad genes).

As one expert summarizes the situation, "The precise causes of these [depressive] illnesses continue to be a matter of intense research."[12] Decoded, that means, "We really don't know exactly what causes depression."

Ancient Indian logic texts distinguish between a "cause" (*hetu*) and a "condition" (*pratyaya*). A "cause" is what's absolutely necessary if there is to be the effect. The cause must be there before the effect will be produced, and if the cause is not there, the effect can never come about. An oak tree cannot grow without an acorn to function as its seed.

But a cause isn't a cause until it's activated by the right circumstances. A "condition" acts as a sort of midwife to help the cause give birth to its result. The acorn is the cause of the oak tree, for without it you'll never get an oak tree. But the acorn needs certain conditions to occur for it to operate as the cause of the oak tree. It has to be planted in the right kind of soil and given water and sunlight. Without the proper conditions, the cause can't perform its function.

When it comes to the origins and treatment of depression and low self-esteem, we should be careful not to mistake what are just conditions for real causes. The so-called external causes for depression listed above—family or interpersonal conflict, loss of a loved one or job, and so on—can't really properly be regarded as such. They certainly can act as conditions for enkindling the true cause. But there are plenty of people who suffer through such experiences in life *without* getting depressed, and depression can arise apart from undergoing such experiences.

And the same is true with respect to the supposedly "internal causes." It's not *necessary* to have had previous negative experiences or some personality defect or a medical illness or a particular genetic disposition in order to succumb to depression.

Here, as in so many other areas of modern, secular life, is where we must push what I call the "Why, Daddy?" question. You know, like that little kid who won't quit asking Daddy or Mommy "Why? . . . Why? . . . Yeah, but why?" As adults, we should ask similar questions of our secular experts:

Why am I so depressed, Doctor?

Well, you just lost your job.

But my friends at work were also laid off, and they didn't get depressed like me. Why am I depressed?

You lost your job, plus you have a genetic predisposition to depression.

Yeah, that's true, but my brother's been through all kinds of terrible experiences in life, and he's never been depressed! And anyway, how come my family has depression genes when other families don't? Why me, Doctor? Why?

And just like the little kid who keeps asking "Why, Daddy?" eventually we get the same answer from the doctor that we give to our inquisitive four-year-old children:

Just because. No reason. It's random. Bad luck.

In my case, it wasn't that I *lost* a job, but rather that I got one that seemed to set off my own depression. For twelve years, throughout college and graduate school, I had been told over and over by my professors that I probably wouldn't get a teaching position in my unmarketable, specialized field. Comparative religion with an emphasis on the religions of ancient India wasn't exactly a lucrative field of study with a huge demand that needed filling.

And sure enough, when I finished my studies and went looking for a job in my field, there weren't many openings. And there were lots and lots of brilliant, well-trained applicants for each one of the very few available positions.

In the year when I was up for employment, I not only landed one of the few jobs advertised, I got the very best of them—a plum position in the Ivy League. And within four months, I was checked into a local psychiatric ward and put on twenty-four-hour suicide watch.

Getting the great job obviously was not what *caused* my depression, but none of the other possibilities I explored with my therapist seemed to sufficiently explain things, either: the difficult relationship with my father, past traumas that had been left unexamined, an "imposter syndrome" that made me afraid I'd be found out to be a sham. No one of these, nor any of the other possibilities that modern therapy could come up with, rose to "acorn" status; they were all just conditions ("soil," "sunlight," "water") that inexplicably came together to precipitate a cause that was yet to be identified.

A depressed person feels like a "real nobody," but, if there is to be a surefire cure for the malady, we should first identify the true source of the ailment.

• • •

It is within the spiritual traditions that we must look for the real causes of our experiences. Religions offer answers to the "Why, Daddy?" questions of life. But if we are to be empowered to really help ourselves, we cannot even here remain satisfied with answers that render us impotent victims. Agreeing to religious explanations like "God's inscrutable will" doesn't get us any further than secular, scientific answers like "genetic predisposition." Both of them end up sounding like "Too bad! Just your tough luck!" and leave us in the same powerless and helpless place.

Fortunately, there are other explanations for what causes depression and low self-esteem. And knowing them gives us power: if we no longer create the cause, the effect will arise no more. But in order to gain the power, we have to accept the responsibility.

The truth of the matter is that we experience depression and low self-esteem because of specific kinds of actions we've done in the past. What goes around really does come around. We do in fact reap what we sow, and this is an absolute truism in every authentic spiritual path: good acts bring pleasant experiences; bad acts bring undesirable consequences.

While the ancient texts offer several candidates for the karmic cause of depression—including anger (animosity toward others boomerangs into hatred of the self) and "idle speech" (talking trash comes back at us as the feeling that we are trash)—there's one that's by far the most glaring: pride. It serves as the cause and then repositions itself as the self-centered perpetuator of our self-esteem problems.

It seems paradoxical only because of our fundamental confusion and ignorance: low self-esteem is the consequence of high self-regard. And what's even less apparent is the fact that identifying oneself as a "depressed person" is just another way, albeit a sad and twisted one, to take pride in being *somebody special*.

BEING SOMEBODY SPECIAL AS NOBODY SPECIAL

Among the many nasty aspects of pride is the fact that it is good at concealing itself from those of us who have it (and, let's be honest, we all have some version of it). "There is no fault which makes a man more unpopular," observes C. S. Lewis, "and no fault which we are more unconscious of in ourselves."[13] Pride can pretend it's not there, when really it has just relocated itself.

And so it is that pride and overweening self-regard can even express themselves through self-deprecation. The individual self, in its desperate attempt to *be somebody*, can stake its claim *to be somebody special because it feels so worthless*—and so it asserts its special status in just that way, as a "depressed person."

As Eckhart Tolle has written, "If you take away one kind of identification, the ego will quickly find another. It ultimately doesn't mind what it identifies with as long as it has an identity."[14] The "somebody self," if unable or unwilling to find confirmation in anything else, will go looking for validation in its own suffering. Physical and psychological disabilities can, as easily as anything else, become the individual's defining quality:

> You can just as easily identify with a "problematic" body and make the body's imperfection, illness, or disability into your identity. You may then think and speak of yourself as a "sufferer" of this or that chronic illness or disability. . . . You then unconsciously cling to the illness because it has become the most important part of who you perceive yourself to be. . . . Once the ego has found an identity, it does not want to let go.[15]

It may seem surprising to those who have never suffered from depression to learn that *nobody thinks of themselves more than somebody who is depressed.* But even those who have only experienced "a bad day" or just "a little case of the blues" will recognize the phenomenon: when you're feeling down, you aren't interested in much else besides how down you feel.

Depression is a caricature of the main cause of depression. *Depression is ultimately caused by thinking about oneself all the time,* and is experienced as *the inability to think about anyone other than oneself.*

Mr. Karma (who is no one other than your own conscience and consciousness) has a sort of sick sense of humor. He notices when we're constantly preoccupied with ourselves—*What about me? What about me?*—and says, "OK. You want to focus on yourself all the time? Try *this*!" We get depressed, unable to get out of our own heads and stop the repetitive, broken record of how bad we feel.

And then, performing another trick from its vast repertoire, the "somebody self" identifies with this "depressed person" it has fabricated. We are so desperate to be somebody that we're willing to stick our heads into even this kind of carnival cutout: *If I can't be a good enough anybody else, at least I can be somebody as a nobody.* The ego tries to solve the problem of low self-esteem by assuming the role of "somebody with low self-esteem."

And tragically, this designation of the self as "a depressed self"—now more self-centered than ever and taking perverse pride in its self-defining misery—re-creates the very cause that brought about this dismal state of affairs in the first place.

Depression is a downward cycle, in more ways than one.

• • •

The culture of narcissism that encourages rampant self-obsession and self-congratulatory pride has had unfavorable ramifications when it comes to the pursuit of true happiness. The precipitous rise in depression and the steep plunge in self-esteem can be directly correlated to living in a society where the unconstrained preoccupation with the self has taken on pathological dimensions.

While we've drawn the karmic correlations between, on one hand, egotism and pride, and on the other hand the calamitous fall into the bleakness of depressed self-absorption, you don't really even have to accept karma to perceive the relationship between the two. Selfishness doesn't make us feel better about ourselves, which we know if we check in on our own experience. And in fact it makes us feel much worse, depressingly so.

The karmic causes of depression—anger; idle speech, either in the form of self-righteous gossiping about others or making promises that aren't kept; and the pride, arrogance, and judgmental mindset that cause us to place ourselves above others—these are all expressions of a more fundamental root problem: self-centeredness. And correspondingly, the real causes of happiness (and the cures for depression) will all orbit around the same foundational source: self-lessness and altruistic concern for our fellow human beings.

In the next chapter, we'll see that the usual forms of self-absorption are in fact based on a grand illusion. While in our culture of narcissism we invest so much time and effort in appeasing the needs of a divinized, egoistic self, the status of that deity is insecure—and for very good reason. The "somebody self," one might say, is in a perpetual identity crisis because it suspects (while at the same time it denies) that it isn't really real.

When we actually go looking for the self we feel so intuitively is there—it makes such constant demands, after all!—a sneaking suspicion starts to grow that there's really nobody home. For the self we are so obsessed with and take such pride in has only an apparitional existence, and our obsession turns out to be no more than chasing a shadow.

This is not, however, the nihilistic tragedy we might fear. When we give up looking for the somebody who's not really there—when we come up empty-handed in our futile search for some unchanging and all-controlling entity amidst our many and variegated personae and appearances—we begin to realize that the nobody we're left with isn't just a big nothing.

Wising up about the real nature of the "somebody self" makes it possible for us to become a happier somebody. It's through accessing the infinite potentiality of being nobody that we can really begin to help and improve ourselves.

Action Plan: Managing Pride

Make a list of personal traits that you are proud of—your looks or physical abilities, acquired skills, natural gifts, accomplishments, whatever. This is not the time to be falsely humble. We're all proud of something about ourselves.

First off, consider whether these traits are permanent and will *always* be with you. Do you really suppose that you will always be beautiful, strong, clever, adept, successful, or famous? How will you feel when what you are proud of is diminished or lost altogether due to the ravages of time and changing circumstances?

Second, check to see whether the pride you take in these characteristics is only in relation to others who don't have them or who have only lesser versions of them. Isn't it always the case that what you're proud of depends on feelings of superiority to others?

Finally, reflect on the fact that there are others who definitely have more or better versions of these traits. Be more realistic about your place in life: are you really the *most* talented, beautiful, rich, skilled, accomplished, or intelligent? Get the fish out of the small pond, at least theoretically, and realize your true place in whatever hierarchy you've bought into!

Notes:

* The five aggregates that comprise the basis for our sense of self are the physical body, the ability to discriminate, consciousness, feelings, and mental imprints.

PART II

MAKING A BETTER SOMEBODY OUT OF NOBODY

3
Clutching at Straws and Chasing Shadows

Knock, knock.
Who's there?
Exactly.

—Author unknown

FREEDOM'S JUST ANOTHER WORD FOR NOTHING LEFT TO LOSE (OR GAIN)

Beneath it all, it is only true contentment—the glorious sensation of being utterly free, unencumbered, and relaxed—that we all desire. The goals depicted in many religions reflect this understanding of what we are shooting for: *moksha* or *mukti* (both meaning "liberation") in Hinduism; *nirvana* (the great "extinguishing" or "sigh of relief" as one becomes free of all troubling thoughts and feelings) in Buddhism; the dropping of the old self and being "born again" into Christ; the release that comes from following God's will and law in Judaism and Islam.

We all want to be free. So what, exactly, are the chains that bind us? What is the nature of the prison that we feel encloses us?

Being free isn't just a matter of doing, saying, or thinking anything that comes into your head. That much should be obvious to anyone who has lived more than a few years in the company of other humans. We've tried that version of "freedom" over and over and over again, to no avail. Whenever some strong impulse arises, unless thwarted by fear of reprisal (or jail!), we usually just give in to it, consequences be damned! We yell back at those who yell at us, try to hurt those who hurt us, plot our revenge when we feel betrayed . . . just because we "feel like it."

Until we have thoroughly trained ourselves, we are enslaved by our negative emotions, our mental afflictions. When anger, jealousy, pride, or lust raise their nasty little heads, we are usually rendered helpless in their thrall. Worse yet, we stick our head into the carnival cutouts of these irrational feelings and say, "*I am* angry! *I am* depressed! *I am* jealous!"

Among the large array of mental afflictions that plague and tyrannize us (the Buddha said we have 84,000 of them!), two lie at the root of our unhappiness and imprisonment.

They are desire and ignorance.

"Desire" here really means perpetual dissatisfaction—with what we have, with the life we are leading, and with who we are. It's like when we have an itchy mosquito bite. We scratch the itch, hoping that by doing so it won't itch anymore.

We're slaves to our itches, and that's one very important way in which we are not free. We get a hankering for a new iPhone and the itch begins: *If only I had the new iPhone! You know, the one with that little computer voice named Siri that talks to you? Then I'd be happy.* Or one or another of the myriad versions of the itch: *If only that girl would pay attention to me. If only I had a better job. If only I were rich, famous, popular.*

I, I, I and *if only, if only*—the repetitive call of incessant yearning and discontent, the "somebody self" always wanting more.

And so we try scratching. We save our money for the iPhone, or try to get the phone number from the beautiful babe or stud-muffin dude, or apply for a different job, or try to be more (more wealthy, more famous, more popular, more attractive) of a somebody.

And every time we scratch, it's in the hope that there won't be any more itches.

We all know what happens next. It's just like those pesky mosquito bites—the more you scratch them, the more irresistibly the itch returns. The relief is at best temporary, and then after a brief respite the desire comes roaring back, more demanding than ever.

And so freedom, we could say, is nothing more than the exalted state of *itchlessness*—being satisfied with everything we have, with "nothing left to lose," as Janis Joplin says in her famous song, and nothing more to gain.

The liberation we seek with all our scratching consists of simply not being beset with new and improved itches all the time. This is called by another name: "contentment," and it is what we hope to attain with every attempt to satisfy our desires. We hope that, by fulfilling this particular craving, we won't want anything more. We hope that each scratch will be the last one; that finally, with this one last scrape, we'll be satisfied.

Maybe there's more than just contentment at the end of our spiritual journey. Maybe there's heaven or a Pure Land with all kinds of rainbows in the sky and unicorns bounding about. And maybe we'll all be angels, blissfully flapping around with supernatural abilities and X-Men superpowers. I can't, in all honesty, say with any certainty that there won't be.

But I do know this: If we shoot for contentment—the Great Itchlessness—it won't matter one way or the other. Once we become content, it will be impossible to be discontented with our lives and ourselves—with or without streets paved with gold and divine bodies made of beautiful light. It's win-win when it comes to contentment! If there's more in addition to that, great; and if there's not, well, that will be OK too, *because we'll be content*!

And, of course, all this itching and scratching is in the service of *being somebody*. We believe that status and personal fulfillment will come through scratching, through obtaining something we don't already have or more (or less) of what we already possess.

This would be far more understandable if we were lacking the necessities of life. But for readers of this book, I'll wager, it's not for want of proper food or shelter or clothing, nor for lack of education or opportunities to make a decent living, nor due to the absence of friends and loved ones that we remain discontented with our lives.

We aren't among the three billion people living on two dollars and fifty cents a day or less, nor are we among the 80 percent of the earth's population subsisting on less than ten dollars a day, nor among the one billion fellow human beings dwelling in slums, nor among a similar number who remain illiterate.[1]

What we really desire is the freedom from endless desires, especially when we already have so much. It's liberation from our incessant whining about how we don't have enough or aren't somebody enough. As for the first, when it comes to wealth, consumer goods, leisure time, access to education and information—the nuts and bolts of the good life—there's really no excuse for folks like us. We're just forgetting the basic facts of our lives; we're just spacing out. Say the mantra:

Om, I have enough, ah hum!

Our problems—our itches—are "First World problems," which hardly deserve the name "problems" at all. Since our "problems," when it comes to what we own and the material lives we lead, are of such an entirely different order than what others face, we do have a real shot at being content with the material circumstances of our lives.

But when it comes to what is termed "self-fulfillment," well, that, you might say, is a different kettle of fish.

So now let us turn to the second of our two great mental afflictions: ignorance. As we shall see, there is a fundamental misunderstanding when it comes to who we think we are, and it lies at the heart of our problems.

THE ROOT OF ALL EVIL

In the Eastern spiritual traditions, ignorance performs the same quintessential role, when it comes to our unhappiness, that disobedience plays in the West. Readers brought up in Western societies all know the story: In the beginning, everything was jake. Adam and Eve lived in the Garden of Eden and swung in hammocks all day long. When they got hungry, they would leisurely pick fruit from the trees that God had generously provided for them. But there was one tree whose fruit God commanded them not to eat. And we know how the story goes from there: of course, they perversely did the one thing they were told not to do, and the rest is history. Adam and Eve were cursed, and they were thrown out of the Garden to fend for themselves. And so, according to the myth, our tale of woe begins.*

In the religious traditions stemming from India, it is ignorance, not insubordination to God's will, that's at the root of our problems. And in these Eastern traditions, there's usually no myth of origins offered to show how ignorance came into our lives.† Ignorance has been with us since time with no beginning, and each of us is simply born with it. It's a standard-issue part of the makeup for us as human beings (not to mention other life-forms).

Because of this ignorance, we make fundamental mistakes about who we are and how to live a good life. We really don't get it when it comes to what's what. And because we don't get it, we're really in for it!

Ignorance (*avidya* in Sanskrit) is not so much *not knowing* as it is *mis-knowing*. Our minds invert things; we mistakenly think things are one way when actually they are another. In the ancient Yoga Sutra, ignorance is (and this is the norm in South Asian scriptures) said to be the "field" or "breeding ground" in which all the other mental afflictions grow. As long as the "root" of these negative emotions remains uncut, we will continue to suffer through life instead of finding true happiness.[2]

The Yoga Sutra's definition of this Mother of All Mental Afflictions is interesting and comprehensive:

> Ignorance is the belief that what is impermanent is permanent, what is impure is pure, what will bring suffering will bring happiness, and what is without an essence has an essence.[3]

This is, I know, quite a mouthful. But it does, I promise you, have direct bearing on both the real cause of our unhappiness and the disastrously wrong view we have about our individual identity.

So let's look carefully at what is meant by each of these four ways in which ignorance works to turn things upside down in our lives:

1. We believe what is impermanent to be permanent.

Does this ever happen to us, do you think? All the time! We are perpetually thrown for a loop when impermanent things, things we thought wouldn't change, actually do change—or else don't change precisely the way we wanted them to.

Our relationships, our financial situation, our jobs, our possessions, our very bodies and thoughts and feelings—everything in our lives is transitory and fleeting. When our partners change ("Don't go changing," sings Billy Joel—but how can any of us not?); when our once-operative computer freezes up; when the boss suddenly alters our job description; when we get depressed, sick, old, or die—what is it but impermanence smacking us upside the head? *Wake up! Did you think this would last forever?*

No, you might protest, *I know that things and people change. But I wanted them to go this way and instead they changed that way!* Well, welcome to reality. We can't govern the specifics of how external things and other people will change any more than we can magically stop change from occurring at all.

We'll return below to the fantasy of the "controlling self," that ignorant sense that we can, in the moment, micromanage our lives and the events and people in them to suit our own whims. But here's the point: *change is*, and the exact direction of how things change is not within our control. Thinking that changing things won't change, or believing that we can decree the precise direction in which change will occur, sets us up for a big fall when reality makes its presence known.

2. We believe what is impure to be pure.

The classic example of this misunderstanding involves the way we normally think about the human body. We sometimes, in our vanity, admire our own body for its good looks; even more often, we lust after the attractive, "pure" bodies of others.

But beauty, as they say, is only skin-deep, and really it's not even that. Even at skin level, up close and personal, we're all pretty much the same, and it's not that fetching. The epidermis of you, me, Angelina Jolie, and Johnny Depp is equally hairy, pocked, flaky, and mole-, pimple-, and freckle-marked.

And when we go subterranean, deeper than skin-deep, well, it's sort of a horror show, isn't it? One Buddhist text describes this "pure" body we're so enamored of as a bundle of "hair, nails, teeth, skin, flesh, sinews, bones, marrow, kidney, heart, liver, membranes, spleen, lungs, stomach, bowels, intestines, excrement, bile, phlegm, pus, blood, sweat, fat, tears, serum, saliva, mucus, synovial fluid [whatever that is—we probably don't want to know!], and urine."[4]

Not a pretty picture, when we actually think about it—which we definitely don't like to do, especially in the throes of either narcissistic self-admiration or sexual longing for another.

One of my teachers used to argue that supermodels, as they promenade down the runways exhibiting their external exquisiteness (*here's me on the outside!*) should also be mandated to carry and display a colostomy bag (*and here's me on the inside!*). But that would sort of spoil the show, wouldn't it? Our attraction to the physical body as something "pure" and desirable requires a dose of fantasy and a dollop of willful overlooking of the disagreeable details.

While it's important to maintain a certain level of self-acceptance when it comes to our own bodies, and while there's nothing intrinsically wrong in being appreciative of or attracted to the physical beauty of another man or woman, our ignorance comes in being unrealistic about what the human body really is. We suffer because of our illusions about our physicality. And these illusions include thinking that beauty, youthful appearance, strength, and flexibility are inherent and unchanging in ourselves and in others. (See above for mistaking impermanent things for permanent ones.)

3. We believe what will bring suffering will bring happiness.

This one is sort of a catchall category that describes our ignorance when it comes to what we think will really pay off for us. Throughout our lives, we scurry about pursuing money, things, experiences, and other people, in the hopes that somehow they will make us happy. But instead, we are repeatedly let down and perpetually left dissatisfied. What we thought would bring happiness ends up leaving us feeling unfulfilled and discontent.

We've set things (and people) up to fail. External things and beings don't have it in their power to make us happy; at best, they can only bring a temporary spike in pleasure. Only we have the power to create real, deep, and lasting satisfaction within ourselves and our lives.

True happiness can only come from within. It's not "out there" somewhere, oozing out from something or someone else. And when we go looking for it in other people or external things, instead of discovering happiness we find ourselves disappointed, disheartened, and sometimes infuriated.

4. We believe what is without an essence has an essence.

When it comes to ignorance, this one's sort of the "root of the root" and will lead us directly to our mistaken view of ourselves: We think that things that have no "essences" (the word in Sanskrit is *anatman*, often translated as "no self") do have some kind of enduring and definitive quality or characteristic (an essential "self" or *atman*).

Here's an example of this kind of mistake. Just imagine that you have an annoying person in your life—an angry boss, an exasperating ex, or a troublesome relative. When we encounter (or even think about) such challenging people, we feel strongly that *it's obvious* to us that they are *defined* by the traits we ascribe to them: they are irritating, exasperating, or troublesome (or provocative, mean, hurtful—pick the adjective that is *apropos* of your own annoying person). Any fool could see it! That's the way they really are—*essentially*.

The proof that there actually are no *essentially* angry, exasperating, or troublesome people in the world is rather obvious, although we choose to ignore it all the time: These people have friends. They have loved ones. They have loads of people in their lives who do not find them angry, exasperating, or troublesome.[‡]

This some find perplexing—so much so that they go to the bother of trying to convince this annoying person's friends, family, and acquaintances how wrong they are. *How can you be friends with her? Let me tell you the real deal about him!* But alas, the annoying person's friends, family, and acquaintances often persevere in their error, don't they?

I once had a student raise his hand in class and say what we all think before the filter goes up that prevents really stupid things from coming out of our mouths: "I know someone who *everyone* would find annoying." Like we should all get on a bus and go on a field trip to visit the one *essentially* annoying person in the world. We'd all file by that innately objectionable person and go, "Ooh, yeah, that's right . . . so annoying!" Like a lighthouse casting its beam, this annoying being would just exude annoyance, and whenever we entered the purview of The Essentially Annoying Person, we could not help but *be annoyed*.

This is a self-justifying fantasy, and one that's often fortified when we find a few other people who agree with our evaluation of the person in question. *See*, we say to ourselves, *she really is annoying. It's a groundswell, a veritable movement, a bandwagon of right-thinking folks, all of whom agree with me!*

Well, in fact, no. It's not that you and your fellow travelers correctly see some definitive unsavory essence that eludes the perception of others. It's that you (and, OK, perhaps some others) *respond* in a certain disagreeable way to some aspect of the personality of another. It's not that someone is annoying; it's that you are *annoyed*.

We don't see the world and the people in it *as they are*; we see them *as we are*. There are no difficult people in the world until and unless you find them to be so.

And as a result of not comprehending this fundamental fact of life, we suffer. Instead of working on what it is in us that is aroused by the annoying person, instead of locating and then fixing the button inside of ourselves that gets pushed, we just complacently assume that the difficulties we experience with our annoying person are the annoying person's fault—because "annoying" is *what they are*, not just what they seem to us to be.

The same error can be made in reverse. Let's say you enjoy Ben & Jerry's ice cream, as I do. Chunky Monkey flavor, let's suppose. Mmmm. Tastes so good! *It is good-tasting ice cream*, and anyone in their right mind would agree!

And then we encounter someone who *doesn't like Chunky Monkey*! Maybe they don't even like the Ben & Jerry's brand. Possibly, *they don't care for ice cream at all*!

If Ben & Jerry's Chunky Monkey ice cream had the essence of being tasty, everyone with working taste buds, and who was not insane, would find it so. But (amazingly to those of us who like B&J's CM), there are people of apparently sound mind and taste buds who don't take a shine to it.

The qualities that we assume are *in* the people, objects, and experiences in life are *not really there*. These qualities are coming *from us, not at us*. We're projecting them, not perceiving them. Sure, we have our reasons. They say this or do that, and this pisses us off. But others hear or see the same things and don't get pissed off. We find a person "difficult" only because *we have difficulties* with him or her. They are not intrinsically, inherently, or essentially "difficult"— in spite of the way they may appear to us.

Thinking otherwise is a serious blunder, and one that we make all the time, much to our detriment. This kind of error is the condition of possibility for the kind of judgmental attitude we talked about in chapter 2, and for all the nastiness that comes in its wake.

This is, bottom line, raw and unadulterated ignorance. Wisdom 101 is the dawning of the realization that we got it all wrong, all back-ass-wards.

THE "WHERE'S WALDO?" SEARCH FROM HELL

There's an even more fundamental application of our tendency to err in our perception of how things and people really are, one that lies even deeper than the mistake of thinking that our "annoying person" *is* annoying, or that Ben & Jerry's ice cream *is* delicious.

If the Mother of All Mental Afflictions is ignorance, the Mother of All Ignorance is the belief in a kind of a "self" that has never existed. What we have called the "root of the root" when it comes to ignorance—thinking things have an inherent essence when they do not—has a root of its own: the "root of the root of the root" is ignorance about the nature of the self.

We believe that we ourselves have a fixed, inherently existing, definitive essence, a self (*atman*)§, when there actually is no such thing (*anatman*). And it is really this foundational error that not only undergirds all our misperceptions but also undermines any chance we have for finding true happiness and real self-knowledge.

The "self" here is not what we've been referring to as the *true* or *higher* self (the Self, Buddha nature, or soul) that we can and do access when we cease thinking we're *somebody* and relax into being *nobody*. What is meant here is an individual, particularistic lower sense of identity—the egoistic self, the *being somebody* self, the little-voice-inside-your-head self.

It's "you" (say your name to yourself) that we're talking about here. It's the self that rises up in defense of itself when falsely accused—"*You* stole my car!" "No, no, *I* didn't!"—it's that "I" we're now focused on. It's the self that has a birthday, and so will have a death day. It's the "itchy self" that's unhappy, discontented, and dissatisfied, and that, fortunately, has no essential existence as such.

And until we see this caterpillar for the chimera it really is, we'll only have a passing acquaintance with our true butterfly nature, that part of us that is free, spacious, and unbounded, that real Self who has never been born and so will never die.

Trying to locate the individual "somebody self" that we're so sure, in our ignorance, is really there is like trying to find that bespectacled little guy with the red-and-white striped shirt and beanie known as Waldo (aka "Wally" in some markets), hidden inconspicuously within a vast crowd of people.

Only it's worse, because in this case "Waldo" isn't there at all. No needle to find in the haystack. Attempting to locate the self that we are so convinced really exists but can't be found is like playing the "Where's Waldo?" from hell!

• • •

When we think of ourselves, who is it that we are thinking about?

Who is it that we think sticks his or her head inside those carnival cutouts: the groups we identify with, the jobs that help define us, the roles we assume in our skein of relationships (father, mother, brother, sister, son, daughter, friend, enemy)? Who is it that we think is angry, jealous, proud, envious, or depressed?

Beneath all the superstructure of personality makeup, memories, emotions, conditioning, and role-playing, who is the "I" that *has* a personality, a past, mental afflictions, an occupation, a set of relationships, and all these various roles to play?

In the Buddhist scriptures, it is said that the self we think exists but doesn't exist is one that (if it truly existed) would have three essential traits: it would be *unitary, independent, and unchanging.* But a particular, individual self—the "you" that your name refers to—with any of these three qualities is totally *unfindable.*||

Now, dear reader, be forewarned: you might not appreciate how the proof for this unfolds. Your egoistic, self-infatuated but ultimately imaginary self will try to protect itself from being exposed for what it is. It will protest; it will feign boredom; it will say,

> **Oh, whatever. Let's take a break from reading this bit and get something to eat!**

However, ignorance is *not* bliss. The truth is what will set you free. But first, as Gloria Steinem once observed, it will piss you off.[5]

So here we go . . .

Unitary means we believe there's only one of us. Unless you have a serious case of multiple personality disorder, you think of yourself in the singular, not the plural. When we think or speak of ourselves, we say "I," not "we" (monarchs using the royal "we" excepted).

The classical analysis when it comes to trying to find this particular Waldo is called "The One or the Many." Is the self one thing, or is it many things? If the self were to exist in the way we think it does—as a real thing, something perceptible—it would have to be either one or the other.

Although we normally assume that the egoistic, personalized self is unitary, we should ask ourselves, "Does this supposed singular thing have parts?" And yes, we could say we are indeed made up of two main components: physical and mental, the body and the mind.*

And we do, at different times, identify with one or another or both of these parts.

If I were to ask you, "How old are you?" and you gave me a number in response, you would have just identified with your body. And if in reply to the question "How are you?" you said "*I am* upset, aggravated, pleased, OK," or whatever, you would have identified with your feelings, with your present state of mind.

So already there is a problem here. How can the one self be *both* the body ("*I am* six feet tall") *and* the mind ("*I am* stressed out")? That's two things, not one—two kinds of selves, one physical and one mental, but not a unitary "I."

And when we look at either one of these two great portions of the supposed individual and indivisible self, we find that they themselves are not really single things either. What we call "the body," as if it were one organism, is itself composed of many constituents—the torso, the limbs, and then all those yucky things inside the body that we talked about earlier in this chapter. And each of these separate parts is infinitely divisible into its own constituent parts. Even a single finger can, upon investigation, be dissected into the part above the knuckle and the part below, the fingernail part and the part beneath the fingernail, the left side of the fingernail and the right side—and on and on, ad infinitum.

There's *no part of us that isn't further divisible into its own parts*. That's what's entailed in saying "a part"; it's something that has a right side, a left side, a top, and a bottom (the parts of a physical object), which makes it different from other parts. And the same is true with a moment in time: a thought arises, lasts for a while, and then ends, and each of those three parts of the moment itself has a beginning, a middle, and an end.

When we say something like "right side" or "beginning," these parts of a part can always be further partitioned: "right side of the right side, left side of the right side, top and bottom of the right side;" or "beginning of the beginning, middle of the beginning, end of the beginning."

And so it is that if we think we *are* the body and/or the mind, that self cannot be unitary, but in fact would be endlessly multiplied and fragmented.

Oh, come on! I didn't really think I actually was my parts. I'm not my body and mind; I have *a body and mind. Now can we please stop thinking about this and get something to eat?*

OK then. So while we might sometimes carelessly identify with one or another of the various constituents of the self, maybe the "I" we think we are is *separable from* those parts. And this would be the second of the three qualities that we attribute to the personal self: *independence.*

The investigation applied to this second kind of misconception about the self is called "The Same As or Different From?" It goes like this: Is the self *the same* as the parts that comprise the self, or is it *different from* (i.e., independent of) those parts? And like "the One and the Many," if the self really and truly exists the way we think it does, it can't logically be both. It's an either/or proposition.

So let's check. If the self were *the same as* its parts, it couldn't be a unitary self, for as we've seen there are lots and lots of parts, physical and mental, that would comprise a self that was the same as its parts. If I were identical to the parts of me, there would be as many me's as there are parts to me.

That leaves the other option, that there's a self that is *different from* the parts. This would be a self that is independent of the parts, a self that *has* a body and mind. And "independent" means "doesn't need them." The body and mind could then be heaped together in London while the self could somehow separately be in New York City.

But that's impossible, isn't it? For one thing, whose mind is it that's thinking about a self that exists apart from the mind that's thinking about such a self? And in any case, that's not the you-say-your-name-to-yourself self we are so sure must be somewhere floating around inside the mind-body complex.

A room *has* four walls, but where is *the room* that has four walls? The self that we imagine has a body and mind is as unfindable as a unitary self that's *the same* as the body and mind. "The self," like "the room," cannot really exist independent of the parts that make its shadowy semblance possible.

Now this is really enough! Why can't he just leave us alone? What about that snack?

Finally, we turn to the third impossible thing that we believe when it comes to ourselves: the idea that there is an *unchanging* personal self. This is sometimes called the "witness self"—an invariable "I" that has observed "me" growing up as a child, graduating from school, getting married, having a family, moving from one house to another, and is presently watching "me" get old and moving nearer and nearer to death.**

We all have this sense that there is an unchanging witness self that carries on continuously as everything else—life as a whole, one's thoughts and feelings, and every individual part of the body—is perpetually and ceaselessly changing. So where's that Waldo? Can we really believe that there's a tangible, perceptible present self that is in any real way whatsoever the same as the self we were when we were three years old?

Yes, we can believe that, as long as we don't have to think about it, so just quit it already! Like Popeye said, "I y'am what I y'am and that's all that I y'am!" Why bother with all this! Let's just stop this thinking about things, OK? I'm hungry . . .

To "The One or the Many" and "The Same As or Different From," we can now add a third kind of analysis to our "Where's Waldo?" search from hell: "Changing or Unchanging?" Where is the individual, particularistic self that remains unchanging as everything else in us and around us changes? Or more subtly, where's the self that *undergoes* change? If there's only a constantly fluctuating self, there's not also an unchanging witness self, let alone an unchanging self that also undergoes change.

So the exercise is now complete. Disoriented? Confused? Filled with objections? Well, it's no wonder. As I warned you above, the ego doesn't like this "Where's Waldo?" game one bit! All kinds of resistance arises in ourselves when we try to find the "somebody self" we think is ourselves!

But I just know I'm somebody! There's probably some trick here. How could it be that I'm really nobody when it feels so obvious that I am somebody? And I still didn't get my snack!

• • •

And there is a trick here, actually. The self can be thought of as *both* unitary and plural, as *both* the same as and different from its parts, as *both* changing and continuous—because *the self is just an idea, not a thing.* From one perspective, the self can be conceptualized as singular, independent, and unchanging; and from another perspective it can be thought of as plural, contingent, and fluctuating. It depends how you look at it—because the "somebody self" is not really there at all apart from our thinking it's there.

When it comes to the little, individual, particularistic, snow-flake, caterpillar self, there is not a findable unitary, independent, unchanging entity either inside or apart from the body and mind. The "somebody self" is not a discrete, discernable object; it is only a conceptualized image.

When we say we have a "self-image" or a "self-conception," we're way more accurate than when we say we have a self or when we claim *to be* somebody.

The "Waldo" we try to find when we go looking for it turns out to be only imaginary. Remember the movie *Harvey*, with Jimmy Stewart? The one whose lead character was always accompanied by an invisible six-foot rabbit? Well, the self we think we are is just as imaginary as Jimmy Stewart's friend Harvey the rabbit.

But imaginary things can feel quite real and can function quite well to bring us a lot of difficulty in life. The Mother of the Mother of All Mental Afflictions—ignorance about what kind of self we think we have—leads to all kinds of problems.

Our belief in the "self-existence" of the personal self—the feeling that Waldo (or Harvey) is *really there* apart from our merely think-ing he's there—inevitably engenders what is called in the Buddhist texts "self-cherishing." We become enchanted with and seduced by an illusory impression of the individualized self, and then we grasp and cling to it for dear life.

All the other mental afflictions—desire, anger, lust, pride, jeal-ousy, envy, greed—arise either to defend or to promote what is, after all is said and done, just a misconception. Ultimately, we are impris-oned not by these negative emotions, but by the imaginary self who is adversely affected by them.

THE CAPTAIN KIRK SELF

There's another false notion we have about ourselves that we haven't examined yet. It's the sense we have that there's *a self who's in control of the present*, a "master self" that rules over the current state of the body, the mind, and, indeed, all aspects of our life.

I like to think of this version of "me" as the "Captain Kirk self."

In the original *Star Trek* television series, the spaceship *Enterprise* was overseen by Captain Kirk, played by William Shatner. He was often depicted sitting in his commander chair—a replica of which I've seen for sale, priced at over two thousand dollars!—on the upper deck of the starship, gazing out at the cosmos through that cool wraparound windshield. And Captain Kirk would bark out orders to his crew: "Scotty, raise deflector shields!" And Scotty would dutifully obey: "Aye, aye, sir! Deflectors raised."

Somewhere ensconced inside the head, just behind the eyes (our own personal windshield of our own personal Spaceship Me) is where we usually locate the Captain Kirk self. And just like the dear captain, that commander self barks out orders: "Legs, prepare to walk!" "Mouth, commence talking!" "Mind, remember to pick up some milk!"

And often enough, our lackey crew obeys. The legs move when ordered to walk, the mouth flaps when instructed to speak (sometimes even before the mind is commanded to think!), and frequently we do remember to get the milk when Captain Kirk enjoins us to.

These kinds of experiences give us a strong conviction that this master self is in charge not only of what the body does and the mind thinks but also of everything else in our lives. And when confronted with incontrovertible evidence that contradicts our conviction, it's usually quite upsetting. When *we don't get our own way*, the old Captain tends to pitch a fit!

If there really were such an all-controlling self, why would that ruler ever decree that we have a bad day, or get upset at an annoying person, or have a headache, or get sick or old, or choose to be anything other than happy and content all the time? If our own personal Captain Kirk truly existed, wouldn't some of his commands seem sort of wacky? "Scotty, let's get really gloomy today. Raise depressors!" Wouldn't Scotty's clear retort be, "Captain, are ye mad? Have ye gone insane?"

In fact, there is no real Captain Kirk self, just as there's no unitary, independent, or unchanging personal self. And here's the real proof of that: *we can't change the present in the present*. If there were a Captain Kirk self, we would command everything in life to be just as we wished. And that's obviously not happening—have you noticed?

As you can probably tell from all my references, I watched a lot of television as a kid. Readers of a certain age might actually remember viewing two shows I used to like from the 1960s—*Bewitched* and *I Dream of Jeannie*. In the first, Elizabeth Montgomery played Samantha, a full-blown witch with all kinds of supernatural powers, married to a pretty hapless ordinary mortal named Darrin. When Samantha wanted to effect some change in a situation (often to fix something poor Darrin had messed up), she would simply wiggle her nose and—*shazam!*—the world would bend to her witchy will.

Bewitched met with some success—it was the second most watched program on television in 1964, and nearly forty years later *TV Guide* magazine included it in a list of "The 50 Greatest TV Shows of All Time"—so it wasn't long before a similar program, *I Dream of Jeannie*, went on the air. The premise again involved a match-up between a magic-making woman (a genie this time) and a normal guy (who was, however, an astronaut, whom his devoted wife called "master"—a patriarchal fantasy, simultaneously subverted by the mismatch when it came to actual power).

In addition to offering a genie instead of a witch in the lead role, the other major difference in the two programs (product differentiation!) was that Jeannie didn't wiggle her nose to magically transform reality whenever she wished. Her modus operandi was to fold her arms and forcefully nod her head such that her long ponytail would flop around a bit. And that was enough to change anything she wanted, right there and then, in the moment.

Most of us go through life wiggling our noses and shaking our ponytails, trying to miraculously transform the present in the present. But things don't work like that; we're not witches and genies, and the confirmation of this is all too apparent. The traffic doesn't unsnarl just because we wish it would; the headache doesn't disappear simply because we don't like having it; and the annoying person doesn't magically stop being annoying when we, metaphorically speaking, twitch our nose or bounce our ponytail. We can't wriggle our way out of tight spots just by wiggling our appendages!

The desire to change the present in the present is perhaps the biggest and most recurring itch of all, but it's the one we clearly can't alleviate by sorcery scratching. That mojo ain't working. The Captain Kirk/Samantha/Jeannie self is really (to switch the pop-cultural reference yet again) the Wizard of Oz, just a humbug behind the curtain, ineffectually moving nonfunctional levers and pulleys.

YOU ARE WHO YOU THINK YOU ARE

The realization that the "somebody self" is *just an idea* should come as really good news. If there were *essentially* a unitary, independent, and unchanging individual self, it would be, well, unchangeable. But luckily, as we've seen, there is no such self. And so it's a good thing that *we are not really the somebody we think we are.*

But, then again, you could equally say that *we are just the some-body we think we are*, and that's all the "somebody" any of us is. It's the conceptualization of somebody that makes us that somebody—and really nothing more than that. As one ancient Indian text puts it, "The one who thinks he is free is free; the one who thinks he is bound is bound. It is true what they say: *You become what you think*."[6]

To say that the "somebody self" we usually desperately clutch to is illusory is not the same as saying it doesn't exist at all. The individual self does, of course, exist . . . but only as an idea, a concept, a label. As philosopher Julian Baggini puts it, "The idea of the self as a construction is one that many want to resist, because it seems to imply that it is not real. But of course constructions can be perfectly real."[††]

And there are different kinds of constructions or conceptualizations of the self, some more beneficial than others. The belief in a unitary, independent, and unchanging self; or the conviction that there really is an all-powerful Captain Kirk self—these are not helpful concepts. Besides the fact that there's no findable "Waldo," the very idea of a self like this leaves us feeling either paralyzed (how could we change such an unchangeable self?) or frustrated (Captain Kirk's commands so often go unheeded!).

The "somebody self" is just like the room we talked about above. The room has four walls, and there's no room without the four walls, but "room" is just a name and a concept that arises due to the empty space enclosed by the walls. And it's just the same with the individual self: *it's nobody that makes somebody possible*.

We're nobody apart from thinking that we're somebody, and when we stop thinking we're somebody, we're left with really nobody. This observation points us to the true methods for "self-improvement," which we'll investigate at length in the next chapter.

The question is not *whether* our individual sense of identity exists. It obviously does; we hear that little voice inside our heads pretty much constantly. The crux of the matter is *how* such a self exists—and how we could improve it.

By recognizing that we're nobody (that is, that we're not a hard-wired somebody who exists essentially and unchangingly), we have the possibility of conceptualizing ourselves as a *better somebody*—a more contented, happy, and fulfilled person.

And by doing so, we will have moved closer and closer to the Great Itchlessness we all desire.

Action Plan: Scratching the Itch

Stop for five or ten minutes each day and pinpoint your biggest desires, your most persistent itches. First identify what it is that you want. Is it more money, a better house or car, or a new iPhone? Or is it an improved relationship with your partner, your family members, or with someone at work? Maybe it's more recognition and popularity, or a holiday in Bermuda. Or perhaps it's losing a few pounds or feeling healthier.

Once you've identified the itch, focus on what you hope will be the outcome if the itch gets scratched—on what you think would happen if you actually obtained what you desire. See if you can't get to the realization that what, in fact, you wish for is actually just contentment—the end of the itchiness itself.

Then revisit the particular desire you've identified. Would getting what you want really bring about the hoped-for satisfaction, or would it just provide some partial and temporary relief from the wanting? While we may not be able to achieve contentment immediately, this action plan helps us train ourselves to be more aware of what it is we really desire.

Notes:

* Overachieving, type-A personalities who are obsessed with their careers might recall that God's curse for humanity as he kicked Adam and Eve out of the Garden was to cause man and woman thereafter to work for a living and look after their children, instead of granting us a permanent holiday.

† There are some exceptions. For stories of how ignorance originated in the Hindu and Buddhist texts, consult Wendy Doniger O'Flaherty, *The Origins of Evil in Hindu Mythology* (Berkeley: University of California Press, 1980).

‡ Another indication that people are not *essentially* the way they sometimes appear to be is that they don't *always* seem to be that way. Sometimes angry people appear angrier than at other times, and sometimes they don't appear angry at all. If the angry person were *essentially* an angry person, he or she would *always* be an angry person, to exactly the same degree. For an "angry person" would always be that and couldn't essentially be that and something other than that at the same time. Isn't that what "essentially" means, after all?

§ In some Indian texts, the Sanskrit word *atman* is used differently than it is here in the Yoga Sutra and in many Buddhist scriptures. Elsewhere it is synonymous with the "true self" as opposed to an individual, egoistic self (which is sometimes designated as the *jiva* to contrast it with the *atman*).

‖ The latest research in the neurosciences is validating the ancient Buddhist observations. As one recent summary puts it, an unchanging and continuous self, a "unifer" self, and an "agent" self (similar to the "Captain Kirk self" talked about later in the book) are all "mistaken beliefs" or "illusions" that "do not withstand scrutiny." See the special issue of *New Scientist* magazine, "The Self: The Greatest Trick Your Mind Ever Played" (February 2013). See also Julian Baggini, *The Ego Trick: What Does It Mean to Be You?* (London: Granta Books, 2011).

\# There are neuroscientists nowadays who believe that the mind's activities—consciousness, thought, emotions, and so forth—can be reduced to the brain and its firing of neurons. While only a few researchers would be so reductive as to say there is absolutely no difference between the mind and the brain (most still acknowledging some sort of "ghost in the machine"), there does seem to be a trend toward the position that ultimately there are *only* physical parts to our being. While such a reductive view of the self does not accord with the assumptions of any of the world's spiritual traditions—indeed, it is the *opposite* of a belief in anything *spiritual*—it has no bearing on our argument here: Are we *one* thing (even if it's just a purely physical thing, just the body) or *many*?

** The "witness self" spoken of here can be distinguished from one of the two "birds" we encountered in the passage from the Upanishads quoted toward the end of chapter 1. The "bird" who looks on impassively as the other "bird" (the individual self) eats and engages with the world, is the true Self—the ocean as opposed to the individual wave; our nameless true nature, not you say your name-to-yourself.

†† Baggini has coined this term "ego trick" to describe the play between the self we think exists and the conceptualization of the self that does exist: "The Ego Trick is not to persuade us that we exist when we do not, but to make us believe we are more substantial and enduring than we really are. There may be an illusion as to *what* we really are, but not *that* we really are." Julian Baggini, *The Ego Trick*, 41, 152.

4
Nobody Makes a
Better Somebody Possible

There is only one corner of the universe you can be certain of
improving, and that's your own self.

—Aldous Huxley

BECOMING A BETTER SOMEBODY

If the individual self is, at bottom, nothing but a conceptualization
of the self, then one important part of the spiritual quest will be to
improve that self-conception. While there may not be a findable
essential "somebody self" to ameliorate—and, remember, the real,
oceanic "nobody/everybody" butterfly self is in no need of improvement at all—the personal self that does exist can and should be
developed into a better edition.

As we noted toward the end of the last chapter, it is precisely
because we are not stuck with the somebody we think we are now
that we can upgrade ourselves into a more self-satisfied model.

And there's nothing wrong with wanting to become a better
somebody. Indeed, without a desire like this, we'll never get to the
point where the Great Itchless State becomes possible, and where
the peace and tranquility of *being nobody* can be fully experienced
and appreciated.

Because it's possible, we should definitely strive for self-improvement. Because we're all really, deep down, nobody, *everyone has the potential to become a different somebody*. We can choose to continue to embrace a depressed, discontented, and perpetually itchy sense of self, or we can work toward creating a joyful and fulfilled personal identity that is nourished by the deep reservoirs of our true identity.

We can change. We can better ourselves. We can create a happier iteration of the self to replace the needy, greedy, twisted version that's driving us crazy. But self-improvement will be achieved not through trying to be *more special* than others, either through foolish pride or through laying claim to an exceptional status due to our suffering.

It's worth repeating: There's nothing inherently wrong with being "self-interested." It's crucial to build a good, healthy sense of the individual self—not as the final goal but as a necessary platform for the higher work of joyful self-transcendence and integration with the world around us. *Enlightened* self-interest entails wising up to what will really work to bring about an untroubled and contented personality, somebody who's ready, willing, and able to be less self-obsessed and self-centered.

Remember, it's not really "self-improvement" if it's all about you.

• • •

The "somebody self" is an artifact of how we presently regard ourselves. And this, in turn, depends on the kind of past we think we had (for *we are who we think we once were*) and our expectations, hopes, and fears about the future (*we are who we think we will become*). The conceptualized "somebody self" is found at the nexus of two times—the past and the future—that themselves only exist as ideas within the present mind.

This "somebody self" is the product of moral training and positive self-development—or the lack thereof. There's a huge difference in the self-perception of someone who has cultivated humility, modesty, and an unselfish and charitable attitude toward others and that of someone who is driven by inborn (and reinforced) selfishness, vanity, pride, and aggressive competition with others.

We've seen in the last chapter that we *can't change the present in the present*. Captain Kirk can't just dictate that things change at will in the moment, nor can any inner witch or genie work this kind of magic. This means that somebody can't just *in the moment* choose to be anybody; the "somebody self" can't *immediately* transform into somebody different. We can't go from zero (selfish, egotistical, and dissatisfied) to one hundred (humble, altruistic, and untroubled) in just a few seconds, or even a few days or weeks or months.

The lower, individual self is an idea of the self, but our self-conception is constantly in flux. This self, we could say, is a *process*, not a thing. To invoke a very common and ancient simile, the self is like a river—let's say the Mississippi. What we call "the Mississippi River" is not an entity or a thing; it is only a name we give to a particular flow of water—to a process. As Paul Robeson famously sings, "Ol' Man River just keeps rolling along."

We mistake changing things for unchanging things. We assume that, because we have *a name* or *a concept* for "the Mississippi River," the word and the idea must refer to some thing, when all it really designates is a flowing current, a movement, an activity.

Well, our sense of personal identity is just like a river. Every part of what we include in our idea of "me"—every physical and mental component of the self—is changing, moment by moment. The kind of idea I have about "me" deceives me. I think my concept of "me" refers to a unitary, independent, and unchanging entity, when all it denominates is a flow.

And so even what we mean by "me" changes over time, doesn't it? What Julian Baggini calls the "autobiographical self" provides a sense of continuity to the self: "The unity and permanence we feel over time depends on our ability to construct an autobiographical narrative that links our experiences over time." "But," Baggini goes on to observe, "individual experiences and sense of self at any particular time can vary enormously. What is more, the autobiographical self is very good at self-revision. In effect, we are constantly rewriting our histories to keep our inner autobiographies coherent."[1]

The self is *mutating* and therefore *mutable*. Otherwise what would be the point of a spiritual practice? If we weren't *changing*, we couldn't *change*! Every authentic spiritual tradition has always assumed that, because the "somebody self" is just a process and not a thing, the process we call "me" can be redirected and differently channeled.

We can transform our understanding and evaluations—not only of ourselves, but also of other people and of everything about our lives. We can train ourselves to change our minds—not in the blink of an eye, of course, but over time. We can gift ourselves with a different set of ideas about both our inner and outer worlds.

And, as we shall see toward the end of this chapter, these two different conceptualizations of our reality—inner and outer—are in a symbiotic relationship.

By cultivating wisdom, we can learn to think differently about both ourselves and the people and things in our outer world (remember, no annoying people or intrinsically tasty ice cream *out there*). With more awareness of the changing nature of the "autobiographical self," we learn to direct that change in a more positive way. Wisdom about the externals will help us act, speak, and think in such a way that we'll improve our sense of self—and this, in turn, will transform our view of the world and the other people in it.

How Karma Really Works

As we saw in the last chapter, we all have a bad case of the "if only" syndrome. We are convinced that *if only* we could adjust the external events in our lives to our satisfaction:

> *If only I had a better job, more money, a nicer home, a new iPhone, a holiday in Bermuda . . .*

And *if only* we could figure out how to make other people in our lives change to our liking:

> *If only my husband or wife were nicer to me . . . if only my boss weren't so demanding . . . if only I could make that annoying person stop being so annoying . . .*

Then, finally, we'd be happy. We're all pretty itchy, pretty much all the time.

In our ignorant and self-centered desire to work our will on the world, we usually just send Captain Kirk out on the case. We hope that the good old Cap'n will micromanage the external world and the people in it so that all will become pleasing instead of so problematic.

But as we've seen, the Captain Kirk self is an ineffectual humbug. It is therefore unsurprising that he is impotent to effect the changes we demand. Events in the outer world aren't modified at our command, and other people don't automatically adjust themselves and their actions in accordance with our mandates.

We are perpetually thwarted in our attempts to work the magic that would change the *present in the present*.

There is, however, a more efficacious method at hand for transforming our lives for the better. We can still hope for a happier future, but we must also accept that there will be a gap between the time of the cause and that of the effect. This gradual method for transformation is what the Eastern traditions would call "changing your karma," or what Jesus spoke about in terms of "sowing what you will reap," or what we colloquially mean when we say "what goes around, comes around."

The basic "laws of karma" can be succinctly stated: "No action in this world goes for naught or brings about a contrary result," as one ancient Indian text crisply puts it.[2]

The first principle—"no action goes for naught"—proclaims that every action will have a reaction; everything we do, say, or even think will have future consequences. And the second rule— "no action brings about a contrary result"—asserts that the kind of outcome one will experience depends on the kind of action that produced it. No cause brings about a "contrary result": nothing bad can come from something good, and nothing good can come from something bad.

These principles are not the creation of any one religious tradition. They are found, in one form or another, in many and various places. In the Yoga Sutra we read, "There is a causal connection between meritorious and blameworthy acts and their respectively cool and pleasurable or scorching and unpleasurable effects."[3] Jesus put forward the same karmic law in more metaphorical terms by noting that you don't get grapes from thorns or figs from thistles:

> You shall know them by their fruits. Do men gather grapes of thorns, or figs of thistles? Even so every good tree brings forth good fruit; but a corrupt tree brings forth evil fruit. A good tree cannot bring forth evil fruit, neither can a corrupt tree bring forth good fruit.[4]

What makes an action "good" or "bad"? An act (inclusive not just of physical acts but also those of speech and even thought) done with a good intention—that is, with a selfless, kind, altruistic, compassionate motivation—will bring about a good (that is, pleasant) result. Conversely, a bad act is "bad" because it is inspired by an intention fueled by one or another of the mental afflictions, all of which are instigated by selfishness. Such a negative action—motivated by ignorance, self-aggrandizement, or the wish to harm others—will bring an unpleasant consequence in the future.

All authentic spiritual traditions teach some form or another of "karma." The fundamental principles we've just discussed form the very heart and soul of every moral system. There's no "system"—and therefore no hope for willed self-improvement—if there's not the assumption that:

1. Every action has a consequence, and
2. The type of result (pleasant or unpleasant) invariably correlates to the nature of the cause (kind or unkind, selfish or selfless).

The first principle denies randomness and therefore empowers us, while the second provides the basic method for governing the direction of one's karma in cultivating a better life.

So far, so good. But while the fundamental rules of karma are both easy to grasp and universally advocated in every ethical system, the actual operation of karma works at a level different from the one we usually think. The project of knowing how to improve the "somebody self" depends upon a belief in moral causality (which gives us confidence that improvement is possible), but also on an understanding of *how* such beneficial transformation can really occur.

Karmic management—creating the causes for a more agreeable life in the future—can easily be misconstrued as just another attempt to magically bend the world and other people to one's self-centered will. When there's only a superficial grasp of karma, the Captain Kirk self is resurrected, albeit in a slightly different guise:

> *OK, I get it now! I can still have my way with the world and with other people . . . I just have to be a little more patient! If I don't hurt others, in the future no one will hurt me. If I am generous, then the boss will someday give me a raise. If I'm patient with my annoying brother-in-law, he'll eventually change into a friendlier person.*

This simplistic, mechanistic, and ultimately narrow-minded and self-seeking understanding of karma is really just the ego grabbing onto a new-and-improved technique in order to once again try to achieve its narcissistic ends. It's the "if only" syndrome at work all over again: *If only others would behave themselves; if only I had more money; if only my brother-in-law were a nice guy.*

The sole difference between this view and the usual version of such wishful thinking is that now we have come into possession of this cool spiritual tool called "karma" in order to realize our longings.

No matter what guise the Captain Kirk self assumes, the egomaniacal assumption persists: We will be able to get whatever we want from the world, and we can make other people behave exactly as we wish, if we can just somehow find and pull the right strings.

• • •

There are some presentations of karma that lend themselves to the mechanistic theory discussed above. But even in those versions of karmic causation, bets are very much hedged. For one thing, according to the texts of Tibetan Buddhism, the precise workings of karma are classified at the level of "very subtle" (as opposed to "obvious" or just plain "subtle") and they're knowable only to enlightened beings, who, unlike us, are supposedly omniscient.

Futhermore, karmic results—becoming famous through practicing humility, or getting money by being generous—are said to ripen in one of three possible times: in this very life (could be tomorrow, could be seventy years from now), in the very next lifetime (when you'll be a dramatically transfigured version of "you"), or (wait for it . . .) in any lifetime after that.

The exact time when one will reap what one has sown is as unknowable as the exact form the reapage might take.

There's a joke that underlines this point. George is magically transported to heaven and meets with God. The visitor is astounded by how dissimilar God's paradise seems from life on earth.

"Wow, it sure is impressive here! So different from where I come from! Say, God," George asks, "how much is a million dollars on earth worth in heavenly currency?"

And God answers, "One penny."

George is, needless to say, quite impressed. Just one of God's pennies is the equivalent of a million dollars!

So he persists in his questioning: "And how long is a hundred years in divine time?"

God replies, "One minute. One minute up here is equal to a hundred human years."

George, suitably dazzled but with his wits still about him, makes a request: "Before I go back to earth, could I get one of your God pennies to take home with me?"

"Sure," God answers. "Just wait a minute."

• • •

It's best not to regard self-improvement through karmic management as a matter of manipulating and upgrading outer events and other people. Positive actions of body, speech, and mind will indeed have positive results. But it's more realistic to think about the fruit of good karma ripening internally, not externally.

As Tolstoy once observed, "Everyone thinks of changing the world, but no one thinks of changing himself."[5]

Karma is not some kind of magical, mystical technique for genetically modifying difficult people or for physically re-engineering events in the material world. Karmic management is primarily a method for *systematically changing one's self-perception*. What we can most effectively, efficiently, and reliably transform is ourselves—and not the world, let alone other people who have their own karma to work out.

In Shantideva's *Guide to the Bodhisattva's Way of Life*, we are given direction as to where to concentrate our efforts when it comes to changing our karma:

> And so, although I am unable to exercise control over external phenomena, *I will restrain my own mind*. What else is there that I can really control?[6]

This verse points us to a more commonsensical understanding of causation and self-improvement. Karma isn't about creating the causes for altering the behavior of other people (*I'm being nice so my husband will change and stop being mean to me*) or directing the processes of the external world (*I'm being generous so more money will come my way*). It isn't about changing the data. The data will change all right, but always in unanticipated, unpredictable, and, as the text says, uncontrollable ways.

In any event, whether other people appear to us as "nice," or whether a particular amount of money is "enough" are subjective *interpretations* and not objective, measurable phenomena. If one's subjective perspective changes, one's perspective on how much money makes you rich or how nice other people are will change as well.

Karma is not like gravity; it is not some kind of invisible external "law of nature." It is first and foremost an internal law governing our own state of mind. And so, karmic management is really about changing our own frame of reference—"restraining my own mind" from creating negative karma—so that our outlook on others and on life itself is not so distorted by our own mental afflictions. It's about transforming our perception such that it is conditioned not by our worst tendencies but rather by virtues like forgiveness, compassion, love, wisdom, and a magnanimous spirit.

When we see ourselves struggling to overcome our own negative proclivities and replace them with goodness, we plant "karmic seeds"—a metaphor for what we nowadays would call "memories" (conscious, subconscious, or even unconscious). And as we know, memory does not simply replay what *really* happened but what we *think* happened, which can and does change over time.

It is what we *think* we have done, said, or thought in the past—in a word, our karma—that defines us in the present. Our concept of our personal identity—*who we think we are*—is a function of *who we think we used to be.* And both our present sense of self and the memories that constitute it are perpetually changing and therefore changeable.

In the Buddhist texts, a big debate rages over where, exactly, the karmic "seeds" we planted in the past were "stored" until they were ready to ripen. Given that we always come up empty-handed in any "Where's Waldo?" search for an immutable and enduring individual self, how does karma persist from the time of its creation to the time of its fruition?

The answer is that karma is conserved in the "simple me"—our basic sense of who we are at any given moment. Karma is memory—again, conscious, subconscious, or unconscious—and it is memory that comprises our current identity. If you don't believe me, try to imagine who you would be if you had no past! As filmmaker Luis Buñuel has said, "Life without memory is no life at all. . . . Our memory is our coherence, our reason, our feeling, even our action. Without it, we are nothing."[7]

The "me" who created my past karma is long gone, but the "me" I presently conceptualize is an idea based on my memories of who I once was and the kinds of things I think I once did, said, or thought.

There's no enduring, abiding self that *has* karma. The conceptualization we have of ourselves *is* karma.

The memories that shape our self-image are called *vasanas* in Sanskrit. They pervade our consciousness in the same way that the fragrance of perfume lingers in a room even after the person wearing it has departed. The "room" that is our present identity is saturated with, and defined by, the aroma of our past karma.

So one way to improve the conception of the self is to rehabilitate the memories we are carrying around. *The past is never like it used to be*. It is forever undergoing reinterpretation. For individuals as for groups, *there's no history except for revisionist history*. As psychologist Mihaly Csikszentmihalyi has written, "The past can never be literally true in memory: it must be continuously edited, and the question is only whether we take creative control of the editing or not."[8]

Since what we call our "past" is really only some part of our present mind, and since our present is constantly changing, our idea of the past is in flux too. Instead of carrying around—and defining ourselves by—a past replete with bitterness, recrimination, and disappointment, we can work at revising our personal histories in such a way that forgiveness replaces anger, gratitude takes the place of resentment, and acceptance supersedes thoughts of sadness and regret.

People who have made peace with their past will have gone a long way toward improving their present sense of self-esteem. Not only will their memories have been altered and improved, but the very acts of forgiveness, gratitude, and acceptance will have modified their sense of self. Rather than thinking of oneself as an embittered, traumatized victim, one can begin to conceptualize the self in terms of the virtues one has practiced in relation to the people and events of the past.

Karma can, in this way, work both retroactively and proactively. By practicing forgiveness, gratitude, and acceptance vis-à-vis our past, we create the causes that will result, over time, in a better self-image. And in the future, we will remember ourselves as someone who was trying to forgive, to be grateful, and to be accepting of all that has happened.

If karma is memory, and memory is what composes our self-image, then improving our sense of self is a matter of acting, speaking, and thinking such that we will look back at our lives with dignity instead of embarassment: *I was the kind of person who tried to live a good life, a life guided by nonviolence, honesty, integrity, charity, and the other virtues.* We practice being a better person today (not just in terms of our past, but in an ongoing way as we interact with the world and other people) so that we will think about ourselves in a better way tomorrow.

Furthermore, by paying more attention to our ethical life, we will have also transformed even our present conception of ourselves. If we can generate conviction in the laws of karma, and if we start living our lives in accordance with what will bring us more happiness and less suffering, we will begin to see ourselves differently in the present. We will regard ourselves as a person who is guided by the karmic laws instead of someone who is just unthinkingly going through life on automatic pilot. Our current level of self-esteem will instantly rise when we become more cognizant of the consequences of the actions we take to enhance our future level of self-esteem.

Karma shapes our perspective of ourselves—and the idea of the self is the only self we have ever had. Trying to manipulate and master other people or external phenomena in order to feel better about one's own life is usually a pretty ineffectual gambit (have you noticed?).

What I can change is myself. And, as the verse says, "What else is there that I can really control?"

"IT'S LIKE THIS NOW"

So now that we're acquainted with the theoretical blueprint of how self-improvement really occurs, it's time to put theory into practice. The secret to feeling better about ourselves and our lives, as we've seen, is not to expect the world and others to be different than what they are. It is rather to accept the hand we're dealt at any given moment, and then learn to play our cards in such a way as to improve our estimation of ourselves as a player.

Here's a little mantra—words of power—that I've found to be extremely helpful for staying focused on the task at hand. It's a kind of acceptance mantra—an embrace of reality as it is, not as we wish it would be. So let's call it "the reality mantra," since it's meant to keep us concentrated on what is actually happening in reality:

Om, it's like this now, ah hum.[*]

Om traditionally marks the start of a mantra. It means, "Here comes a mantra." And *ah hum* signifies the end of the incantation.

"*It's like this now*" are words of absolute truth, and this is one aspect of their power.

Because it is always the case, right? It's always "like this now," isn't it? The hand we've been dealt at any given moment is the only one we have to play.

Please note that the mantra is *not* "It's like this now, and I wish it weren't." That's the usual spurious mantra of discontentment and non-acceptance. Nor is the mantra, "It's like this now, and I wish it would stay like this forever." That's the fanciful mantra we recite to ourselves in those (relatively rare) times when things are going just the way we want them to.

So the mantra has to be continually repeated, because the "now" in "It's like this now" is perpetually on the move. If we are to stay in reality rather than drift off into fantasy, we have to keep up with the ever-changing present.

The first element of the actual practice of self-improvement is accepting *what is* rather than either wishing that it were different or that it would freeze-frame and stay the same.

Now for the next step: *Since it's like this now, what would be my most intelligent response? How to best play these cards I've been dealt?* Instead of just unthinkingly reacting to situations, we try to stay mindful and rational and think:

What can I do, say, and think in this situation that would enrich rather than diminish my self-image? Will what I do now be something I will regret in the future, or something I can look back on with satisfaction that I did my best?

Because we misunderstand the nature of our "somebody self," we habitually respond to difficult situations and people with our untrained feelings rather than with an educated view of how the personal, individual self exists—as a constantly changing and evolving idea or conception based upon karma.

We think of the self in an erroneous way, and therefore want always to preserve and enhance the identity we think truly does exist as a unitary, unchanging, independent, and Captain Kirk self. So when faced with difficult situations or people, we respond defensively or aggressively. Instead of using the rationality of our heads and the compassion and love in our hearts, we acquiesce to our selfish instincts and untrained habits.

When someone is angry with us, we respond with anger; when someone hurts us, we feel we must strike back. When we are faced with an unwanted event, we flail about, trying to avoid or change it in the moment instead of thinking about how we could best preserve our present peace of mind and create better memories with which to define our future.

But in order to make the smart choice in any given situation, we have to fight our tendencies to succumb to our selfish negative feelings, our mental afflictions. The guidelines for an intelligent and compassionate response to any situation can be set out as simply as the laws of karma themselves:

❧ Do unto others as you would have them do unto you.
❧ Do not do unto others as you would not have them do unto you.

Just as you don't want to suffer, others don't want you to return anger with anger, hurt with hurt, lies with more lies, untrustworthiness with some version of the same. Changing our habitual responses to the events and challenging people in our lives involves shifting the focus from what *seems* to be "good for me" (and harmful to others) at any given moment and concentrating instead on what will *really* be the best way to improve my sense of self—here and now and also in the future.

And from the karmic point of view, what's actually best for us will also be what's best for the others around us. *Om, it's like this now, ah hum.* So how, in every moment, can we act, speak, and think in such a way that we'll be happier and make the lives of those around us better, not worse?

The way to improve our self-image, the truly efficacious method for upgrading the "somebody self," is to train ourselves to stop reacting negatively—defensively or aggressively, protecting or promoting the self-centered ego—and instead respond in such a way as to increase our sense of self-worth.

We must use our "best friend" self to overcome our "worst enemy" self. If we really want to improve and help ourselves, we must side with the angel inside of us, not with our demons.

Who else will overcome your unhappy, depressed, discontented self if not you? Who else besides you will make you a better "somebody self"?

THE BIG SMACKDOWN, RAGE IN THE CAGE

Because self-improvement really is possible, it's our responsibility to make efforts to accomplish it. And it will take effort. It's naïve to assume that responding wisely and kindly to difficult events or annoying people will be easy. Our contrary habits are deeply engrained. Our habitual responses are like knee-jerk reactions.

When the mental afflictions arise—rage, vanity, lust, jealousy, resentment, annoyance, self-deprecation, and so on—there's a strong air of inevitability about them. We feel, in the moment, *compelled* to do, say, or think things we soon regret (or at least *should* regret). We excuse ourselves or apologize to others by saying, *I'm sorry, but I just couldn't help it!*

We all know how it goes. Someone says or does something that we don't like—something that insults or injures or provokes our "somebody self." A force is awakened, an energy that seems to have a life of its own. Like in the *Alien* movies, the affliction feels like an aroused monster that just pops out of our gut.

And then the alien power starts to surge through our being. The negative feeling seems to rise up in us (one old expression for getting angry is that "the ire rises"). Left unchecked, the mental afflictions move from the solar plexus area and make their way up through our tightening chest and throat and quickly hijack our heads.

The negative emotion takes possession of us. We "lose it," meaning we "lose our temper" or basically go temporarily insane. We become the puppet of the affliction and do, say, and think unpleasant, hurtful, and damaging things.

If we wish to free ourselves from the negative emotions—if we are to change these foolish and self-destructive responses—we must prepare ourselves for battle. Old habits are hard to break. We must gird our loins and train for the Big Smackdown, the Rage in the Cage, with our mental afflictions.

•   •   •

I was a big wrestling fan when I was a kid (*professional* wrestling, not the more staid and rule-governed collegiate or Olympic version), and so was my grandfather. We'd watch televised matches between characters called "Gorilla Monsoon" and "Dick the Bruiser" and marvel at the feats of violence: one combatant would jump off the top rope in the ring and smash his elbow into the throat of his opponent lying prone on the mat—stuff like that.

Both my grandfather and I were totally convinced that this kind of wrestling was real. It drove my dad bonkers! We would watch eye gouges, "sleeper holds" (pinching some "nerve" in the shoulder that would render the opponent instantly unconscious), death grips, and elbows to windpipes—not to mention the fully illegal bashing with chairs and attacks with smuggled blackjacks, brass knuckles, and razor blades. All this, my dad adamantly maintained, had to be fake.

You know the adage? Grandparents and grandchildren generally get along so well because they share a common enemy. My granddad and I derived a certain perverse pleasure in the apoplectic response we got from my father as we held firmly to our faith that wrestling was a real "sport" and not just athletic "theater."

If we are to defeat our mental afflictions, we have to be like the professional wrestlers. We need to get ready for the Big Smackdown. We have to be ruthless and brutal with our negative emotions, for they are our true foes. While our human "enemies" have lots of other things to do when they're not harassing us—sleep, eat, carry on relationships, tend to business, pursue hobbies—our mental afflictions have nothing else to do but destroy our happiness.

There's a big misconception about the spiritual life. There is a widespread assumption that the spiritual practitioner should always remain in a sort of otherworldly and catatonic state—tranquilized, muted, and peacefully inert.

But the true spiritual renegade is not some namby-pamby navel-gazer, looking vague and flashing the peace sign at his or her negative emotions. It may come as a surprise to some that many spiritual texts use the language of violence and war in relation to the project of self-control.

The Buddhist classic *Guide to the Bodhisattva's Way of Life* by Shantideva, for example, urges us to be "fierce warriors" when it comes to overcoming what the text refers to as our "congenital enemies." Just like soldiers on the battlefield, we should be brave when it comes to our own personal Rage in the Cage. Knowing that the struggle will not be easy, we should steel ourselves and resolve to persevere no matter how difficult it may be:

> In the heat of battle, fierce warriors are able to swiftly kill those who, ignorant and unhappy, will die anyway. Although tormented by countless wounds from arrows and spears, they do not turn away until they've accomplished their goal.
>
> When I am intent on slaying my congenital enemies, the causes of all my continuous suffering, why am I now depressed and dejected, even if I must put up with hundreds of difficulties?[9]

Warriors on the battlefield, boxers in the ring, and, yes, professional wrestlers in their smackdowns get even more psyched when injured. And we too should become even more maniacal when the opposition puts up resistance in our personal struggle with our own worst inclinations.

The *Guide* also urges us to be not only strong-willed but also merciless when it comes to the Big Smackdown. We all have the tendency to make excuses for our thoughtless reactions. Even worse, we defend, justify, and rationalize our afflictions:

> **So what if I got angry and yelled? She deserved it! I just had to set her straight!**

And worst of all, we go so far as to identify with our negative emotions—and thus define ourselves through them:

> **I am jealous; I am proud.**

In order to live happier lives, we must stop pampering, excusing, rationalizing, and identifying with the enemies of our peace of mind. If we leave the door open even a crack, they will surely rush in. If we continue to mollycoddle these nasty demons, they'll beat us every time.

That's why Shantideva exhorts us to *get medieval* on the little buggers!

> Let my guts ooze out and my head fall off—whatever! But I will never, no matter what, bow before my enemy, the mental afflictions.[10]

Nothing namby-pamby about that, right?
Let the Rage in the Cage begin!

• • •

What are the weapons we'll need to fight the mental afflictions? What kind of wrestling holds can we apply the next time one of them raises its ugly head? And what sort of "illegal" implements can we smuggle into the Rage in the Cage that might give us a fighting chance in our efforts to defeat our worst enemies?

Recognition

Just acknowledging the mental afflictions as harmful, rather than as necessary or even desirable constituents of our being, will go a long way toward helping us beat them.

A smoker friend of mine refers to cigarettes as his "little friends." They're always there for you, he explains. First thing in the morning with your coffee, all day long as you work, with a drink at the end of the day, after meals or sex—you can always count on your "little friends" to help you get through life.

Many of us regard our mental afflictions as our "little friends" instead of our worst enemies. Labeling them more accurately will help get us psyched for the Big Smackdown.

Understanding

Mental afflictions always justify themselves. It is, in fact, part of the negative emotion's modus operandi to appear to be a reasonable response to a difficult situation. But this is a serious mistake. The mental afflictions are not rational at all; they are harmful emotional outbursts that reduce us rather than lead us to a better self-perception.

I had a student who once told me that she was having a hard time breaking her habit of getting angry. "I get such clarity when I'm mad," she reported. "With anger, things really come into focus and I feel such certainty."

And yes, as we all know, there is the sense of great lucidity that comes with a strong emotion like anger. Everything is indeed quite starkly black and white: *I'm right; they're wrong.*

But when the spell of the affliction is broken, we often realize that the seeming clarity that came with the negative emotion was actually a distorted, skewed view of the actual situation. A powerful feeling, wholly in service to the ego, was masquerading as a hyper-rational, objective evaluation.

The mental afflictions do not actually bring us real lucidity, and they do not arise out of rational, objective calculation. No one in the cold light of day chooses to have a mental affliction attack. No one, when faced with a problematic person or situation, judiciously, cogently, and reasonably considers their options and then elects to have a big meltdown.

This person just said something I didn't like. Hmm. I wonder what would be the best thing to do here, for my own present and future happiness and peace of mind? Oh, I know! I'll increase my blood pressure and heart rate, get all knotted up and tense inside, go red in the face, and say things—maybe really loudly with lots of four-letter words—that I'll probably regret a few hours from now!

So another major weapon we can develop and then bring into the Big Smackdown is wisdom and understanding. Remembering how karma works to create our sense of self, we remind ourselves that if we want to have a better self-conception we'll need to avoid the temptation to give in to the siren song of the afflictions. And so we dispel the affliction's spell of pseudo-rationality.

With wisdom we understand that *it is never in our self-interest to be anything other than cool, calm, and collected.* It's never intelligent to capitulate to a mental affliction. Giving rein to our worst inclinations is neither rational nor advantageous.

Self-improvement derives from self-control, not from self-indulgence.

De-identification

Disassociating from the negative emotions gives us more power over them. We are *not* our jealousy, pride, envy, anger, or depression. A mental affliction may have arisen, but regarding it as an alien power will reposition it as something other than "you." You will be fighting them, not integrating and identifying with them.

Determination . . . by any means necessary

We've already seen how important unwavering resolution is in our battle with our negative emotions:

Let my guts ooze out and my head fall off—whatever! But I will never, no matter what, bow before my enemy, the mental afflictions.

Any other attitude we take with our afflictions will only sustain and invigorate them. The "by any means necessary" determination is perhaps the most powerful arrow in our quiver as we wage war against our inner enemies.

And like the professional wrestlers I used to watch on television, we can't be too scrupulous about what methods we use to try to win the match. Full nelsons, scissor holds, kicks to the head, but also blackjacks, folding chairs, and razor blades—we have to resort to whatever weaponry will help us emerge victorious from the Big Smackdown.

Once more, we let the *Guide* be our guide. In order to aid our good intentions, resolution, and determination to become a better, more self-controlled person, the text recommends a truly radical method, one that bends the usual rules. We are told how to smuggle the blackjacks and brass knuckles into the ring.

We are charged to use and direct the mental afflictions against themselves. As in some of the martial arts, we take the energy of our opponent—and make no mistake about it: anger, jealousy, pride, and strong desire have great energy—and we turn it to our own advantage.

And so Shantideva draws a distinction between the mental afflictions that function as our enemies and the very same energies when utilized as our allies. The *Guide* recommends, for example, that we abandon patience (the usual antidote to anger) and *get angry at our anger*!

Stationed within my own mind, they are perfectly situated to destroy me. And yet I do not get angry. To hell with this inappropriate patience!

I will be tenacious and intent on revenge! I will wage war against my mental afflictions—except for the kind that are designed to obliterate mental afflictions.[11]

Get angry . . . about being a slave to anger![12] Be proud . . . of efforts to overcome pride.[13] Be envious . . . of those without envy!

And be strongly desirous. Desire the defeat of the opponent in the Big Smackdown, the Rage in the Cage. Desire self-improvement. Desire a better self-image, the reward of self-development through self-discipline and karmic management.

And finally, desire with all your heart the end of desire, the Great Itchlessness that is the end of desire, contentment itself.

• • •

"I count him braver who overcomes his [negative, selfish] desires than he who conquers his [external] enemies," said Aristotle, "for the hardest victory is over self."[14]

It has been recognized since at least the ancient Greeks that it is hard to change self-destructive habits and replace them with beneficial ones. It's difficult for the self to overcome the self. It's totally worth doing—and we should fervently desire it—for it's the only way to really improve our self-esteem. But no one is saying it will be easy.

And so, as we engage in our regimen of self-improvement through karmic management, we have to expect setbacks.

We won't always emerge from the Big Smackdown victorious. There will be plenty of times when the mental affliction du jour will defeat us, even when we put up our best fight. We may offer resistance, but there is a point of no return where we just capitulate:

Oh, the hell with this! I don't care if this affliction is bad for me! I don't care who I hurt—myself or others!

And we give in to the urgent demands of the affliction, and the negative emotion wins that round of the wrestling match.

When we are temporarily vanquished by our own worst inclinations—when we submit to the powerful wrestling holds of anger, desire, jealousy, resentment, and prideful arrogance—it feels like we're a character in a cartoon. The affliction grabs us by the throat, and we become a rag doll as we are bounced against the wall and swung up and down and right and left for a while. We are in the throes of a force that is currently greater than the potency of the weaponry we are using to combat it.

We then must switch into a defensive rather than aggressive strategy. We cover up and try to protect ourselves the best we can in order to minimize the damage.

The first line of defense is to break our opponent's hold as soon as possible. Many of us are accustomed to letting our mental afflictions have their way with us for hours, days, weeks, or even months and years. A spiritual warrior will wait until the overwhelming force of the affliction lessens its death grip a bit. But when it does, he or she will immediately shake it off:

OK, that's enough now. I gave in to my resentment, my arrogance, my anger, or my jealousy, but I will not let it ruin another minute of my life! I may have lost this round, but I will not concede the match!

Freeing ourselves from its hold, we get back on our feet and ready ourselves for the next encounter with the enemy. We go back to the spiritual gym and work out some more. We fortify our weaponry in preparation for the next bout. We *recognize* that the afflictions are the real and only enemy to our happiness; we *understand* that self-improvement is a matter of fighting old habits and replacing them with new ones; we *de-identify* with these nasty tendencies; and we *determine* to be victorious in the next round of the Big Smackdown.

A second defensive strategy to employ when we lose the Big Smackdown is to not use the setback as just another way to feel bad about ourselves. Regret, yes; but guilt, no—and there's a difference. Feeling guilty about our failures, like the depression that often feeds on such guilt, is really just another form of narcissistic self-absorption. It doesn't help, and in fact it saps the energy we need to feel better about ourselves.

Regret, on the other hand, is the acknowledgment that giving in to the mental afflictions hurts oneself and others. Regret always entails the resolve to try harder not to do that kind of thing again in the future. While guilt debilitates, regret inspires us to strengthen our willpower to become stronger and better prepared for the next confrontation.

And a third defensive tack: we (once again) de-identify with whatever mental affliction has temporarily defeated us. We don't join enemy forces; we don't surrender to the provisionally victorious affliction and become its prisoner of war.

Even Shantideva, Mr. "Be a Spiritual Warrior," knows we won't always win the battle with our bad habits. And so we read,

> Whenever you fail, your cheeks should burn in humiliation and you should think: "What can I do so that this doesn't happen to me again?"[15]

When you fall off the horse, you dust yourself off and get back up on it for the next ride. This is called "practice." We renew our efforts and strengthen our will. And this is the only road, rocky as it may sometimes be, to real self-improvement.

Remember the "reality mantra":

Om, it's like this now, ah hum.

Given that this mantra is perpetually relevant, we can deploy it also in those times of failure:

It's like this now. So what can I do now to avoid future defeat at the hands of my mental afflictions?

PLAYING FOR BIG STAKES

There is a very helpful spiritual maxim—perhaps the most effective of all the tools we can employ in our laborious undertaking of self-improvement:

If you can't do it for yourself, then do it for others.

There's a tremendous power in altruism. I'm reminded here of news stories that tell of a small child pinned under a car. The child's mother, filled with adrenaline due to her panic and desperate wish to rescue her beloved offspring, just lifts up the car by the bumper, snatches the kid out of harm's way, and then drops the two tons of steel back on the ground.

In the next section of this book, we'll learn more about both the power and joy of self-forgetfulness. But even in our quest for self-improvement, thinking about others and not just ourselves is ultimately our greatest resource.

Creating a better "somebody self" involves understanding how karma really works in order to gradually give one's self-image a makeover. And our self-conception begins to change immediately upon making the shift from ignorant self-indulgence to informed self-rehabilitation. We start to think of ourselves as someone trying to be a *better* somebody rather than as someone addicted to becoming *more* of a somebody. We begin turning our attention to others and how we can help rather than hurt them.

We focus on our ethical behavior and wage war against our mental afflictions, our true enemies who both destroy our current happiness and plant the seeds for an unhappy "somebody self" in the future. We hone and deploy the weapons of recognition, understanding, de-identification, and determination in our internal battle with our demons, and we do not get discouraged with the setbacks and failures that will inevitably be part of our path. We remember our mantra—*it's like this now*—and we play the hand we've been dealt with wisdom and skill, remembering that self-improvement is possible and knowing how it will be effectuated.

We try to play our cards smartly, but we should also recognize that the stakes are high. We are in every moment creating the causes for who we will be in the future. For our future happiness, or its opposite, depends on what we do, say, or think in the ongoing present.

But here's the real rub. Here's how high the stakes really are. Your world, and all the people in it, will change when you change.

Change you, change the world.

• • •

This, I fully acknowledge, is extremely hard for any of us to believe. It is virtually inconceivable to think that we as individuals have this kind of power, as it is sort of overwhelming to be laden with this kind of heavy responsibility.

It's one thing to think that we can change and improve ourselves. While most of us assume this is possible, it seems far-fetched indeed that there's any correlation between an inner transformation and a change in the outer world.

But what we make of our lives has repercussions far beyond what we ordinarily believe. What we do, say, and think defines not only who we are but also what kind of world we live in and what sort of people we encounter. If we truly wish to help others and create a better world, helping ourselves turns out to be the best way to do that.

And if we are to come to actually believe this, we'll have to very carefully go through the logic for why this is so, and we'll have to repeatedly rehearse the syllogism.

Ready?

None of us has an objective view of our external world.

When we aren't actually thinking about it, we all feel that we see things, events, and people *as they really are*. But this is an illusion, another trick of the egoistic self. Nobody has a "God's eye" view on reality.

If we're honest with ourselves, we can't help but admit that we are human beings and not digital cameras or recorders. And as humans, we're not like detective Joe Friday in *Dragnet*, who gathers "just the facts, ma'am." None of us is privy to "just the facts"; we're only privy to what we *think* "the facts" are.

And as psychologist Mihaly Csikszentmihalyi writes, "How we feel about ourselves, the joy we get from living, ultimately depends directly on how the mind filters and interprets everyday experiences."[16]

Since none of us has an objective take on things, each of us necessarily has only a subjective view of the external world.

Because we're not machines but living organisms called "people," our respective perceptions of the world, events, and other people come from a subjective, and not an objective, perspective.

Put otherwise, all the data received by our senses is strained through our subjective filter. We don't see, hear, feel, taste, or touch the outside world in an unmediated fashion. We *interpret* what we experience in order to experience it.

And the way we interpret things, events, and people is determined by our conditioning, by our karma. There are a multitude of factors that constitute the subjective filter through which all the external data must pass in order to be comprehended. The language we speak and the linguistic categories with which we think, the cultural and historical conditioning and assumptions of our place and time—these form one part of the subjective filter. But additionally there are even more individual factors, such as our personal history, the ideology or belief system we adhere to, our psychological make-up, even how we are feeling on any particular day, and the prejudices and biases that derive from and are shaped by all of these conditions.

The "subjective filter" is really just another name for what we've been calling the "somebody self." And so it is that we see the world not *as it is* but *as we are.*

If you change your subjective perspective, you change your experience of the external world.

If you accept the above two premises, then here is the first of the necessary logical conclusions: when you change your interpretive lens, you change your perceptions. Change you, and you'll change your viewpoint on external events and other people.

We all have experience of this. One day you wake up on the "right side of the bed" and the world looks pretty good—you're relatively happy with your life and the people in it. But the next day, when you wake up on the "wrong side of the bed," that same world takes on a different hue.

George Eliot wrote, "Will not a tiny speck very close to our vision blot out the glory of the world, and leave only a margin by which we see the blot? I know no speck so troublesome as self."[17] Our "somebody self" blocks out much of the range of possibility and permits us to see only a fragment of potential reality. But when we alter the "troublesome speck of the self," we gain a different perspective on the world around us.

So self-improvement improves not only your sense of who you are, but it also cleans the filter through which you process what's outside of you. When you feel better about yourself, the world and other people seem more approachable and less problematic.

As we've seen, the individual self is nothing other than the sum total of our karma. When we change our karma, we change our sense of self, and thereby also change the subjective filter through which we apprehend the world.

OK so far?

If you have followed me through these first three steps of the reasoning, then here comes the real kicker.

If you change your subjective perspective, you change the world.

Wait a minute! What happened? That couldn't be. I've been tricked!

No, you've just followed the logic of the syllogism. Since none of us has an objective view of the external world, and since all of us only experience the world from our subjective perspective, if we change our subjective perspective, we change our perspective on the world.

And the world seen from the subjective perspective is *the only knowable world there ever has been, is, or will be for any of us.* So we might as well just call it "the world."

Change you, change the world.

Get it? No? Review the steps. We all need to work through it over and over again. Because if we have even an inkling of how self-improvement goes hand in hand with the amelioration of the world we live in, it will supercharge our efforts to better ourselves.

The stakes are high when it comes to self-improvement. And so, once again, when the going gets tough—when the Big Smackdown with the mental afflictions seems too daunting—remember the maxim:

If you can't do it for yourself, do it for others.

Action Plan: The Daily Rage in the Cage

Single out your worst negative emotion, your number-one mental affliction. (If you need some help, ask someone who knows you well; they'll tell you!) Begin your own daily Rage in the Cage with the affliction, employing the techniques we've discussed in this chapter—recognition, understanding, de-identification, and determination. Don't be discouraged when the negative emotion wins the Smackdown. Review the defensive strategies above, and get back into the ring for the next round!

And remember, your indulgence of the mental affliction is not making the lives of those around you more pleasant. Take strength in your consideration for their well-being. *If you can't do it for yourself, do it for others.*

Notes:

* I believe this mantra—at least the "it's like this now" part—originates with Buddhist teacher Jack Kornfield, although he may have gotten it from someone else too.

PART III

LOSING THE "SOMEBODY SELF"

5

Being Nobody for Others

Whatever suffering there is in the world
comes from the selfish desire for happiness.
Whatever happiness there is in the world
comes from the desire for the happiness of others.
—Guide to the Bodhisattva's Way of Life

WHAT CAN I DO FOR YOU?

Any task is easier if it's done selflessly rather than egotistically, and that very much includes the big life project of improving the "somebody self"—and thereby improving the world we live in.

The means to real self-improvement is, paradoxical as it might seem to the controlling, Captain Kirk self, a function of self-forgetting. We are happiest when we leave off assessing and evaluating our own relative happiness and become absorbed in something or someone other than ourselves.

In this section, we will examine two interrelated techniques for discovering more of the joy and fulfillment that *being nobody* can bring to our lives. Both methods involve losing the "somebody self"—either by fully engaging in unselfconscious action (that's in the next chapter) or, as we'll see here, by freeing the ego from its endless itching through empathetically thinking about someone else and their wants and needs.

It is not through incessant self-consciousness but rather through dissolving ourselves in something or someone other than ourselves that we access the greatest source of transformational power we have available. It is when we can *drop the demands of the "somebody self" and be available for others* that we create the karma for improving our self-conception and the quality of life we lead.

Karmic regulation, far from being just another method for ego-enhancement, is the only effective method of self-help. And at the very heart and soul of self-improvement through karmic management is t*he ability to put others and their interests first.* Contrary to our usual unenlightened beliefs, *the best thing we can do for ourselves* is to consider how we can help others.

At first, it might seem a bit like driving a car with the accelerator floored while simultaneously stomping on the brake. Two apparently opposite operations occur simultaneously: we forget ourselves and turn our attention to others, all the time knowing that thinking about others and their needs is the best and only way to our own personal fulfillment.

• • •

"The most satisfying thing in life," writes Pierre Teilhard de Chardin, "is to have been able to give a large part of one's self to others."[1] We all know that some of our deepest and most rewarding experiences in life come when we can forget ourselves in service to another. We derive much of our joy in life from caring about and for other beings: our children, parents, lovers, friends, and even our pets.

As we witnessed in the last chapter, we usually can't trust either our untrained instincts or the mental afflictions they inspire. Or, it could also be said, we *can* trust them—*to be 180 degrees wrong.* Just check for yourself: What responses do your instincts immediately advocate when someone hurts, offends, insults, or betrays you? These habitual reactions are in need of retraining, and this is the first task of self-improvement.

Fortunately we have certain instincts that we *can* trust, and those are the ones we should nurture and strengthen. Our deep-seated need to connect with others, to love and empathize with fellow human beings, is surely one urge we should cherish and nourish. The affection and concern a parent has for a child; the gratitude, respect, and responsibility a child feels for his or her parents; the heart-felt and intimate sense of union between lovers; the bonds of loyalty and camaraderie we share with close friends—these are inborn positive emotions that our relationships with others inspire and call forth.

The inner angel strongly desires the self-forgetfulness—or perhaps we should say, self-expansion—that can accompany these kinds of links with other people. But the inner demon—concerned only with the lower, egoistic, caterpillar self—misconstrues and, often enough, subverts this aspect of our lives.

As we know all too well, the relationships we maintain with our significant others not only deliver the joys of interconnection and freedom from alienation; they can also inflict on us our greatest disappointments, aggravation, and animosity. That which is potentially one of the sources of our highest happiness can be (and, sad to say, often is) the cause of considerable frustration.

The spiritual project—and the path to true contentment—require that we tutor our self-destructive inclinations such that they can align with our deepest desire and purpose in life: to achieve the "Great Itchless State" so that we can help others achieve it too.

We ally ourselves with the inner angel—that part of us that longs for the freedom that comes from relinquishing the purely egoistic orientation—and we disavow the self-preoccupied "me-first" demon that keeps us tethered to our lower, individual self.

Grasping to our individuality, to the little self we're so attached to, we invite unpleasant feelings of separation and isolation. Good relationships hinge on our ability to set aside the individual self's insatiable need to be venerated. The tiresome chant—*What about me?*—is replaced with a different incantation—*What can I do for you?*

RELATIVITY THEORY

None of us is an autonomous, disconnected little island. We are inevitably and perpetually engaged in interactions with the other people in our world—physical or mental, and for better or worse. These relationships not only affect our sense of self, they constitute it. Just as we don't *have* karma but *are* our karma, we also don't *have* relationships but are *defined* by them.

The personal self does not exist independently, only dependently. It is dependent on the body and mind that acts as the basis for the idea of the self (as we have seen in chapter 3), and on the karma or memories that fashion our self-conception (as we noted in chapter 4).

But we also exist in relation to our relationships. Every role we inhabit is made possible only *in relation to somebody else*. What Zen teacher Thich Nhat Hanh calls "interbeing" (as opposed to the "illusion of our separateness")[2] describes not just our interpersonal relationships but our reality as a whole.

• • •

We have already encountered a *negative* description of how the world really exists: Things and people are *not* perceived by any of us objectively. Just as we ourselves do not have a hardwired "self" in the way we think we do (recall the "Where's Waldo?" search), it is also not possible to identify some kind of unchanging and definitive essence for anyone or anything. Remember our examples from chapter 3? There are no *essentially* aggravating people in the world, and there is no *essentially* tasty flavor of ice cream.

But this negative assertion must be carefully distinguished from the nihilistic idea that what's external to us doesn't exist at all, that it is some kind of fantasy conjured up by "me" (whoever *that* is!). The external world and other people in it *do* exist—and here's the positive articulation—*dependently*. There *are* aggravating persons, but this depends upon others being aggravated by them. Ben & Jerry's Chunky Monkey ice cream *is* delicious, but only to someone (like me!) who judges it so.

And it's like that with everything. Everything, without exception, depends on something else, and that something else depends in turn on something else! And so this positively stated depiction of reality is more accurately put like this: everything and everyone exists *interdependently*, not independently.

You know that old puzzle? If a tree falls in the forest and no one is there to hear it, does it make a sound? The answer is *of course not*! And here's why:

There is nothing perceivable in the world until and unless it is perceived. There can be, for example, no *audible sound* like that of a tree falling in the forest until and unless it is *heard* by someone. And while we may have all kinds of objections to such an apparently audacious statement, what would it really mean to assert that a sound occurs when no one hears it? Wouldn't such a position have to posit an *inaudible* (that is, not heard by anyone) audible sound?

We're not talking here about a sound's *potential* to be heard. *Potentially*, all kinds of things are possible. What we're discussing here is how things really are. Something is audible only when it is heard by a hearer, and not until. Right?

Similarly, there is no visible object until and unless it is seen by someone—for if there were, there could be an invisible visible object! There's no odor until and unless it's smelt, there's nothing tangible that isn't felt, there's no tasty thing (like ice cream!) without a taster. And there's no thought that exists independently of a thinker who thinks the thought.

An unthought thought, an invisible visible object, an inaudible sound, an unsmelled smell, an intangible tangible thing, an untasted taste—these are impossible things, totally inconceivable!

Too theoretical? Here's the cash-out.

This truth of interdependence buttresses the startling conclusion of the last chapter: *Change you, change the world.* Because the external, perceivable world exists (for any of us) only in relation to being perceived (by any of us), the way it exists (for any of us) depends upon us, on the perceiver. If you want to perceive the external world—things, events, and other people—in a better way, adjust the perceiver, the lens through which the world comes into existence. *Change you,* and you will *change the world.*

But here the other shoe drops: in accordance with the interdependence of things, it's not just that perceptible objects depend upon a perceiver in order to be perceptible; because things exist *interdependently,* it is also the case that *perceivers become perceivers only when they perceive something.*

For a seer to be a seer, he or she must see a visible object, right? Can't be a "seer" if you aren't seeing something! And you can't be a "listener" until and unless you hear some sound. In what sense are you a "seer" or "hearer" (actually, not potentially) until and unless you see or hear something? And the same is true with the smeller, feeler, taster, and thinker; they exist dependently on what they sense—a smell, a tangible thing, or a thought—just as what they sense depends on being sensed in order to exist as such.

And here's the relevant consequence of that dropped shoe. It's the inverse of our previous formula: *Change the world, change you.* If our sense of self—the perceiver—depends upon what is perceived, then if we learn to perceive things, events, and people differently we will change as well.

We see things and people not as they are but as we are. But because of interdependence, it is also the case that *we are what we see* (and hear, smell, feel, taste, and think). The perceiver is defined by what is perceived, and vice versa, and that's another reason why "it's all relative"—everything and everybody exists within the matrix of interdependence.

If, for example, we see "problems" as "opportunities," we will feel less embattled and thwarted, and will instead view ourselves as more engaged and empowered. If we focus on the good qualities of our aggravating person, we will be less aggravated. And if we engage with others with love and compassion, we will experience those relationships, and ourselves, in a much more positive way.

"I AM BECAUSE YOU ARE"

Because everything exists interdependently and not independently, our sense of self is inextricably entwined in and constituted by our relationships with others. We depend upon other people to be who we are.

There's an African concept called *ubuntu*, which is summarized in the proverb "I am because you are" and explained by Archbishop Desmond Tutu in this way:

> My humanity is caught up, is inextricably bound up, in theirs. We belong in a bundle of life. We say, "A person is a person through other people." It is not "I think, therefore I am." It says rather: "I am human because I belong. I participate, I share."[3]

None of us is somebody without other somebodies. All the roles we play—every one of the carnival cutouts we stick our faces in—are made possible by our relationships with others. We are fathers or mothers dependent upon having children; we're children only because we have parents. We're "a friend" because there is someone we're friends with, and we're "a lover" because there's someone (other than ourselves!) to love.

Our professional identities are likewise always relational. A "doctor" can only be so because of patients, a "teacher" because of students, and a "car mechanic" because there are car owners whose vehicles need servicing. And as we observed in chapter 2, we also define our individual selves in relation to the communities we identify with—our nationality, race, religion, or whatever.

Group identities, no less than individual ones, exist only in relation to others; they are forged in opposition to those who belong to different communities. As we've seen, we conceptualize ourselves as "American" because we're *not* "Canadian"; if we're "Buddhist," it's dependent on us *not* being "Christian." And so it is that we are also defined even by relationships with those we don't consciously identify with. We are annoyed because there are people who annoy us; angry and upset because others seem provocative; resentful or envious because of another's actions or status.

We are tied to those we dislike just as we are to those we more willingly associate with. Relationships fueled by negative emotion keep us chained to a self-conception marred by disaffection and unhappiness. As writer Ursula K. Le Guin observes, "To oppose something is to maintain it."[4] We can only think of ourselves as victims because we think of others as oppressors.

We can't be *somebody* all by ourselves, and the kind of "somebody self" we think we are exists dependently on the quality of our relationships. If we establish and maintain pleasant, loving, supportive relationships, we feel one way about ourselves. But if we are continually hassling with others, our self-image will suffer and our lives will continue to be troubled by these interpersonal difficulties.

· · ·

The mental afflictions we spoke of in the last chapter almost always arise in relation to someone else. While we sometimes get angry, greedy, or prideful in relation to inanimate objects or events, it's when there are other people involved that we really get our backs behind the negative emotion.

We've talked about some of the tools available to us to combat those disturbing feelings as they rear their ugly heads:

* Recognition: "This mental affliction is not my 'little friend.'"
* Understanding: "It's never in my self-interest to give in to such destructive emotions."
* De-identification: "This affliction is *not me*."
* Determination: "I will combat this feeling with all my might!"

All of these methods involve turning inward. We introspectively identify and combat the negative feelings within ourselves as part of the project of self-improvement. The Rage in the Cage occurs within ourselves. But we also realize that, by changing ourselves through this kind of self-mastery, we will alter our perceptions of the people and situations that once evoked such destructive sentiments in us. We purify the subjective filter through which we perceive external things and beings and thereby clean our karma:

Change you, change the world.

But as we've seen, there is a second method for transformation that stems from the theory of relativity and interdependence. Instead of focusing within, we turn our attention outward. If we can learn to perceive the things, events, and especially the other people in our world as beneficial instead of problematic, as targets of our positive feelings rather than our negative ones, we'll automatically gain a happier sense of self:

Change the world, change you.

And there is one powerful emotion, one virtuous state of mind, that we can direct outwardly in order to transform our perception of other people and thus our relationships with them.

FIND SOMEBODY TO LOVE

There's an old song made famous by Dean Martin, "You're Nobody 'til Somebody Loves You":

> *You're nobody 'til somebody loves you*
> *You're nobody 'til somebody cares.*[5]

Dino croons on about how you might "be king" or possess all the riches of the world, maybe even the world itself, but no amount of riches can bring you true, lasting happiness. These lyrics convey a certain truth about the most important source of our self-esteem and self-worth. It's not our wealth, possessions, or professional achievements that now or in the end, when you're growing old, are of the greatest importance. We are indeed nothing without the meaningful, loving relationships we establish and maintain with others.

When my dad was a resident in an assisted-living facility (what used to be known as the "old folks' home"), I would travel to visit him once or twice a year. It was not much of a sacrifice for me—a couple days out of my life—but it was a big deal for him. He would parade me around, introducing me to his friends at the facility, showing me off—not so much for how special I supposedly was, but for the very fact that I was there at all, that I had come to visit him.

In conversations with my father and other elderly people at the old folks' home, I learned that what really mattered to them was not their former professions (no one spoke much about what or who they "used to be") or the possessions they had once acquired (now, for the most part, gone) or the exotic holidays they once enjoyed (just fading memories and tattered photographs).

None of this was that important to them anymore—and none of it will be important to any of us if we're lucky enough to grow old before we die.

What mattered to the elderly was who loved them. What was of greatest import was who cared about them enough to come visit, to spend a few hours of their lives with those who had been stripped of the more tenuous ego props we often rely on to feel like we're really somebody.

And, of course, the old folks also talked a great deal not only about who loved them, but about those they loved. When the "somebody self" has been reduced to being just another inhabitant in a retirement facility, much of life is lived vicariously. The activities of the children and grandchildren, the nieces and nephews, take on greater significance. The focus in such a situation, almost by necessity, tends to turn away from the self and toward others.

It's like that, too, in times of crisis. When the chips are really down, we humans often rise to the occasion, break out of our self-imposed egoistic confines and instead think about how we can help those in need. There are, unfortunately, countless examples of such terrible times. The great tragedy of 9/11 brought out the best in many New Yorkers, who selflessly aided and supported each other in the darkest of times. And there have regrettably been more recent and continuing incidents where a disaster elicits heroic responses of self-sacrifice and concern for others.

But it's not necessary to wait until old age or a crisis situation to exercise our greatest instinctual drive—to love and care for someone other than ourselves.

• • •

"You're nobody 'til somebody loves you," as the song title states, but the lyrics continue to take things in a different direction:

> You're nobody 'til somebody loves you,
> So find yourself somebody to love.[6]

The orientation shifts here. Instead of focusing on receiving love, we are advised to give it. "Find somebody to love"—a recommendation put into our pop-cultural consciousness not just by Dean Martin, but also in tunes by Jefferson Airplane ("Wouldn't you love somebody to love? You better find somebody to love") and Queen ("Can anybody find me somebody to love?"), among many, many others.

Instead of dwelling on ourselves and our own need for love, we think of others and how we can love them. *Change the world*—through the power of love for someone else—and you will *change you*.

• • •

The centrality of love is reflected in the fact that our popular culture continually shapes and gives expression to our deep need for it. From television shows and movies to Hallmark greeting cards, from the novels we read to the music we listen to, the theme of love recurs over and over again.

But the message we receive—and often resonate with—is not always helpful for a proper understanding of this all-important human emotion.

In preparation for remarks I was to give as the officiant at a wedding, I did some research and found a database that had compiled a comprehensive list of popular song titles. When I searched for those whose messages might be relevant for a couple that was getting married, I found that many of our so-called love songs conveyed a rather screwy idea of what love is.

I found out that 191 songs have in their title the phrase "you belong to me," and lots of others have variants on this theme:

"You Belong Here"

"You Belong Here with Me"

"You Belong in My Arms"

"You Belong inside My Heart"

"You Belong to Only Me"

There is one song with the title that really cuts to the chase: "I Own You." There are two, according to the database, with the title "You Own Me."

Two songs are entitled "I'm Your Woman."

Five claim "You're My Woman."

Six are called "You're My Man," while forty-five say "I'm Your Man."

And no less than 137 songs have titles that begin with the words "you're mine":

"You're Mine, I'm Yours"

"You're Mine, Heart and Soul"

"You're Mine Alone"

"You're Mine Tonight"

"You're Mine Forever"

"You're Mine Only"

"You're Still Mine"

And on it goes, the epitome of the genre being "You're Mine, Mine, Mine."

Real love is not about owning or possessing another. And love is also not about coercion, about "making" someone love you. Again, our popular so-called love songs reinforce this mistaken idea. Tunes with titles like "I'm Gonna Make You Love Me" or "What Do I Have to Do to Make You Love Me?" create the idea that we can somehow compel another's love for us.

Or, much more often, we believe that the other can or should "make us" something or another, that our emotional life is putty in the hands of others. Sixty-seven songs begin with the phrase "you make me":

"You Make Me Feel Like a Natural Woman"

"You Make Me Feel Like a Man"

"You Make Me Want to Be a Mother"

"You Make Me Feel Like Dancing"

"You Make Me Feel So Young"

"You Make Me Feel Brand New"

And, interestingly, "You Make Me Real."

Consider this title, a combination of both of the erroneous ideas about love—as ownership and as compulsion: "You Make Me Want to Make You Mine."

We are especially encouraged to think that a loved one has the power, and therefore also the obligation, to "make us happy"—a message famously conveyed in the Blood, Sweat & Tears song "You've Made Me So Very Happy."

If we believe that others have it within their power to "make us happy," then soon enough we will also believe that they are capable of "making us unhappy." Instead of taking responsibility for our own happiness and unhappiness, we cede it to others. We saddle them with a task they cannot perform ("you make me so very happy") and blame them for what they do not in fact have the ability to do ("you make me so very unhappy").

True love—whether it is romantic, fraternal, parental, filial, or whatever—is neither about "owning" another person nor about what the other can or should do for you. Rather, it is about what you can or should do for another.

Real love is about giving, not taking. It is the cessation of the "me" orientation and the generation of a selfless concern for another's happiness and well-being.

• • •

The mental afflictions we've been discussing can all be viewed as self-centered perversions of love. Anger ("You're not loveable at all!"), lust ("I love you so much, I must have you to love me!"), jealousy ("You love somebody else and not me!"), envy ("You have something I don't that makes others love you more than me!"), pride ("I am so very, very loveable, don't you think?")—we can view the whole list of negative emotions in terms of our egotistical demands that *others should love us*.

While we all want to be loved in order to feel like a real some-body, we also need to love in order to be loved—and to do the latter, we must exercise self-forgetting. For it is when we suspend our self-centeredness and give ourselves over to others that we tap into the real power of love, the Higher Power, the god (or God) that is love.

The love *of* another is gratifying and helps us feel like a better somebody; but it is the love *for* another, premised on self-abnegation, that gives us a glimpse of our true nature and the real strength and bliss that come from *being nobody*.

You're nobody 'til somebody loves you, so you'd better find somebody to love. And when you do, *you will truly love not as a* somebody *but as a* nobody. As Bhagwan Rajneesh (aka Osho) remarked, "When you love a person, you have to become a no-self."[7]

EMPATHY, OR THE ART OF PUTTING YOURSELF IN ANOTHER'S SHOES

True love—again, not just romantic love but love in all its forms—is an exercise in selflessness, the leap out of the stifling confines of our own individuality and into another's life and their desires, their cares, their difficulties.

The world's spiritual traditions have, in one voice, extolled such altruistic substitution for myopic self-absorption. This is not only because it's "nice" or "good" to be concerned with the well-being of others. It's also because, when we are able to think about somebody other than ourselves, we by necessity must drop the egoistic demands of the "somebody self." The little voice inside stops its *me, me, me* refrain and a different mantra is heard: *What about you? What can I do for you?*

The essence of, and precondition for, selfless love is empathy, the ability to put oneself in another's position, to feel what they must be feeling and to relate to what they must be thinking. While the degree to which we are able to do this varies, the more we empathize with another, the less we are preoccupied with ourselves—and therefore, the more relief we get from the isolation and burden of our disconnected individuality.

Empathy, the prerequisite of altruistic love and compassion, itself depends upon the assumption that others are essentially no different than us. This is why this kind of self-sacrificial emotion is relatively easy (although by no means always practiced) with our families, lovers, and friends. Because we identify with them, we can relatively easily love them "as ourselves"—to "love your neighbor as yourself," as Jesus put it.*

But it's not just those close to us who are like us. We saw way back in chapter 1 that "we're all in the same boat": we all equally are suffering, and we all equally have the desire, innate capability, and right to be happy.

This recognition of the fundamental equality of all human beings (or maybe it would be better to say of all living beings, for animals also share in these two big facts of life) lies behind the invariable principles that should guide all of our responses to others and their actions. We've mentioned them before; they are universally extolled and sometimes referred to as the Golden and Silver Rules:

✢ Do unto others as you would have them do unto you.
✢ Do not do unto others as you would not have them do unto you.

Because we know how we feel when others treat us either kindly or poorly, we know how we should treat them. It is the assumption of our basic equality that makes empathy possible, and, in turn, informs us about how to interact with others with love and respect—friends as well as enemies.

• • •

It is also our ability to empathize—to put ourselves in another's shoes—that provides another clue as to why and how karma really works when it comes to our actions vis-à-vis others. Why is it a karmic "law" that what goes around *unfailingly* comes around? Why couldn't something bad come from something good, and vice versa?

Karma, as we argued in the last chapter, is not operating "out there" as a "law of nature," but rather works to determine our perception of ourselves and of the external world.† Karma as an explanatory system is not about why and how other people are the way they are, or about why and how events occur the way they do. It explains how and why we experience people and events (and also, of course, ourselves) the way we do.

Karma in its causal dimension depends on *intention*. Because we know how it feels to be hurt, for example, we can formulate the intention to hurt others. Similarly, we know how to show compassion, goodwill, and respect because we have been on the receiving end of others' positive actions toward us. We know how it feels to be loved, and because of that we know how to love.

But, as in our previous discussion concerning interdependence, we have to again drop the other shoe: because we know what it feels like to intend to hurt others, we know what it feels like to be hurt.

Suffering and pain don't come so much from the words of another—they're just syllables and decibels until they are *interpreted* as words *meant to be hurtful*. Even when it comes to harmful physical actions done to us, although the body itself may be injured, we are nevertheless much more liable to excuse and forgive if we believe the damage has been done accidentally or unwillingly. It is, again, the cruel motivation that makes the deed most upsetting and least pardonable. The deeper pain is not in the words spoken or even in the physical abuse, but in the belief that it was the other's *intention* to hurt us.

And on the positive side, we know what it feels like to be loved by another because we have loved others. The warmhearted intention we project onto the other is what makes us feel loved, and we can project that intention onto the other because we've already had that same wish ourselves.

This is interdependence when it comes to karma and our relationships with others: (1) Because we know how it feels to be hurt or loved ourselves, we can formulate the intention to love or hurt others; and (2) because we know what it feels like to intend to hurt or love others, we also know what it feels like to be loved or hurt, as we presume the same intention on the part of another.

Karmic management therefore entails another principle: *Think the best of others*—allow for the possibility that they are basically well-intentioned. Because of this assumption—because of interdependence—you'll think better about yourself, and you'll be more likely to formulate better intentions in your interactions with others. This, in turn, will promote the habit of assuming that others' intentions are fundamentally good, like yours are, and on it goes . . . in an upward spiral.

The usual proverb can be inverted: It is *the road to heaven*, and not to hell, that is *paved with good intentions*.

• • •

We should pause here to emphasize something about empathy. Empathy infused with love is not some chuckleheaded, naïve, Pollyanna-ish attitude. Our capacity to put ourselves in another's position allows us to think well of others—repeat this mantra: *we're all just doing our best*—but it also recognizes that others are just like us in another way.

We're all equally fallible; we all make mistakes; we all are liable to succumb to our worst tendencies and to do and say things that we know, when the mental afflictions don't have their death grip on us, are wrong and hurtful.

"*Homo sum, humani nihil a me alienum puto,*" wrote the playwright Terence nearly two thousand years ago. "I'm a human being. Nothing human is foreign to me."[8] And that refers both to our human capacity for virtue and to our common inability to always exhibit it.

And so empathy also inspires us to consideration, tolerance, and forgiveness when it comes to the other people in our lives. Just as we hope others will cut us a break when we fail, similarly we can use empathy to give others the benefit of the doubt. This too is a form of seeing the best in others, for, as we all know, "doing our best" does not always mean we win the Big Smackdown with our own negative emotions. Sometimes our best when it comes to a particularly challenging situation does not reflect our idealistic best.

The smartest response to others' mistakes and shortcomings is guided not by self-righteousness rooted in pride and egoism; rather, it is guided by the exercise of our wisdom and compassion, both of which are grounded in a recognition of our common humanity.

We can both appreciate the goodness in others as well as acknowledge our shared failings if we exercise empathetic love. Such a perspective brings us closer to one another rather than keeping us apart. Such a point of view is essential for overcoming the separation we feel when we over-identify with the "somebody self" as if it were somehow cordoned off from other beings who are essentially just like us.

Reflection on the nature of our relationships with others helps us understand the artificial, and therefore porous and expandable, boundaries of our own selfhood. We all have the capacity to stretch the borderlines of our identity such that the small individual self encompasses others. And in the process, the ego is subsumed within a larger whole.

When we lose ourselves in empathetic identification with others—with our children or parents, our lovers or friends, but also with those we find difficult (and these are not mutually exclusive categories!)—we get an inkling of the joys and benefits of dropping the "somebody self" and *being nobody*.

THE DOORMAT SYNDROME AND THE MYTH OF "COMPASSION FATIGUE"

There are two objections I often hear when it comes to the spiritual teachings on selflessness in relation to others.

The first objection concerns dysfunctional relationships involving repeated incidents of abuse. Our closest relationships can, unfortunately, be our most traumatic when they've gone seriously awry. *Should I stay or should I leave* is a question I'm often asked. And the inevitable answer is, "It depends."

It is not a compassionate act to allow yourself to be a doormat. Obviously it's not good for you. Being the repeated object of another's aggression places you in the role of "helpless victim"—and this is neither a pleasant nor beneficial carnival cutout to stick your face in. We are all equally entitled to respect from others—and that includes you!

But a relationship characterized by such abuse is also not good for the one who's using you as the doormat. Entering into and perpetuating an association where we allow another person to hurt us over and over again is not good for that other person. Hurting others is wrong, and those who hurt others are creating some very nasty karma for themselves. Out of love and compassion *for both yourself and your partner*, you must put a stop to it.

Empathy can once again guide us. People who hurt other people are not happy people. We know this from our own experience. When we are deeply troubled inside, we often seek relief by taking it out on others. Misery, as they say, loves company. The proper response to the suffering of others—even or especially the suffering that causes people to lash out in violent speech or actions—is compassion.

Compassion: to suffer together. And with such empathy for the other's pain, we can determine the best course of action should we find ourselves in an abusive relationship.

Stay or leave? It may be possible to stay and try to work things out, perhaps with the help of a good therapist, such that the cycle of mistreatment is broken. But it might also be necessary to leave in order to end an unhealthy codependency where negative karma for all concerned continues to be reproduced.

In either case, empathetic love will help point us in the right direction. Instead of basing our decision on what we think will be most advantageous for ourselves, we turn our attention to the other:

What's best for him or her? Can I really help this person end the abusive behavior by staying, or do I need to vacate the relationship in order to stop perpetuating this unhealthy codependency?

Don't forget: *being nobody* does not mean being a worthless nothing; *being nobody* is not the same as being a victimized, traumatized, doormat somebody. What is called for is the willingness to drop our inveterate self-centeredness. And also remember, if it doesn't bring the release that comes from laying down the burden of selfishness, it ain't really being nobody.

The other objection many of us have when it comes to losing the "somebody self" in our love for others is what has been labeled "compassion fatigue." People in the helping professions, or just overtaxed parents and caregivers, sometimes claim to be burned out or drained from "too much compassion." *I give and I give and I give, and now I'm exhausted. I need a little "me time"!*

But if we examine the notion of "compassion fatigue" from the karmic point of view, it turns out to be an oxymoron. One of the invariable principles of karma is that nothing bad can come from something good. Assuming that "fatigue" is not a welcome feeling, and that "compassion" is indeed a virtuous state of mind, the former cannot actually derive from the latter.

Any "fatigue" we experience when engaged in helping others comes from self-concern, not from self-forgetfulness. Once we have truly lost ourselves in service to others, we tap into a source of energy and strength far beyond what the "somebody self" is capable of. Like the mother who lifts the car under which her child is trapped, when we give ourselves over completely to others we gain access to a tremendous reservoir of power—the power that comes from *being nobody*.

It is not often, however, that we are able to be so completely self-effacing in our relationships. The demands of the hungry ego are very, very compelling. It is an extremely self-assured, self-confident person who can summon the courage and daring to willfully and completely set aside the imperatives of the "somebody self."

In the next chapter we'll discuss the nature of selfless action—activity that encompasses a kind of relaxed presence and playfulness quite different from what we think of as "work." If we experience "fatigue" or "burnout" from our compassionate actions toward others, it ceases to be truly compassionate and truly selfless. It's no longer a choice but a chore.

And so, with the understanding that it's not the compassion that fatigues you, when you feel the need, you must rest. When your charitable service to others threatens to subvert the virtuous inclination that led to it, it's time to take a break . . . before *you* break! Go ahead and grab some "me time" so that you can return later, refreshed, to the aid of those who need you.

Many of the world's religions share the tradition of regularly observing holidays ("holy days") in order to rest and revitalize. In the Western religions, this is the purpose of the "Sabbath," one day of vacation every week. And in the Eastern traditions, we find similar injunctions to nurture and protect our altruistic inclinations from burnout. Here's one such admonition:

The forces for helping us accomplish the goals of other living beings are willpower, steadfastness, joy, and taking a break when needed.[9]

The text lays out the "forces" that keep us going even when the temptations to quit are great. Willpower—the determination to overcome the stifling limitations of selfish egoism by "finding someone to love." Steadfastness—sticking with our resolution to pursue our *enlightened* self-interest through cultivating empathetic love and altruistic behavior. Joy—being happy to have the opportunity to create the causes for our own true happiness by promoting the welfare of others.

Finally, "taking a break." The word I've translated as "taking a break" is *mukti*, which means "freedom, release, deliverance from"—here in the sense of "leaving off" or "releasing" oneself from the task. This means taking a holiday—or at least some "down time"—in order to safeguard our charitable, altruistic inclinations from the self-preoccupation that can undermine them, and to restore ourselves such that we can think more clearly about the value of service to others.

WHAT IF GOD WERE ONE (OR ALL) OF US?

Losing the self in service to others is a time-honored spiritual method for overcoming our innate egoism. An opposing inborn predisposition is called up: the desire to connect and identify with other people and rise above and beyond the arbitrary limitations through which we imprison ourselves.

It is because of the fact of interdependence, the truth that we are inextricably bound to others, that we can acknowledge and make use of interdependence to improve the quality of the relationships that, in their turn, define us. One of the two formulas of transformation is employed—*change the world, change you*, the twin of the equally potent recipe: *change you, change the world*—and we work the magic.

We think about others with the empathy that evolves from an assumption of basic equality. We wish that others be free from suffering and that they find happiness, just as we wish it for ourselves; and we interact with others with that kind of intention rather than with the more egoistic and injurious desires our mental afflictions motivate. And we also recognize that others, like us, are fallible and don't always live up to their highest ideals—an exercise in empathy that invokes in us compassion rather than anger or judgment, forgiveness rather than resentment and a thirst for revenge.

Overcoming our preoccupation with the self and its perverse misunderstanding of "love," we realize that our love *for* another is the karmic cause of feeling loved *by* another—for what goes around *will* come around. And we are wise enough to understand that empathy sometimes requires tough love and tough choices toward others (to avoid the "doormat syndrome") and the careful preservation and maintenance of our own efforts (to avoid associating "compassion" with "fatigue").

In the next chapter, we will see how our activities in general can be pursued more selflessly—and joyously! Losing the self in the ongoing flow of life itself—in our solitude as well as in our interactions with others—provides us with another opportunity to *be nobody* in our everyday lives.

But let's conclude here with what has been called the greatest secret, the most esoteric and powerful practice, when it comes to our relationships with others:

Hear once more My highest words, the most secret of all, for you are surely dear to Me so I will tell you for your own good. Keep your

mind on Me, be devoted to Me, sacrifice to Me, prostrate to Me.
I promise that you will come to Me, for you are dear to Me.[10]

These verses are from one of the world's religious classics, the
Bhagavad Gita. Krishna is speaking to his friend and student Arjuna
at the very end of the long dialogue that comprises the text. At
one level, the "highest words, the most secret of all," that Krishna
communicates relate to the transcendence of the lower self and the
realization of the Divine, the Great Unity that lies beneath all diversity that is the ultimate experience of *being nobody*.

But another dimension of Krishna's supreme teaching offers us a
formidable strategy when dealing with others. It is one that we all can
utilize in order to improve—*radically* improve—our relationships.
In the Eastern traditions, this practice is called "guru yoga"—seeing
another person as a divine manifestation in your life, an emissary
sent from HQ and assigned specifically to your case.

There's a lot of misunderstanding about the nature and function
of the "guru"—the Sanskrit term for the spiritual teacher—so it is
important to be clear about what this practice really entails before
we can benefit from it.

First of all, a guru is not essentially or objectively a guru, any
more than the aggravating person is. A guru *becomes* a guru when a
student voluntarily enters into this special relationship with him or
her—and not until. The guru-disciple bond, like all other relationships, functions interdependently: for the guru to act as a guru, he or
she must have a student; and for a student to be a student, he or she
must have a teacher.

A second important point about the guru follows from the first.
Your guru could literally be anyone. There's no factory that produces
gurus, and there's no "Gurus R Us" website from which you could
order yours. The guru comes into being *when we designate someone*

to act in that capacity for us. And in a sense, that choice is arbitrary. Your guru could be a minister, rabbi, priest, imam, monk, or nun; but he or she could also be your wife or husband, boyfriend or girlfriend, son or daughter, father or mother, friend or relative— or even (maybe especially!) whoever that aggravating person is in your life.

And so it is that we can put into practice this most esoteric, secret technique for making our relationships extraordinary. We begin with the admission that we really don't know who other people are. We know how they *appear* to us, but we also acknowledge that *we don't see others as they are, but rather as we are.*

And who we are is a complex bundle of possibilities. We alternate, even moment to moment, among a vast array of potential identities. We stick our faces into all kinds of carnival cutouts, and as we've observed in this chapter, we also define ourselves through our relationships with others.

The core of guru yoga involves *intentionally deciding to see another as the reflection of our Highest Self.* "I am seated in the hearts of everyone," says Krishna.[11] God is within us as well as without, a notion that is common to many of the world's spiritual traditions, especially in their more mystical strands.

And so guru yoga can be understood as a mechanism for using another person as a mirror for catching a glimpse of what is best in us. By tapping into the truth of interdependence, we connect with our innate divinity by working to see the divine in another. Perceive it without, and you will recognize it within.

But now for a third crucial observation about guru yoga: Constituting someone as your guru does not mean that everything they say or do will automatically be "good" or "right," and that the student's job is just to agree and obey. This is a dangerous misunderstanding of the practice and has gotten a lot of people into a lot of trouble!

The essence of guru yoga is to be constantly learning; the guru is the teacher and teachings can come in many forms. Sometimes teachings are easy, but sometimes they're hard. Sometimes teachings make us feel better about ourselves, but perhaps the most beneficial lessons are those that challenge us to look at what we need to change. Sometimes teachings make it easy for us to like the teacher, but sometimes they are presented in the form of a negative exposure—cautionary examples about what we need to avoid in our own lives. There are even instances when the teaching the guru gives is that it's time to find someone else to fulfill that function—a lesson in detachment that can be particularly hard.

But in every case, a teacher can only teach if a student learns. The proper practice of guru yoga always requires the student to take personal responsibility for the relationship and to think for him- or herself. One reflects on whatever the guru says or does and struggles to come to his or her own determination:

What am I to learn from this?

• • •

Some of us may choose to formally enter into a relationship with an "official" guru—someone who represents a spiritual lineage and teaches us what has been handed down in a particular tradition. But all of us have the opportunity to avail ourselves of the power inherent in the practice of guru yoga. Whether one works with an "authorized" spiritual teacher or chooses to remain a "none," guru yoga is the most efficacious way to transform our relationships and make quick progress in our spiritual journey.

We often have this somewhat naïve notion that a *real* spiritual teacher should look and act in a particular way. They should, perhaps, wear certain clothing, adorn themselves with religious artifacts, or have a distinctive hairstyle (or lack thereof). They should, we might think, be capable of miracles, or at least have all kinds of charisma and charm. They should, we may assume, have some sort of signature "spiritual" demeanor, only speak softly and significantly, and (here's what we really hope!) always be nice to us.

But with the understanding that the guru could be anyone, what if we decided to bring the personage who occupies that special role for us a little closer to home? What if we took the guru off the pedestal and put him or her inside our living room? What if we tried to imagine that a divine being had moved in with us in order to help us improve ourselves?

What if God were one of us, trying to help us see the divine that is in all of us?

Here's the way it works—and kids, do try this at home! Just make a decision that from now on someone in your life will serve as your guru. Just decide that your husband or wife, your flatmate, your son or daughter, your best friend, or even a very difficult person with whom you have a close relationship will function in this special way for you. From now on, you assume that this person is a divine being, working undercover (sometimes it will seem that they are *deeply* undercover!), trying to help you.

From now on, everything this newly appointed guru says or does *will be interpreted as a teaching meant especially for you.*

And then let the games begin! Occasionally things will indeed seem magical. Words and actions that you once paid little or no attention to will take on deep meaning. The relationship will assume the enchanted quality of our dreams:

Wow! I can't believe what she just said to me! Amazing!

But far more often, the practice will be a lot more challenging:

Why did he leave his dirty underwear on the floor?

Why did she forget my birthday?

And why oh why did my guru just insult me?

In fact, it probably won't be but a few minutes into this practice that your newly appointed guru will do and say what will seem to be very "un-guru-like" things!

Then it's up to you to think, "What's the lesson here? What is this divine being trying to teach me?" Maybe it's to be more like him or her, to imitate the positive qualities you have become keenly aware of while engaging in this practice of seeing the other as divine. But maybe it's to learn patience from a teacher posing as an irritating person; to learn to be more thoughtful of others as the teacher displays what it looks like to be selfish; to be careful that you're not doing to others what the teacher is now doing to you.

No matter whether the lesson is presented positively or negatively, the relationship becomes an ongoing opportunity to learn and grow. And that's the real magic inherent in the practice of guru yoga.

While it's probably easiest to begin with one person you already see as sort of special, someone you love and who loves you, guru yoga has the capability of revolutionizing any relationship. It can be employed with equal benefit with loved ones and difficult people alike. It is the ultimate extension of thinking the best of others, of giving others the benefit of the doubt; of seeing the transformative possibilities inherent in any relationship; and of exploiting to the fullest the fact that if we alter our perception of others we will change our understanding of ourselves.

Action Plan: Working with a Guru

Pick one person in your life to function as your "guru." As we've said above, it could theoretically be anyone, but it might be best to start with someone close to you who you love—a wife or husband, boyfriend or girlfriend, mother or father, sister or brother, son or daughter, or a very close friend.

The practice is simple to describe, but difficult indeed to stick with. Just decide that from now you'll regard this person as a kind of divine being—an angel who is only trying to help you—and everything, without exception, that this special person says or does is meant to be a teaching for you. What is it you need to learn about yourself from what the "guru" just said or did?

Notes:

* When asked which of the commandments were most important, Jesus said: "You shall love the Lord your God with all your heart, with all your soul, and with all your mind. This is the greatest commandment. And the second is like it: You shall love your neighbor as yourself." Matthew 22:37–39.

† In philosophical terms, we might say that karma isn't a *metaphysical* system but rather an *epistemological* one.

6

Going with the Flow

To be too conscious is an illness—a real thoroughgoing illness.
—*Fyodor Dostoyevsky*

GETTING INTO THE ZONE

You must lose the self, as Jesus said, to find it.* Or, to put it in the terminology we've used here, you must rise above the "somebody self" in order to gain some kind of access to the joyful unselfconsciousness of *being nobody*.

The empathetic expansion of identity to encompass others in our lives is one of the principal methods provided by our spiritual traditions to overcome the confines of mere individuality. But there is another spiritual technique designed to help us drop the self-consciousness and self-centeredness that are the ultimate sources of our unhappiness.

The method we'll explore in this chapter is designed to help us lose the self in action of all sorts—not only in our relationships with others, but in each and every one of our everyday activities, alone or in company.

We use various colloquialisms to speak of being engrossed in action. When we're "really into it," or when we're in "the zone" or "the pocket" or "the groove," or when we're "going with the flow," we're describing what it's like to *be nobody* because the "somebody self" has been wholly absorbed in an endeavor.

We all know what it feels like to be really consumed in an activity. When we say a book was a "real page-turner" or a movie was "riveting," we are referring to this experience. When the concert was "mind-blowing" or the football match kept us on the "edge of our seat," it's this sensation we're pointing to.

We are attracted to our hobbies, recreational activities, and games because they tend to launch us into this special state of mind. We're captivated by puzzles, and we love challenges at work for their capacity to bring us there. The rush we get while engaged in stimulating activities, especially those with a hint of danger (for me, it's riding my motorcycle), or when we're in the midst of an emergency—these too can evoke this feeling. And, of course, it is this state of self-forgetfulness and ecstasy (derived from the word *exstasis*, "standing outside of the self") that lies behind the powerful attraction of heightened sexual experiences.

It's the feeling of *not being there*, or, we could also say, of *totally being there*—of dropping the mental narrative and fully integrating with the experience itself. The inner play-by-play commentary on life ceases. Instead of the usual voice-over we superimpose on unfolding events, we are fully engrossed in the activity itself. The mind's monologue is silenced as unmediated awareness takes over.

We're all familiar with this unselfconscious state of consciousness that arises when we fully inhabit the here and now. It's the joy of being fully integrated into life itself. It's the exhilaration and elation we feel when we are deeply engaged in what we're doing. And it's another way we gain access in our everyday lives to the rapture of *being nobody*.

• • •

Mihaly Csikszentmihalyi has observed that we're happiest when we're in this condition of pure awareness. He has famously labeled it "flow," defining it as the state "in which people are so involved in an activity that nothing else seems to matter; the experience itself is so enjoyable that people will do it even at great cost, for the sheer sake of doing it."[1]

"Really getting into it" is the opposite of being "out of it," of just spacing out and living life on cruise control. The flow state is characterized by extraordinary concentration on a task one finds captivating. "Concentration is so intense that there is no attention left over to think about anything irrelevant, or to worry about problems," writes Csikszentmihalyi.[2] When we are fully in the moment, completely occupied with the task at hand, we are unable to be simultaneously preoccupied with what comes next or "post-occupied" with what has already happened.

The flow state is the thorough engagement with the present, the utter embrace of reality as it's happening. *It's like this now*—entirely accepted and embodied.

Most importantly for our theme, this state of heightened awareness—full absorption in what one is doing—is also characterized by the loss of a sense of self-consciousness. "Happiness," notes spiritual teacher Krishnamurti, "is not something that you can seek; it is a result, a by-product," of self-abandonment:

> If you pursue happiness for itself, it will have no meaning. Happiness comes uninvited; and the moment you are conscious that you are happy, you are no longer happy. . . . Being self-consciously happy, or pursuing happiness, is the very ending of happiness.

There is happiness only when the self and its demands are put
aside.[3]

The "somebody self" disappears when we are truly happy; the
inner voice shuts up. In fact, it is precisely the degree to which one
loses the self in the activity that defines how deep the flow really
goes.[†] Such "peak experiences," as Abraham Maslow designated
them, are moments of self-transcendence and contentment: "Perception in the peak-experience can be relatively ego-transcending,
self-forgetful, egoless, unselfish. It can come closer to being unmo-
tivated, impersonal, desireless, detached, not needing or wishing."[4]

These optimal, self-transcending states of mind are the bread
and butter of religious mysticism. The "oceanic feeling" occurs when
the individual feels herself or himself subsumed within some greater
whole: "God," "ultimate reality," "the Ground of All Being," one's
"Buddha nature," or whatever one wishes to call the nameless.

In the Eastern religious traditions, we are given a method
designed to bring some version of this exalted state of mind into all
our actions. In Taoism and Confucianism, the practice is called *wu
wei*, or "effortless action," and in Buddhism it's spoken of in terms
of "awareness" and "mindfulness" in each and every one of our pursuits. In the Hindu tradition the phrase describing this spiritual
technique for getting into the zone is particularly apt: *karma yoga*, or
"disciplined action."

These spiritual traditions posit that even in the ordinary activities of our daily lives we can enter the flow state. We don't need to
wait for some extraordinary gift of grace to get a taste of the bliss,
or sequester ourselves in a cave somewhere in order to bring about
a mystical trip. And we don't have to continually and desperately
search for exceptionally titillating "peak experiences" before we can
get into the groove.

Every experience in life has the potential to be "peak"; every moment and every activity has the latent capacity to be "optimal" if we learn to let go of the "somebody self" and live in a more integrated and less self-conscious way.

There is, however, a difference between being mindlessly absorbed in an activity—passively watching television or a movie or staring at the computer, for example—and what we might call *mindful unselfconsciousness* in our actions. Karma yoga assumes both the disciplined "mindfulness" and the joyful "unselfconsciousness" that comprise "being in the zone" as opposed to just "zoning out."

There's also a difference between hoping that some activity or another will seem captivating enough to push us into the flow, and the learned ability to put ourselves there. We all know and desire the joy of being completely engaged in what we're doing. But in between such "optimal experiences," few of us stop to reflect on why and how they happen, and how we could potentially enter into any activity with this same intensity and attention.

Washing the dishes offers the same potential for getting into the zone as motorcycling or rock climbing do. There's nothing in any Himalayan cave that's missing from the office when it comes to getting into the flow. Any action done with mindful unselfconsciousness can take us there.

• • •

The unexamined life, it has been said, is not worth living—and that's true enough. It's important to be self-aware, in part because it is through self-awareness that one can come to realize that it is *too much* self-awareness that blocks us from the source of our greatest happiness. For the over-examined life can perpetually defer the actual living of it. "Ask yourself whether you are happy," wrote

J. S. Mill, echoing the Krishnamurti quotation cited above, "and you cease to be so."[5]

Our deepest joy arises only when we cease taking our own temperature and, like the old Nike slogan says, *just do it*. Life does not run best when it's in neutral—stalled out in continual self-analysis—but when it's fully engaged.

GETTING UNBUSY

Yeah, but I'm already "fully engaged," and it's totally stressing me out! I've got a million things to do—so many responsibilities! I'm just so busy!

Nowadays most of us do indeed often feel the tension that accompanies having a lot to do. We have homework to complete, exams to pass, diplomas to acquire, and paying jobs to land. There are tasks at the office to accomplish, business problems to solve, and professional promotions to earn. The bills must be paid, forms must be filled out, and taxes must be filed.

The housework needs attention, the kids have to be driven to their soccer game, and there are birthday parties to be organized. There are home repairs that await us, meals to be prepared, and dishes, clothes, cars, and bodies to be washed. And there are, for some of us, book manuscripts to complete in order to meet the publisher's deadline.

Our social lives can also sometimes seem a bit overwhelming, what with all the appointments, meetings, engagements, rendezvous, dinner parties, and lunch dates there are to juggle. We even fill our leisure time with plans, projects, schedules, and itineraries so as to not run the risk of—gasp!—boredom, the characteristically modern abhorrence of not having *enough things to do*.

And the younger you are, the more likely that you're freaking out about all of this. A survey done on behalf of the American Psychological Association found that half of all "millennials" say their angst keeps them awake at night, and 39 percent of them said that their stress levels had increased in the past year.[6]

We've done a good job of passing on this kind of anxiousness about life's tasks to our kids. When I was a teenager, I looked forward to sleeping in on Saturday morning (and we all know the amazing talent most teenagers have for sleeping in—especially, I guess, if they've been kept awake the night before by stress!). But invariably my dreams were literally shattered as my father woke me at some ungodly hour (like maybe around 10:00 AM) with the "to do list"— the chores I was expected to get through that day.

Idleness, I was told, was the devil's playground, and there would be no such demonic tomfoolery in this house! *Let's get to work, son!*

And so most of us have internalized the idea that our self-worth consists at least in part in how busy we keep ourselves, with all the pressures and strains that come from such an attitude. Now more than ever before, we feel it's crucial to keep ourselves constantly occupied—or at least thinking about all the things we have to do—in order to be a real somebody.

Even though such perpetual worry and frenetic activity is wearing us out and down, we nevertheless revel in what has become a *cult of busyness.*

Our communications these days are often just to let each other know how much we've all got going on. Have you ever phoned up a friend and asked them how they're doing, only to sit there on the other end of the line, listening to them talk for fifteen minutes about how busy they are? Maybe you've found yourself doing the same when someone else asks after you. Our catch-up conversations turn into contests to see who's busier.

And what's the unspoken message behind such tedious sharing and cataloging of our many activities?

I'm really, really busy—so see how important and valuable my life is?

In an article published in the *New Statesman*, Ed Smith writes that busy people "are not rushing to arrive somewhere, still less to achieve anything. They are rushing because rushing is how they display how hard they work." The cult of busyness has become "a cultural malaise." We're all trying to convince ourselves and others that our lives are significant because we are so busy working:

> In every area of public life, we demand not only that people work harder, but, crucially, that they be seen to work ever harder. This is the age of professional martyrdom.[7]

One of my spiritual teachers once pointed out that super-busy people are actually the very ones—talented, energetic, and intelligent people—who, if they paused their nonstop spinning long enough, would realize how relatively insignificant much of what they're busy doing actually is.

Busyness for its own sake can keep us unaware of and unfocused on the more consequential things we have to do in life. And the busyness stresses us out, which often enough triggers major mental-affliction attacks. Anxiety about how many things there are to do does not help us do them better or more efficiently, let alone more wisely and calmly.

Instead of putting us in the flow, busyness just sweeps us away in the current. Instead of the mind*ful* unselfconsciousness that characterizes being in the zone, the cult of busyness instills a self-conscious mind*less*ness that keeps us stewing about how much we have to do instead of concentrating on what we are actually doing.

• • •

Staying busy for the sake of busyness is not a spiritual technique for self-transcendence, happiness, or contentment. It is, rather, a recipe for agitation and turmoil, in addition to often being just another ploy to accentuate one's self-importance.

The spiritual methods for self-forgetfulness in action are quite different than this kind of hectic, chicken-with-its-head-cut-off urge to just keep busy all the time. And it's not mere inactivity that serves as the real antidote. Another cause of stress derives from worrying about all the things we should be doing that for one reason or another we are unable or unwilling to do.

The opposite of busyness is not paralysis. It's remaining active and engaged in life, but in a calm and relaxed manner. We must do what there is to do, but most of us need to get way more *unbusy* as we're doing it.

Getting unbusy can mean cutting back on nonessential or meaningless activity in order to create a more uncluttered schedule. Reprioritizing what is really important puts what is not so essential in its proper place.

It can also mean taking more time off or simply enjoying the free time we already have without diluting it with obsessive worry, nonstop checking of email and text messages, and treating our days off and holidays as if they were just another opportunity to stay busy. We don't need to bring our work into our leisure time, and we don't need to turn our leisure time into work.[8]

Getting unbusy can also include introducing a relaxation or meditation practice into the daily schedule—a time where you just sit and do nothing (except grabbing some peace of mind!), which is perhaps one reason why so many of us resist it. To the busyness fanatic, meditating seems so . . . *unproductive*.

But the main thing about getting unbusy is a change in one's attitude. Our duties in life, no matter how many or even how onerous, will not seem so overwhelming if we are not overwhelmed.

Stress does not arise in reaction to some quantifiable number of things one has to do. There are plenty of people—I've personally known several—who remain constantly occupied all day long without evincing much or any anxiety. And then there are folks who have, like, two things to do in the day and get themselves all balled up:

> *Oh, I'm so busy! I have a doctor's appointment at 9:30, and then this afternoon, I have this other thing to do!*

There's a difference between staying active—physically doing what needs to be done in the here and now—and the mental feeling of being too busy. It's not that there aren't things in our lives that need attending to. There certainly are. What's being suggested here is definitely not that we ignore our jobs, our family obligations, or any of our other responsibilities. But these duties need not be a perpetual source of unhappiness by being regarded as drudgery instead of as opportunities for *getting into the flow*.

Assuming an unbusy mindset allows for relaxed action instead of frenzied movement. Bhagwan Rajneesh ("Osho") has drawn a distinction between "activity" and "action." "Action is not activity," Rajneesh argues, and "activity is not action."

> Action is when the situation demands it, you act, you respond.
> Activity is when the situation doesn't matter, it is not a response;

you are so restless within that the situation is just an excuse to be active. Action comes out of a silent mind—it is the most beautiful thing in the world. Activity comes out of a restless mind—it is the ugliest.[9]

When the situation demands it, we act—*it's like this now*, so we do what needs to be done. The opposite of busyness is not simple indolence or immobility, and it is certainly not shirking our obligations. But the agitation and restlessness—the chronic *impulse to just do something, anything!*—that accompanies what Rajneesh labels "activity" is the source of tension and anxiety.

Indian deities and Tibetan Buddhist enlightened beings are often depicted with multiple arms to indicate the many beneficial ways they act in the world. They are portrayed as industrious—it's a big job keeping the universe going and all! But none of them is pictured with brows all furrowed in angst. They're all totally Botoxed!

Actively and skillfully engaged, but not crazy busy—this is the model for action in our own lives. Getting unbusy entails doing what there is to do efficiently and happily but without the incessant demands for frenetic activity associated with a stressed-out lifestyle that accompanies the cult of busyness.

FREEDOM FROM COMPULSIVE ACTIVITY

True freedom, as we've been emphasizing, does not consist of just doing anything our untrained impulses suggest. Such an understanding of "freedom" keeps us locked in a prison of our own making. The happiness associated with spiritual goals depicted as "liberation," "deliverance," or "release," requires first and foremost the end of this sort of bondage to our unrestrained mental afflictions, not the unconstrained expression of them.

So if you really must be busy, maybe it's best to get busy subduing these negative emotions that are the source of all our unhappiness. We feel more or less constantly a compelling need to change the way things presently are.

But living freely also mandates that we shake ourselves loose from the obsessive need to constantly accomplish, fix, or improve things through manic activity. We are enslaved not only by our mental afflictions but by our continuous attempts to direct future outcomes instead of fully concentrating on what we are doing in the here and now.

And so the controlling, Captain Kirk self makes yet another appearance! Reinforced by the misguided idea that we need to keep busy in order to be of value, we feel compelled to be perpetually working to alter and change things. Motivated by stressful discontentment, the good old Captain turns out to be a full-blown neurotic!

This obsession with work and achievement is another way we try to scratch the perpetual itch of dissatisfaction—in this case, the itch of always feeling like we *have to do something in order to be somebody*. It is the antithesis of the Great Itchless State.

The opposite of freedom, contentment, and perfect happiness is what the Eastern religions call *samsara*, the cyclical reproduction of suffering in our lives. And while there are many dimensions to what constitutes and causes this recurrent unhappiness, one definition of *samsara* found in the ancient texts is particularly striking for our present subject.

"Samsara," it is said in the Ashtavakra Gita, "is nothing other than *having something that needs to be done*."[10]

The crucial Sanskrit word in the verse, *kartavya* ("having something that needs to be done") refers to the *compulsion to act*, the niggling dissatisfaction that instigates panicky activity. The statement is rather radical and adamant, that this feeling of being *compelled* to act, and nothing other, keeps us from contentment.

At first blush, such an assertion might seem rather extreme—
But there are things I need to do! If I don't feed the kids, who will? If I don't go to work, how will I pay the bills? There are, of course, responsibilities that we all have to fulfill. But we'll complete them a lot more efficiently and happily if we lose the feeling that we are doing so under duress. It's not the obligation to act that's the problem. It's the *neediness* that spurs activity that causes us stress.

The idea that we are unhappy owing to a *compulsion to act* actually does pretty accurately sum up our unrest. We more or less constantly feel a compelling need to change the way things presently are. We are kept dissatisfied by our perpetual itchiness—the desire for what we don't already possess and the yearning to rid ourselves of something we do have in our lives. These are the two forms of discontentment, and it is the cessation of both that brings us tranquility and peace.

It is the wish that things were *not like this now* that defines our unhappy state—what we've called the "if only" syndrome. And in response to this discontentment, we feel the compulsion to *get busy* and *start scratching* all those nagging itches in the hopes of getting what we want and getting rid of what we don't.

Jesus, among many other great spiritual teachers, advised us long ago *to just relax already*. "Therefore I tell you, do not worry about your life, what you will eat or what you will drink, or about your body, what you will wear." Constant fretting and stressing out about the future just ruins the present and, in general, spoils the limited time we have here on earth:

> Is not life more than food, and the body more than clothing? Look at the birds of the air; they neither sow nor reap nor gather into barns, and yet your heavenly Father feeds them. Are you not of more value than they? And can any of you by worrying add a single hour to your span of life? And why do you worry about

clothing? Consider the lilies of the field, how they grow; they neither toil nor spin, yet I tell you, even Solomon in all his glory was
not clothed like one of these. But if God so clothes the grass of the
field, which is alive today and tomorrow is thrown into the oven,
will he not much more clothe you—you of little faith? Therefore
do not worry, saying, "What will we eat?" or "What will we drink?" or
"What will we wear?"[11]

This famous passage from the Bible—its message can be put succinctly: *Don't worry, be happy!*—concludes with the following useful
summary: "So do not worry about tomorrow, for tomorrow will
bring worries of its own. Today's trouble is enough for today."

We've got enough to take care of in the here and now without
polluting our lives with anxiety and fear about future difficulties.
There will be "worries" and "troubles" tomorrow—let's rename them
"challenges," shall we?—and when they arrive we'll need to deal with
them. But the best way to prepare for tomorrow is to concentrate on
today, for it is in the present that we are creating the causes that will
govern our relative ability to deal with the events of the future.

There's another potential teaching on this subject that may be
floating, so to speak, in your head somewhere.

Row, row, row your boat, goes the song. We have things to do and
responsibilities to fulfill, so keep rowing! The converse of keeping
busy in compulsive activity is not slothful inactivity. But row your
boat *gently* down the stream (and also *merrily, merrily, merrily!*) for
life is but a dream—and one day it will end.

Flailing about with the oars in a frenzy of compulsive activity,
worrying about what might be around the next bend, we forego the
opportunity to leisurely enjoy the boat ride and do what we need to
do in the present—gently, merrily, and in a way that doesn't take the
"dream" so very, very seriously.

KARMA AND ACTION FOR ITS OWN SAKE

It is important to do what we can to ensure a pleasant future. But such preparations are best accomplished through mindful attention to the present. The future will fall into place if we create the appropriate karmic causes in the here and now. And the most effective means for doing so is neither through harried busyness nor the compulsion to fix and change things that distracts us from what there is to do right now.

The compulsion to act is motivated by a perceived need to effect an "improved" situation in the future. It's just another instance of the "if only" syndrome. We ignore the present and the opportunities it affords when we obsess too much about the future. We feel compelled to *get busy* and *start scratching* in the hopes that we'll later obtain something better than what's going on now.

It was John Lennon who famously said, "Life is what happens while you're busy making other plans."[12] We become oblivious to the possibilities inherent in each moment of our lives when we're preoccupied with what *will happen* instead of centering on what *is actually happening*.

There is a spiritual technique to help us concentrate mindfully on what we're doing now. It is to act, not to gain some future reward, but simply because the task is there to do. This is the essence of what in the Bhagavad Gita is called *karma yoga*, the "discipline" (for this is what "yoga" really means) of action.

To do this sort of yoga there's no need to get a high-performance mat or buy expensive attire made of free-range organic cotton. A practitioner of karma yoga is defined as "one who does what needs to be done while remaining unattached to the results of this action."[13]

Most of our actions, most of the time, are carried out as a means to achieve a desired end, expedients for reaching a desired goal. To be sure, every action will achieve some result—there's a beginning, middle, and end to everything. But being "in the flow" puts our full attention on the action as it's happening—on the middle bit, in "real time"—and not on trying to arrive at an outcome as quickly as possible.

Losing oneself in the activity at hand is by definition not "goal-oriented." This is not to suggest that there isn't an end to be reached or a result to be eventuated. But in karma yoga, the means and the ends collapse so that the focus is on the action in and of itself.

This attention on the task at hand rather than on some projected result we hope to bring about is what we might call *action done for its own sake.*

"Action done for its own sake"—it's the very definition of being "in the flow."[‡] And while we are all happiest when we're *mindfully unselfconscious* and in the zone, the compulsion to act in order to attain a future objective tends to rule nearly every aspect of our everyday lives.

It's the inner angel and devil locking horns once again. We long to submerge ourselves in an activity and go with the flow, but at the same time we tell ourselves that such action for its own sake is somehow *irresponsible*. Given our desire to improve our own lives and the lives of those we love, we may think that losing ourselves in our present is somehow reneging on our obligation to try to create a better future.

Here's another way to put this apparent quandary: There may seem to be a contradiction between action for its own sake and what we've talked about above in terms of "karmic management." Can we simultaneously be fully and unselfconsciously absorbed in an activity while at the same time be working to create a better life for ourselves, for our loved ones, and for the world as a whole?

We observed in chapter 5 that according to the laws of karma every action will definitely have a corresponding reaction—good acts bring pleasant consequences for our sense of self and happiness, while bad acts bring unpleasant results. The self-improvement enterprise—which we've also argued is the best and really the only method for helping others (summed up in the formula *change you, change the world*)—depends on wisely manipulating the karmic system.

But laboring to create the karmic causes for a better future might seem to be inherently goal-oriented; indeed, the whole concept of "self-improvement" might seem so. And neither would appear to mesh very well with a vision of "action for its own sake."

To resolve this apparent contradiction, we'll need to review a few things about karma and then introduce some new observations pertaining to how the system really operates. And perhaps we will see that effective karmic management and action for its own sake turn out to be two sides of the very same coin.

We've already encountered one reason why there is actually no real conflict between creating new good karma—acting in the present in order to create a better future—and karma yoga, acting without attention to the fruits. The "good" acts we do are "good" to the degree that they are motivated by a selfless intention. The more we are motivated by self-interest, the less "good" that act is, and therefore the less pleasant will be the result.

To really work the karmic system, we must silence the demonic inner voice that always asks, *What's in it for me?* It is only a seeming paradox that the more *selfless* the intention behind any particular action the more beneficial that action will be to *oneself*. It's actually the very principle for generating good karma. It is intrinsic to the most effective management of karma that one *loses oneself in action*.

Perhaps the easiest way to take the selfishness out of any activity is, as we've seen, to *do it for someone else*. Compassionate and empathetically inspired action—*What can I do for you?*—is a very effective surgical instrument for performing the ego-ectomy, extracting the self-interest out of the act.

When we take our self-centered motivations out of the equation, we are able to concentrate more fully on the action itself instead of diluting it with futuristic projections of what we hope to personally gain from it. So from this angle we can see that karmic management—directed by altruism and empathy—entails the self-forgetting necessary for action done for its own sake. We can act *unselfconsciously* because our *attention is focused on another*.

• • •

But there's another dimension of why action for its own sake is built into the very system of karma. It is not the perpetual dissatisfaction with the present—"I'll do *x* so that I'll later obtain *y*"—that lies at the heart of the karmic enterprise. Creating the karma for a better future actually necessitates an opposite assumption.

The most effective karmic management assumes some version of contentment, and with contentment we have the possibility for pure action—action done truly for its own sake.

What goes around, comes around—this is Karma 101. But for "it" to come around, "it" must go around first—and herein lies an important secret when it comes to karma. We have to have some kind of sense that we already have "it" sufficiently before we become comfortable enough to give "it" away.

Let's take one example. The feeling of prosperity or abundance— for it is indeed a "feeling" and not a quantifiable commodity—is the karmic result of generosity. Give and you shall receive, right? We may not always believe it, but we've heard the maxim plenty of times, from plenty of sources.

The example is a salient one, for generosity is one way of describing the whole karmic program. It is the willingness to give to others—not just money and things, but also time and energy, love and compassion, respect and protection—that lies at the very core of the care and maintenance of one's karma.

Karmic management assumes some awareness of *present fulfillment*. Before we can even think about giving to others, we must believe we have enough to give—enough material things, enough time, enough emotional gratification. We know that there will be future rewards—that it will "come around"—but even in the present there must be a certain sense of sufficiency, even excess, for us to first let it "go around."

Even the most self-interested, naïve, and mechanistic understanding of karma has some degree of this sensibility that *I have enough already*. Even karma simplistically regarded as a kind of investment scheme—"I'll give this so that I'll get that in the future"—has some element of the notion that *I have something I can afford to give right now*.

And a more informed understanding of how karma really works will bear an even deeper appreciation of this underlying secret: It is the feeling of plenitude and abundance, not the constant craving for more, that makes for truly efficacious karmic management.

Do unto others as you would have them do unto you. Because I believe I have adequate material prosperity, I feel free to donate my money or things. Because I think I have enough time, I share my surfeit with others. If I feel a basic contentment within myself, I then feel able to give others the love and compassion that might help them feel more contentment too.

Such a recognition of self-sufficiency also helps us restrain ourselves from generating bad karma—*do not do unto others as you would not have them do unto you*. If I feel safe and secure, I have no interest in harming others. When I am content with what I possess, I do not think of stealing. Because I feel enough love within, I am not tempted to infringe on others' relationships. And when I am satisfied with my own life I am not inclined to be envious or resentful of what others have.

Karma yoga, in one sense, simply means disciplining one's actions in order to do good instead of bad, to be kind instead of cruel, to be other-oriented instead of egotistical. But we've also noticed that this method presupposes the latent assumption behind all karmically beneficial and unselfish activity. It is encapsulated in our contentment mantra:

Om, I have enough, ah hum.

Action done without expectation of personal reward presumes the recognition that one has been rewarded enough already. According to the Bhagavad Gita, "No one becomes a yogi" or true practitioner of karma yoga "who has not renounced expectation of selfish advantage."[14]

Because we don't need or expect recompense, we complete the action with the purest intention and the fullest attention on the act itself—which, as we've repeatedly underscored, is the most powerful way to ensure that the act will have a positive karmic result.

• • •

There is no contradiction between karmic management and action done for its own sake. In fact, we do the former best when we are doing the latter. But, needless to say, we have a resistance to engaging in either.

The mental afflictions—all of them revolving around egoistical self-cherishing—militate against relying on the self-sacrificing principles of karma in our actions. The Big Smackdown, the Rage in the Cage, recurs over and over again as we fight our selfish inclinations in our attempts to live more wisely and joyously.

And because of this same clinging to the self we resist, even while we yearn for, the experience of losing ourselves in an activity. *Who would I be if I weren't somebody?*—a question we'll actually attempt to answer in chapter 7. But some part of us fears the very unselfconsciousness that brings us the euphoria of being in the flow—of doing what needs to be done selflessly, efficiently, and with attention to the act itself and not to the fruits.

Karma yoga as a *discipline* requires repeated practice. Our battles with the inner demon of egoistic self-centeredness are ongoing and arduous. And so in our quest to lose the self-consciousness and get into the flow of things when it comes to our everyday actions, we'll need to recall, over and over again, the benefits of doing so in order to strengthen the inner angel.

To reinforce our desire to act without selfish intention, we must remind ourselves how much pleasure there is in being in the zone, in the bliss of *mindful unselfconsciousness*, the exuberance of acting *as nobody*.

LIFE AS ART, WORK AS PLAY

Karma yoga, or action done for its own sake, is a revolutionary method for living one's life. It is a radical procedure for removing the self-interest from our daily activities and becoming more attentive to what we're doing while we're doing it.

One of the principal ways of practicing karma is to replace the drone of *What's in for me?* with *What can I do for you?* Already this inverts our usual self-centered motivation and begins the revolution in our thinking about our everyday acts.

Understanding the deeper principles of karma, we tune in to our own sense of self-sufficiency in order to give to others. Willfully suspending and foregoing any future personal rewards of action, we do what there is to do to the best of our ability, but for its own sake—just because it's given to us to do.

And there is another way of describing karma yoga that further highlights its revolutionary implications: Action done for its own sake is *purposeless action*.

Every action comes to an end and serves as the cause for a future effect. But action done for its own sake is focused not on the result but on the action itself. When the means and ends collapse, there is no particular purpose for doing something, other than that's what there is to do. The activity is enough in and of itself, not for what it achieves or brings about.

Purposeless action does not imply that the activity is *meaningless*, and it certainly does not suggest that it need not be done at all or without giving it our full attention. If you're like me, you're accustomed to associate "purposelessness" with indifference and apathy. *If you say there's no purpose, well, I guess there's no point.*

Action done for its own sake is purposeless but not pointless. To better understand this aspect of karma yoga, let's turn to two familiar examples of purposeless action: play and artistic expression.

• • •

"This is the real secret of life," declares Alan Watts—"to be completely engaged with what you are doing in the here and now. And instead of calling it work, realize it is play."[15]

Watts is by no means the first or only person to recommend that we concentrate fully on the task at hand; and he's also not alone in advising us to conceptualize all our activities in life as "play" rather than "work." We naturally and easily do the first—engage thoroughly with what we're doing in the here and now—when we do the second, dropping the stress and compulsion to act and adopting instead a relaxed, playful attitude toward our daily tasks.

When we are at play, it is not because we *need* to do something, but because we really *want* to do it. As opposed to the onerous demands associated with the idea of "work," we play simply because it's *fun*. In play, we continue to row our boats—and we do so quite assiduously and even strenuously—but we also row *merrily*, because it's fun to play.

One of the reasons so many spiritual teachers, theologians, and secular scholars have taken play quite seriously is that when we are at play we don't take things so seriously. We relax (without losing focus) and shed the stressful anxiety that comes when we obsess about the outcome rather than really getting into the process.

It's been said that we should lighten up on our way to enlightenment, and thinking about all our activities in terms of "play" rather than "work" can help us to do this.

Johan Huizinga, the author of the classic scholarly study on this subject, *Homo Ludens: A Study of the Play-Element in Culture*, refers to the irreducible "fun element" lying at the heart of play: "Now this element, the fun of playing, resists all analysis, all logical interpretation. As a concept, it cannot be reduced to any other mental category."[16] The essential purpose of play is that it has no purpose, which makes it both "fun" and quite different from our usual compulsive need to act. Play, Huizinga writes, "stands outside the immediate satisfaction of wants and appetites."[17]

The importance of the concept of play has been recognized for millennia in the world's spiritual traditions. In one branch of the religions of India, the concept of "play," or "sport," is known by the Sanskrit term *lila*, and it was originally introduced as a stratagem for solving a perennial theological question: Why did God create the universe? Did God—who lacks for nothing and is complete in Him- or Herself—nevertheless have some *need* to create, some *purpose* behind bringing the world into existence?

In response to the accusation that God can't be the creator of the world, since God, being God and all, has no motive or reason to act, it was countered that God did create the world—but "merely in play."§ As William Sax writes in his aptly titled *The Gods at Play*, "The idea is that God's creation of the world is motivated not by any desire or lack, since these would be incompatible with his or her self-fulfilled and complete nature, but rather by a free and spontaneous creativity."[18]

In the Bhagavad Gita, we are explicitly advised to imitate the divine in our own actions, in the ongoing creation of our own lives. Krishna tells Arjuna, his student and friend, to act—to do what needs to be done—but to act like God does, not out of a compulsive need for self-aggrandizement, but totally and selflessly unattached to the results:

> Arjuna, throughout the three worlds there is nothing whatsoever that I need to do. There is nothing unattained that I need to attain, and yet I still engage in action. . . . While those who are ignorant perform actions out of attachment, the wise one, unattached, acts in order to maintain the world.[19]

Lila describes action done out of freedom rather than necessity, out of a sense of prior and ongoing contentment rather than the neediness of the "if only" syndrome. It is the paradigm for action done for its own sake, the blueprint for karma yoga.

The purity of play has been seriously diluted in our modern, grown-up versions of "games" and "sports" and must be distinguished from them. The overweening emphasis on winning as the purpose, especially in professional sports, where fame and fortune depend on victory, have compromised the "action for its own sake" nature of play in its essential form.

The quaint old aphorism "It's not whether you win or lose but how you play the game" has largely been forgotten and replaced by football coach Vince Lombardi's famous dictum: "Winning isn't everything; it's the only thing."[20]

This preoccupation with victory is thoroughly tied up in the culture of narcissism we spoke of in the introduction. We're encouraged to think we're not "somebody enough" unless we're a real "winner." And winners require losers. We often believe that we'll be a real somebody only if somebody else is less of one.

I once met a professional speed skater who was very, very good at what he did—so good, in fact, that he was sent to the Olympics, where he did very, very well. He came home with a silver medal. He was *the second best skater in the world* in his event.

And guess what? He was disappointed, because he was *only* second best.

Play in its uncorrupted sense isn't about trying to be better than others. But it also does not preclude healthy competition. Action done for its own sake, whether done alone (competing against ourselves) or in the company of others (competing against competitors), can bring out the best in all of us.

What the Tao Te Ching calls the "virtue of non-competition" is not about no competition, as the text makes clear. It is rather doing one's best—and wanting others to do their best too—all in the "spirit of play":

> *The best athlete*
> *wants his opponent at his best . . .*

All of them embody
the virtue of non-competition.
Not that they don't love to compete,
but they do it in the spirit of play.
In this they are like children
and in harmony with the Tao.[21]

And so it is that to act in the "spirit of play" we are pointed to the example of children. Children, before they are taught that the point is to "win," exemplify the pure version of playful activity. If you've been around small children (or if you remember being one), you know that kids get totally and tirelessly absorbed in what is, after all, purposeless action.

Imagine going to a playground and asking kids why they're doing what they're doing—that is, asking what the *purpose* of the activity is. "Why are you sliding down the slide, little girl? What is the purpose of all this swinging back and forth? Why the teetering, then the tottering? What is your objective in going around and around in circles on the merry-go-round? And what exactly is the reason for climbing up and down that jungle gym?"

The kid would probably run away screaming to her mom or dad, terrorized and confused by such stupid questions coming from such a crazy grown-up!

The point of play is found not in the completion but in the process. As always, there's a beginning, middle, and end to the activity. You climb up the stairs of the slide and slide down, thus getting to the ground. Sliding ends when one reaches the bottom, but it's not in order to reach the bottom that one slides. In play, *it's all about the sliding,* not the *having slid.*

The kids got it right when it comes to action for its own sake. Play is not puerile or childish in the sense of being fatuous or foolish. But it is childlike to the degree that it embodies the simple, unencumbered sense of wonderment and joy involved in acting mindfully and unselfconsciously in purposeless action.

It is this simplicity in behavior, purity in action, and humility rather than self-promotion—not believing that "winning is the only thing"—that led Jesus to answer the way he did when asked by his disciples, "Who is the greatest in the kingdom of heaven?"

> He called a child, whom he put among them, and said, "Truly I tell you, unless you change and become like children, you will never enter the kingdom of heaven. Whoever becomes humble like this child is the greatest in the kingdom of heaven."[22]

As an Indian text asserts, the wise spiritual practitioner "does whatever comes to him to do, no matter if it's pleasant or unpleasant."[23] The adult version of childlike simplicity entails facing every responsibility—"pleasant" or "unpleasant"—with the same playful and lighthearted attitude. And so, the text continues, she "who is without desire in all undertakings behaves in a childlike fashion. Acts done by a pure one like this are without stain."[24]

One final note about play. A *serious* person might, once again, object that using this analogy of "life as play" is immature and irresponsible. But as the ancient Greek thinker Heraclitus observed, "Man is most nearly himself when he achieves the seriousness of a child at play."[25]

For all those good-hearted but perhaps overly earnest people out there, remember what's been said above about the relationship between karmic management and action for its own sake: There's no contradiction between working to improve oneself and the world, on the one hand, and selflessly losing oneself in action—making work into play—on the other. As we've seen, the former is actually done best when the latter occurs.

Acting as if it were all "just a game" ("life is but a dream") is neither irresponsible nor uncompassionate, and we can once again return to the theology of *lila* to understand why. The "sportive" activity of God's play does not preclude the "supportive" or compassionate element of God's grace, as Norvin Hein has cleverly put it. They are reconciled in that they both are defined by the same absence of "calculation of any selfish gain":

> God's sportive acts and his supportive acts are one because both are done without calculation of any selfish gain that might be made through them. Both are therefore desireless . . . and between God's lila and his grace there is no inconsistency.[26]

• • •

Many forms of artistic expression also exemplify the purposelessness of action done for its own sake. It's not usually to fulfill some practical function that one paints, dances, sings, writes poetry, plays an instrument, or sculpts—although professional artists need to make a living too!

While the artistic endeavor often results in a product—a picture is painted, a form is sculpted, a dance has been danced—even the finished "work of art" is aesthetic, not utilitarian. Andy Warhol once remarked, "An artist is somebody who produces things that people don't need to have."[27]

And the process of artistic creation is arguably more important than the product. "The object isn't to make art," observed painter Robert Henri. "It's to be in that wonderful state which makes art inevitable."[28] The purpose of artistic creation is to get into the flow of artistic creation. Like play, artistic activity in its pure form has no purpose other than itself.

In some instances, art is clearly created as ephemeral and transitory in order to highlight the importance of the creative process over the created product. Tibetan Buddhist monks labor for days, even weeks, painstakingly pouring colored sand to construct a mandala, an elaborate geometrical representation of the cosmos—and then completely destroy it upon its completion. In a similar fashion, Andy Goldsworthy assembles equally intricate designs over the course of many hours, with icicles that melt in the sun, twigs that are blown away by a gust of wind, or rock structures that are swallowed by the sea when the tide comes in.

Graffiti art (aka "street art") is also often quite detailed and time-consuming to create, but usually with the expectation that sooner or later the civic authorities will scrub it off or paint over it. And performance art of all sorts is by definition, well, *performed*—it's the activity itself that's essential; not something else that is brought about by the activity.

Music and dance are particularly salient examples of artistic expression done purely for its own sake. There's no real purpose to either playing or listening to a piece of music other than the pleasure of aesthetic expression and appreciation. And we dance or watch others dance not because doing so produces some result or attains some goal, but simply because it's enjoyable to do or watch.

The meaning and purpose are in the music and the dance themselves. As Isadora Duncan memorably quipped, "If I could tell you what it meant, there would be no point in dancing it."[29]

"A strong relaxation and calm comes over me," reports another dancer. "I have no worries of failure."[30] Like with pure play, there's no winning or losing, success or failure, involved in pure artistic expression. While others might judge the dance or the poem to be "good" or "bad" according to some criterion or another, the creative *experience* of dancing or writing poetry is rewarding in and of itself.

As one nonprofessional dancer elegantly observed, when we give ourselves over to the dance, our mental afflictions temporarily evaporate, our sense of individual isolation dissolves, and we feel fully integrated with our surroundings:

> While I dance, I cannot judge. I cannot hate. I cannot separate myself from life. I can only be joyful and whole. That is why I dance.[31]

Art imitates life, it is said; and it's also said that life imitates art. From the point of view of karma yoga, we might also put forward the idea that life *should* imitate art, just as "work" should best be regarded as "play."

"Art," declared philosopher Friedrich Nietzsche, "is the proper task of life."[32] And to fully engage in life as art, the artist loses him- or herself in the ongoing process of creation.

VIRTUE IS ITS OWN REWARD

Any activity can be made much more enjoyable and rewarding if it's done for its own sake. Any act undertaken calmly and *unbusily*, free from the *compulsion to act*; any chore that's reconceptualized as play; any pursuit that's reconstituted as a kind of *performance art*—in sum, any endeavor we do with *mindful unselfconsciousness*, can get us into the flow.

I wish I could tell you that I knew of some quick and easy tricks for getting into the zone—especially when the activity does not seem that intrinsically magnetizing. It's relatively easy for me to get into the flow when riding my motorcycle or playing in the waves at a beautiful beach. I too would be stoked to learn of some magic that would effortlessly launch me into action when it came to taking out the garbage, mowing the lawn, or doing my taxes.

But karma yoga, as we've mentioned before, is a form of "yoga" or "discipline," and the main feature of this yoga is not physical. Karma yoga is a method that depends on mindfulness and awareness. The essence of this technique is continuously remembering our simple but always relevant formula:

Om. It's like this now. Ah hum.

The only "trick" to karma yoga is to constantly recall this mantra. "This is what's happening now; this is the task I have to do at present." There's no point in starting up the "if only" whine again. *It's like this now*, so let's *just do it*!

It is the complete acceptance of whatever the next scene is in the ever-changing drama of life that serves as the precondition for losing oneself in the play. Karma yoga is the discipline of integrating the "somebody self" into what we are doing in the here and now, and thereby assuming the guise of the "nobody self" when acting.

So among the other descriptors that characterize action for its own sake, the most important of them is *egolessness*:

Whether he is seeing, hearing, touching, smelling, eating, walking, sleeping, or breathing, the disciplined one, who knows how things really are, would think, "I'm not doing anything at all."[33]

It's just the "seeing, hearing, touching, and so forth" that's happening. The "I" that's doing the "seeing, hearing, touching" is subsumed in the activity itself. "I'm not doing anything at all" because the self-consciousness required for awareness of the conceptualized "I" has been lost in complete engagement with what one is actually doing. The separation between the self and the world evaporates, and we become one with the life we are living.

. . .

Before concluding this discussion on "losing oneself in action," it's important to emphasize that the kind of "action for its own sake" we're speaking of here is *not* a morally neutral exercise. There are better and worse ways to be "in the zone." It's totally conceivable, to take one grisly example, that an ax murderer could really get into the activity of chopping up his victims.

While our secular psychologists have extolled the "flow state" for the pleasant and rewarding feelings that naturally attend it, our spiritual teachers have always emphasized that it matters not only *how* we do what we do, but also *what* we do and *why* we do it.

The discipline of karma yoga assumes that we understand the "karma" part. It presupposes wisdom about how karma really works and the direction such wisdom moves us when determining what we will do with our lives. Most importantly, karma yoga assumes that we are clear about the *why*—the intention or motivation behind any activity. The more aware we are that it is the selfless motivation that creates a happier life, the happier our lives will be—in both the present and the future.

The ancient Stoic philosopher Seneca remarked, "The real compensation of a right action is inherent in having performed it."[34] Virtue, in other words, is its own reward.

But virtue is virtue only *if* it is its own reward. Virtuous actions pay off only to the extent that we forego the explicit and conscious expectation of future personal benefit and concentrate on doing what needs to be done—to the best of our ability and out of the best of intentions.

There is pleasure to be found in any activity that puts us in the flow. But the rewards of virtuous action done for its own sake are doubled. Selfless action creates the karmic causes for future happiness: what goes around will come around. But action guided by karma yoga also entails contentment with our present situation and the opportunities it provides for acting wisely and happily in the here and now.

"The one who abandons attachment to the results of action," it says in the Bhagavad Gita, and "who is always satisfied and independent, does nothing at all, even when he is engaged in action."[35] Once again, with the loss of the "I," it's nobody who's doing anything when action is done for its own sake.

When we practice going with the flow, guided by karma yoga, we obtain relief from incessant self-consciousness, the inner chatter of the "somebody self." We are also at least temporarily liberated from the itchiness of the "if only" syndrome. And we are propelled for the length of our mindful unselfconsciousness into an experience of the Great Itchless State, the place where the "somebody self" stops cogitating and scheming ("I'm not doing anything at all") and allows the "nobody self" to take over and play.

Action Plan: Who's There When You're in the Flow?

Make a list of the activities you engage in that bring you the most pleasure—gardening, going to the beach, playing with your children, dancing at the club, getting absorbed in a challenging and enjoyable task at work, or whatever yours might be. When you are fully engaged in these happiness-producing activities, are you self-consciously monitoring yourself, or are "you" not really there at all?

Then pay attention to the experience of doing what you truly enjoy next time you have the opportunity to do it. Check to see whether it is precisely the degree to which you can "lose yourself" in the activity that produces the joy and satisfaction you attribute to it.

Notes:

* "If you cling to your life, you will lose it; but if you give up your life for me, you will find it."
   Matthew 10:39.

† "In flow, a person is challenged to do her best and must constantly improve her skills. At
   the time, she doesn't have the opportunity to reflect on what this means in terms of the
   self—if she did allow herself to become self-conscious, the experience could not have been
   very deep." Mihaly Csikszentmihalyi, *Flow: The Psychology of Optimal Experience* (New
   York: Harper & Row, 1990), 65–66.

‡ Compare Csikszentmihalyi's fancier label for this same idea: "The term 'autotelic' derives
   from two Greek words, *auto* meaning 'self' and *telos* meaning 'goal.' It refers to a self-
   contained activity, one that is done not with the expectation of some future benefit, but
   simply because the doing itself is the reward." Csikszentmihalyi, *Flow*, 67.

§ The earliest example of this argument in Sanskrit literature is found in Badarayana's *Vedantasutras*, 2.1.32–33. The author answers the objection that God can't be the creator of the
   world since God has no motive or reason to act (*na prayojanavattvat*, 2.13.2) by saying
   God does so "merely in play" (*lokavattu lilakaivalyam*).

PART IV

EVERYBODY
IS NOBODY

7

Living as an Ordinary Joe

We have the choice of two identities:
the external mask which seems to be real,
and the hidden, inner person who seems to us to be nothing,
but who can give himself eternally to the truth
in whom he subsists.

—Thomas Merton

WHO DA HELL AM I?

In the futuristic movie *Total Recall*, the protagonist, played by Arnold Schwarzenegger, purchases a brain implant designed to endow him temporarily with a completely new persona. The procedure goes haywire and Arnie becomes seriously confused, wandering through the movie trying to remember his former, and real, identity.

At one point, the frustrated, amnesiac Teutonic hero cries out in anguish, "If I'm not me, who da hell am I?!"

This is the million-dollar question for all of us: "Who da hell am I?" And there's one thing that the world's spiritual traditions and modern science and philosophy agree upon when it comes to the self: *We are not who we think we are.* We are all amnesiacs like the Schwarzenegger character, wandering through life, trying to find ourselves.

Julian Baggini has summarized the state-of-the-art findings in psychology, neuroscience, and modern philosophy in *The Ego Trick*, noting first that we're all pretty damned sure that there must be a real "me" in there somewhere: "People almost invariably believe that there is such an essence, a core of self that holds steady through life," he writes. "This is sometimes called the 'pearl' view." But the pearl inside the oyster is impossible to find: "The problem is that no one seems to be quite sure where to locate this precious gem."[1]

Despite our certainty that there must be "a core of self," we've seen that the "Where's Waldo?" search from hell for a unitary, unchanging, independent, Captain Kirk, essential pearl of a self inevitably leaves us empty-handed.

The Buddhist tradition has coined the term "no-self" (*anatman*) to describe this absence of the kind of "me" I think I am. But the recognition of the illusive nature of the personal, individual self is neither the sole discovery of any one religion nor nowadays even of religion itself.

It's become common knowledge that our commonsensical ideas about the self are in no way obviously or self-evidently true.

The self we think we have turns out to be just a kind of imaginary friend—or, perhaps even more often, an imaginary enemy. So we can all join our voices with Arnie's and cry out in unison: "*If I'm not me*"—if I'm not the "me" I think am—then "*who da hell am I?*"

• • •

Here's what we've discovered so far:

Each of us is, in fact, a unique individual; we're all equally "special," worthy of healthy self-respect and deserving of basic human rights. These are the givens when it comes to the question of personal identity—*I am somebody!*

Yes, each of us is somebody, and we're all fundamentally equal as somebodies. We're all the same in that we suffer and have problems in life, and we're all equally entitled to and have the capacity for attaining true happiness. And we all, equally, make mistakes—the worst of them stemming from our ignorance about who da hell the somebody we are really is.

But we delimit ourselves when we overidentify with the temporary and changing roles we play—when we mistake the revolving series of carnival cutouts, which we employ to constitute either our individual or group identities, as being fully and essentially definitive of who we actually are. And we especially suffer when one or another of these cutouts pits us against the cutouts into which other people are sticking their faces. This desperate, if futile, quest to be a *real somebody* quickly devolves into the divisive competitiveness of trying to be *more of a somebody* than somebody else.

Our ongoing culture of narcissism—stretching from the "Me Decade" right through to the present "iEra"—has magnified our attachment to the ego and its insatiable need to be admired and inflated. The elevation of self-centeredness as a culturally acceptable obsession has had obvious consequences, for what goes up must come down. The rampant pandemic of depression (and its less virulent but nevertheless serious twin, low self-esteem) can be directly linked to the excessive self-preoccupation that is both the real cause and the tragic expression of this debilitating disease.

Real self-improvement is founded upon first wising up about the question of "Who da hell am I?" I'm not the "me" I think I am— unified, changeless, independent, and a Master Controller of the present in the present. Who I am—as somebody—is an *idea* of me based on my parts: my body (can't be me without it!) and my mind (I'd really be in trouble without a mind!). "We are *nothing but* our parts," writes Julian Baggini, "but we are more than just our parts."[2]

This "more" that makes us who we are is simply a label, a name, an idea. I am, in sum, a conceptualization made possible by the conglomeration of multiple physical and mental parts that are forever changing.

I myself (!) have been many different *me*'s (both internally and externally) over the course of lo these sixty years—child *me*, rebellious youth *me*, family man *me*, academic *me*, surfer bum/biker *me*, monk *me*, spiritual teacher *me*, and retired man-of-leisure *me*. In some of my interactions, I'm "Dr. Smith, PhD," and in others, "Brian K. Smith." In yet other circumstances I'm "Lama Marut," but to friends and family, I'm just plain "Brian." Each *me* is a different persona, each a different conceptualization of the self and role, which I (whoever *that* is!) assume depending on the context and type of relationship I have with others.

And because who I am is merely a conceptualization on the basis of constantly evolving mental and physical parts, I can learn to re-conceptualize myself so as to become a happier me, no matter what role "I" am playing.

We've spoken in this book of many methods that function to help us improve our sense of self. Since who we think we are at any given moment is dependent on who we think we once were—on our memories or past karma—if we practice forgiveness, gratitude, and acceptance vis-à-vis our past, we will think of ourselves differently now. As we battle our selfish, destructive, and irrational mental afflictions in our own inner Rage in the Cage, we begin to think of ourselves as someone who is at least trying to be a good person, someone who is working to tame the worst of our habits.

When we drop the egotistical *me, me, me* chant and substitute the *What can I do for you?* mantra, we advance the process of self-improvement ever further, knowing that the best thing we can do for ourselves is to think about how we can help others. Lovingly and empathetically putting ourselves in other people's places, we gain freedom from the artificial limitations we place on our self-identity. And when we lose ourselves in action and concentrate on joyfully doing what needs to be done rather than calculating what we personally will get from doing it, we practice *mindfully unselfconscious* living all day long, in each and every situation.

If we wish to think of ourselves as a better somebody, we must act, speak, and think in more selfless and less selfish ways—in our relationships with others and in our everyday activities. We gain a better sense of self when we're not thinking about ourselves—and this is the seemingly paradoxical key to true "self-improvement."

So who da hell are you? And if you don't like the answer, make the necessary changes! "Your worst enemy cannot harm you as much as your own unguarded thoughts," asserts the Dhammapada. "But once mastered, no one can help you as much, not even your father or your mother."[3]

There's no one who makes you "you" other than you, and you now have the necessary tools for the creative process of self-reinvention.

• • •

The question for us at this point is not "*If* I'm not me, who da hell am I?" I may not be the "me" I ordinarily think I am. But I am also *no other than the "me" that I think I am*. That's all the self there is when it comes to the particular, individual "me"—the "somebody self" is a self-conception.

The really pertinent question at this concluding stage of our inquiry is "*When* I'm not me, who da hell am I?" We're nobody apart from thinking that we're somebody. And when we stop thinking we're somebody, we're really left with nobody.

We've said it before, and it's worth repeating: It's nobody that makes any and all somebodies possible. If we were *really* somebody—if there were a hardwired, permanent, essential "somebody self"—we'd be forever saddled with a static, unchanging, unimprovable, and very bored "me."

So let's put it positively: *because* we really are, have always been, and will always be nobody, *we can be* the ever-changing somebody we are now, have been in the past, and will be in the future.

It's getting in touch with the nobody that we really are that helps us improve the somebody we think we are. Thomas Mann once said, "No one remains quite what he was when he recognizes himself"[4]— and this is especially true if we know which self is changed when which self is recognized.

It is in the close encounters of the third kind with our "nobody self"—when we drop the self-consciousness, the self-grasping, and the self-centeredness—that we plug into our true being and the real power that transforms us. It is by losing the little self that we discover the Higher Power that is our Higher Self. And it is those moments when we commune with our true nature that function to make us a better and happier somebody.

So in this concluding chapter, we'll be exploring the final frontiers of the question of self-identity:

Who are we when we're not somebody?

We'll first look a bit more closely at who this "nobody self" we've been talking about really is. We'll then investigate the relationship between our personal identity and our universally shared true nature. Finally, we'll conclude with some tips on how the "somebody self" can further integrate with its real nobody-ness as it learns to live, not as someone desperately striving to be somebody special, but rather contentedly, as just an Ordinary Joe.

THE SELF THAT HAS NO NAME

What we've called the "nobody self" has various names in different traditions: it is our "true self" or "Buddha nature," the immortal soul, the Ground of Being, the *atman*, or the Tao. And the different traditions describe it in comparable ways, albeit with somewhat different vocabulary—that is, when they are willing to describe it at all.

The "true self," says one Hindu text, is "pure, awake, dear, complete, unmanifest, and faultless."[5] It "has never been born and never dies," says another ancient Indian scripture. "It has not come from anywhere, nor has it become anyone. It is unborn, unchanging, eternal, and primordial. It is not killed when the body is killed."[6]

All of these descriptors point to the fact that *the "nobody self" is the exact opposite of the "somebody self."* When our true nature is depicted, it is as a kind of reverse image of the limited, flawed, mortal, and basically disgruntled self we are so attached to.

And in many of the world's religions, there is also the recognition that the "nobody self" can't really be depicted or characterized at all. It is the unspeakable, the inconceivable. The "nobody self" is, by definition, *nameless*:

> *The tao that can be told*
> *is not the eternal Tao*
> *The name that can be named*
> *is not the eternal Name.*

> *The unnamable is the eternally real.*
> *Naming is the origin*
> *of all particular things.*[7]

Whereas the particular, individualized, lower self is really nothing other than a "name"—an idea or concept—the "nobody self" is the self that has no name . . . and is eternally unnamable.

In the ancient Indian traditions, this ultimate state is sometimes said to be *nirguna*, "without qualities or characteristics," and from this point of view the only way to refer to it is negatively. It is *neti, neti*, "not this, not that." "Ultimate reality is indescribable and cannot be signified," as one text puts it. "The blissful experience of one's own innermost self is accessible only when conceptual thought ceases."[8]

Or as another text declares, "It is unseen, unattainable, ungraspable, and without distinguishing marks. It is unthinkable, indefinable, and its essence is the perception of only itself. It is the pacification of all projections—peaceful, auspicious, non-dual. This is the true self; this is to be known."[9]

What is labeled our "Buddha nature" in the Buddhist tradition is similarly depicted as "beyond conceptualization" and description:

Because of its inexhaustible qualities, in nature it's like nothing else. Limitless, it acts as the only real refuge for living beings. It is always non-dual, beyond conceptualization. It has an indestructible quality since its true nature is uncreated. It is not born because it is permanent. It does not die because it is immovable. It is not harassed because it is in a state of peace. It does not decay because it is eternal.[10]

Turning to the Western traditions, in Islam there are said to be ninety-nine names for Allah ("The Merciful," "The Creator," "The Bestower," and so on), but the hundredth name is the "name that cannot be uttered." Jewish theologian Lawrence Kushner also declares that "there is yet a higher Name for the One of Being," and this name is "Nothing":

Beyond One there is only Nothing, for only Nothing can comprehend both good and evil, being and becoming, unity and duality,
sea and dry land. Already hinted at in Kabbalistic tradition by the
ultimate Name, *Ayn Sof*: literally, without end or utter Nothingness.
It is here that our consciousness and the Name of God while still
discrete, are no longer separate.[11]

And in the Christian tradition, this negatively enunciated depiction of what cannot be accurately or fully depicted is called the *via
negativa*, "apophasis" (from a Greek word meaning "to say 'no'"), or
"negative theology" (describing God or ultimate reality only by saying what it *is not*). Such an approach to the truly real can be found in
many other ancient traditions as well—including certain strands of
modern Western philosophy.[12]

"When you come to the ultimate," writes Rajneesh, "when you
come to your deepest core, you suddenly know that you are neither
this nor that, you are no one. You are not an ego. You are just a vast
emptiness."[13]

So there's not much to be said about that of which we cannot
speak. We, as particular somebodies, can really only point to the
universal nobody we all really are, like so many fingers pointing to
an indescribable moon. The great mystics have often said—when
they're talking about what can't be talked about at all—that silence is
probably the best strategy when it comes to our attempts to describe
the "nobody self."

But we can definitely say this: *Being nobody is not being nothing.* It
is an absence (no-body) and not a presence (some-body), but it is the
emptiness that makes the plenitude possible. It is the hole in the middle
that makes a donut what it is; it is the empty glass that can hold whatever is poured into it; it is the undifferentiated ocean from which all
particular waves arise, last for a while, and then return to their source.

This absence is the space in which all manifestation and life forms take place. It is nobody from which any and all somebodies arise and into which we are all reabsorbed. Nameless but not a non-entity, the ultimately real is the silence from which all sounds, words, names, and concepts emerge and back into which they dissolve.

And there's another thing we should say about the inexpressible: in its presence, we stand in reverential wonderment. It is the ultimate Great Itchless State of pure bliss. If we space out on those times when we commune with the infinite spaciousness of our true being—the self that cannot be named, conceptualized, or described—we miss out on the possibility of being *awestruck* . . . and therefore *dumbstruck*.

It's like the difference between appreciating the awe-inspiring beauty of a gorgeous sunset and coldly calculating the angle of the light rays as they filter through the atmosphere. The latter is driven by curiosity and utilizes words and concepts; the former captures the wonder of open-mouthed astonishment and wordless stupefaction.

As Rajneesh says, if you haven't experienced that which is beyond words, you haven't really lived at all:

> Even in ordinary life you feel the futility of words. And if you don't feel the futility of words, that shows that you have not been alive at all; that shows that you have lived very superficially. . . . When for the first time something starts happening which is beyond words, then life has happened to you, life has knocked on your door.[14]

• • •

Throughout this book, we've talked about the opposition between the "somebody" and "nobody" selves as a tension between our sense of individuality and our longing for absorption into the universal.

We've reviewed some of the various battlegrounds on which this inner war is waged, and we've spoken of the debate between the "devil" and the "angel" within. While we cling to our unique snowflake self, at some level we also long to merge into the cosmic avalanche—or to melt away altogether, vaporized into what is truly real.

But these two fundamental aspects of our being—the nameable "somebody self" and the unnamable "nobody self"—need not be at war with each other, and we needn't feel torn between them. The inner house need not be divided, but can live in harmony.

And to achieve this détente between our two selves, it's helpful to recognize that one does not exist without the other.

THE IN-BETWEEN STATE

In the Tibetan Buddhist tradition, the concept of the *bardo* is meant to explain where we go in between lives. In a system that presupposes rebirth, the *bardo* is thought of as a sort of a purgatory, betwixt and between the end of one life and the beginning of another.

But there is also a larger and more inclusive understanding of the term *bardo*. While living, we are in between birth and death; when we're middle-aged, we're in between youth and old age; when we're asleep, we're in between the end of last night's waking consciousness and the beginning of tomorrow morning's. And in this very moment, we're in between the past and the future.

So, from this point of view, we are *always* in some *bardo* or another. We're always "in between."

The "somebody self" is who we are in between experiences of being nobody, and the "nobody self" is who we are when we are in between being somebody. That's the simplest way to answer the question "Who da hell am I when I'm not somebody?" You're nobody when you're in between being somebody.

The remarkable ancient Indian scripture that we'll use for the meditational exercises at the end of the book points to any number of these in-between states where we drop into our true nature of being nobody. What the Vijnana Bhairava Tantra calls "the omnipresent state of ultimate reality" is continuously available: it is "on the radar even of ordinary people."[15] Between the polarities and dualities—between "this" and "that"—is the potential for the "highest realization":

> One should meditate on the perception of two things, and then place oneself in the middle between them. Dropping the two of them simultaneously, reality appears.[16]

Or:

> When the mind leaves one object and then is restrained from wandering to another object, being in the middle between two objects the highest realization then unfolds.[17]

All day long, every minute, we have the opportunity to revisit and commune with our nobody self. It is who we are in between being aware of ourselves as somebody. This state is even findable in the gap between every breath we take in and let out.

It is in those in-between moments, in the gaps between being somebody self-consciously doing something, that our ever-present true nature shines through.

• • •

The two kinds of self, somebody and nobody, are mutually exclusive when it comes to our awareness of them. We can't be conscious of being nobody when we're thinking we're somebody, and we aren't consciously somebody when we've dropped the self-awareness and become nobody.

And although we really *are* nobody all the time, we can't *be* nobody all the time. Our somebody and nobody selves exist, like everything else, interdependently—you can't have one without the other.

We're the kind of somebody we are—a changing, conceptualized self—because we really are nobody. But it's also true that we can only *be nobody* when we stop being somebody.

And we have to be somebody in order to *stop* being somebody!

The point is not to attempt to be nobody all the time. That's impossible. We'll always be somebody in between being nobody, because we're always in between. We alternate between our two selves, and each serves an essential purpose. We self-consciously plan our schedule and, if we're practicing karma yoga, unselfconsciously but mindfully carry out each task with our full attention, wholly integrated into the activity, like a child at play. We might make a decision to read a book, but, if we are self-consciously reading each word instead of getting into the flow of the story line, we're not really enjoying what we're doing.

Alternating between the somebody and nobody selves is just in the nature of change, and our lives are in constant flux. Things arise, last for a while, and then end. And then there is the gap—the in-between state—before a new cycle begins.

People who completely lose touch with their individual sense of self over a long period of time are, to put it bluntly, crazy. Clinical psychology calls such an unfortunate malady "depersonalization," and this condition is "associated with such unpleasant states of mind as fatigue, sleep deprivation, sensory deprivation, anxiety, depression, temporal lobe migraine, temporal lobe epilepsy, and so on."[18]

It is healthy and normal to identify, at least to some degree, with the somebody self, and to rotate between it and the always present, unchanging, and eternal nobody self. As enjoyable as it is to be "in the flow," if we were *always* in the flow there would be no one to emerge from the experience refreshed, revitalized, and energized. If we were in a state of self-forgetfulness all the time, the experience of self-loss would not result in any kind of self-transformation, for there would be no return to the self that could be transformed.

Neuroscientist Susan Greenfield remarked in an interview, "There are moments in most of our lives when we want to 'let ourselves go,' 'blow our minds.'" But such Dionysian experiences of self-transcendence, enjoyable and rejuvenating as they are, cannot realistically be extended indefinitely, any more than it is healthy to only remain in the Apollonian state of uptight self-control:

> If someone said to you, "I want to do that all the time, I want to go to the rave every single moment I'm alive," on the whole, we'd feel rather sorry for someone like that, just as we'd feel sorry for someone that proudly declared they'd never let their hair down, they'd never let themselves go, they'd never had a sensational time in their whole lives.[19]

No one really knows what happens to us after we die. Perhaps then we permanently merge into the nobody state forever and ever. But in this life—and in future rebirths, if there are any in store for us—we will always be somebody when we're not being nobody.

So the spiritual goal is not to somehow disappear the "somebody self" but rather to know it for what it is and detach from the belief that it's the only self that there is. Depictions of the enlightened state—the person who is "liberated in this very lifetime" (*jivanmukta*) or one who has gone into "nirvana with something left over" (i.e., one who still has a body and continues to appear in this world)—do not suggest that somebody who is free ceases to be somebody entirely.

But such a person is not only free from the illusions the rest of us carry around, he or she is also free from the grasping onto and full identification with those illusions. The liberated person has realized the true nature of both the individual self (transient, changing, finite, and restricted) and the universal self (eternal, unchanging, infinite, and universal).

The free man or woman lives "like an ordinary person" but also "is completely different."[20] And the difference lies in how they think of themselves—or, we might say, how they *don't* think of themselves. The liberated person has emancipated herself or himself from the prison of a restricted self-conception that completely identifies with one's own individuality, distinctiveness, and separation from others—and also from all the unhappiness that attends such a delimited understanding of the self.

• • •

The spiritual quest is ultimately not the freedom *of* the individual; it is the freedom *from* the individual. And one of the main reasons we are not free is that the "somebody self" resists its own dethronement as the sole monarch ruling the Kingdom of Me.

"You" (say your name to yourself) will not somehow gain liberation as "you." The "somebody self" will not become some supersized version of itself in nirvana or heaven; such a fantasy is just spiritual megalomania.

As the great modern Tibetan Buddhist teacher Chögyam Trungpa Rinpoche famously observed, enlightenment will be the ego's "ultimate and final disappointment."[21]

Actually we cannot attain enlightenment until we give up the notion of me personally attaining it. As long as the enlightenment drama has a central character known as me, who has certain attributes, there is no hope of attaining enlightenment, because *it's nobody's project.*[22]

Awakening is not *somebody's* project but *nobody's.* Salvation or liberation is freedom from both the complete association with the "somebody self" and the alienation from the "nobody self." "He who knows the true self is blessed," says one Indian text, and "because of who he is"—because of this radical de- and re-identification—"when acting in everyday life he does not suffer like ordinary people."[23] He or she has discovered and abides in the Great State of Itchlessness.

Such a person continues to "act in everyday life"; he or she remains "a somebody" in the world—going to work, interacting with others, leading a life. But the liberated man or woman is a completely *happy* somebody, knowing he or she is just in between being nobody, and not grasping onto an illusory version of his or her identity:

One whose mind is completely at peace stays happy in his everyday life. He sleeps happily, he comes and goes happily, he speaks happily, and he eats happily.[24]

THE TWO SELVES IN HARMONY

We are all split personalities when it comes to our identity. There are two of us within each of us—the ever-changing "somebody self" that exists only conceptually, and the "nobody self" that truly exists but cannot be named.

Remember the two birds sitting on the same tree we encountered back in chapter 1? They are described, you may recall, as "inseparable friends," not as irreconcilable antagonists. One of them is actively engaged in the world (that's the lower, individual self) while the other only passively "looks on" (that would be the Higher Self). When the "somebody self" birdie perceives the "nobody self" birdie and "realizes that all greatness is his, then his despair vanishes."[25]

The personal self, being changing and therefore changeable, is improvable. But as we have seen, improving the "somebody self" is not accomplished through further inflating the ego in the attempt to *become more of a somebody*. Rather, it is by systematically deflating the self-centered self, and accessing the ever-present reality of *being nobody*, that we move forward in the reconceptualization of who we think we are.

It's when our two selves are reconciled and coordinated that we truly become complete. The two birds then sing in harmony; somebody and nobody peacefully coexist as inseparable friends.

• • •

Our dual selves are spoken of in the Mahayana Buddhist tradition as two versions of our "Buddha nature," that "element" (*dhatu*) or "propensity" (*gotra*) within every living being that serves as the "womb" for birthing an Awakened Buddha (*tathagata-garbha*). As it says in the Uttara Tantra,

> It should be understood that the propensity comes in two types. . . . There is the propensity that is naturally present from time with no beginning, and that which has been perfected through cultivation.[26]

The "somebody self" possesses the "developable" Buddha nature—"perfected through cultivation"—which is said to be like a seed. When watered and given sunlight—when we cultivate the virtue that pivots on the development of humility, kindness, empathy, selfless action, and compassion and love for others—this sort of Buddha nature is nurtured and propagated. We improve ourselves by learning to let go of our selfish needs and wants and the mental afflictions inevitably associated with them. The inner potential is activated little by little as we drop the ego's *What about me?* imperative and turn our attention to the *What can I do for you?* directive.

The second sort of Buddha nature is said to be "innate" and is in no need of improvement or development whatsoever. It is always and unchangingly present, eternally perfect, but also usually unrecognized. It's said to be like an undiscovered treasure trove of riches buried under a poor man's home.

Although we may be unaware of its existence, we all have within us this precious treasure, which is our true nature, our "nobody self." It is always with us, right under our house; it is always available and accessible. But we need to notice, embrace, and identify with it if we are to partake of this inner abundance.

"There is nothing whatsoever that needs to be removed from this, and nothing whatsoever that needs to be added," the text says. The innate Buddha nature within us—our "nobody self"—is always and already perfected. Simply by fully realizing who we truly are, we are freed from the monopolizing tyranny of who we think we are: "It is from seeing reality that the seer of reality is really and completely liberated."[27]

The integrated self is less fully identified with somebody and more with nobody. It is only our desperate clinging to the ego, and its insatiable desire to be a "real someone," that keeps us from realizing our deeper identity and the balance that comes when the two selves are in harmony.

EMPTYING AND FILLING

When we commune with the "self with no name," we immediately gain what Jesus called the "peace that surpasses understanding."[28] Realizing who we are when we're not being ourselves, experiencing the great relief and itchlessness of *being nobody*, is thus more a matter of emptying than filling.

When it comes to the deeper answer to the "Who da hell am I?" question, less is in fact more.

It is important to honor the personal self and its "developable" Buddha nature, and to continuously cultivate its transformation. But the less we grasp onto our particularity and individuality, the more we make ourselves available to our universal, eternal, blissful, and perfect "nobody self."

In the Christian tradition, the relinquishing of the exclusive identification with the individual self is called *kenosis* (from the Greek word for emptiness)—the "self-emptying" of one's own ego in order to become entirely receptive to the divine. In a passage from the New Testament, we are admonished to renounce the ego's "selfish ambition" and "in humility" lose ourselves in service to others:

> Be of the same mind, having the same love, being in full accord and of one mind. Do nothing from selfish ambition or conceit, but in humility regard others as better than yourselves. Let each of you look not to your own interests, but to the interests of others.[29]

The more we are able to let go of thinking about "me," the more we are able to think of ourselves as "we." Self-emptying allows for the recognition not only of our true self but also of our commonality, of the bonds we share with all other somebodies. When somebody is emptied out and nobody remains, the space is created to refill and *be everybody.*

This passage from the Bible goes on to say that the self-emptying process also entails a kind of "mind meld" with Christ—not with the Jesus Christ Superstar version but rather with the one who truly voided himself of all conceit and pride:

> Let the same mind be in you that was in Christ Jesus, who, though he was in the form of God, did not regard equality with God as something to be exploited, but emptied himself, taking the form of a slave, being born in human likeness. And being found in human form, he humbled himself . . .[30]

The "somebody self" becomes more like nobody when it practices humility rather than pride, modesty rather than arrogance, connection rather than haughty (and unhappy) isolation. It is when we empty ourselves that we are filled with plentitude and realize the Great Commonality we share with all others.

The more we can put the "somebody self" aside, the more affinity we feel for all others and for life itself. We become more like Jesus—humbled by his humanness rather than prideful about his divine origins—and by doing so become more attuned to both the common humanity and universal divinity each of us shares with all others. As we are told in the Biblical passage cited above, it is through practicing "looking not to your own interests, but to the interests of others" that we train ourselves for increasingly melding our minds to that of the divine.

• • •

When we empty ourselves completely, we automatically slip into our "nobody self." As we've seen, we are nobody when we are in between being somebody. But even as a self-conscious somebody, we can practice taking on both the identitylessness and the sense of interrelationship with others that is entailed in *being nobody*. When a "somebody self" learns to be more of a nobody, they increasingly actualize their capacity to identify more with everybody.

As we have noted, selflessness and empathy lie at the very heart of what it means to create good karma rather than bad. The practice of karma yoga, you will remember, is action done without self-regard or personal reward—action done for its own sake, knowing that virtue is its own reward. If our intention is motivated by selflessness and altruism, our activities will have a beneficial result on our self-image and on our outlook on the world.

We've discussed several methods for improving our self-image, all of which revolve around the premise that it is *nobody that makes a better somebody possible*. When we drop into our true nature and in one way or another turn off the self-centered inner narration—through love and compassion for others, mindful unselfconsciousness in our actions, or virtuous action done for its own sake—we experience the power and joy of *being nobody*.

The self-emptying project can be thought of not only as a hollowing out but also as an infusion of our true selfless nature into our "somebody self" identity. The latter gets itself out of the way and, in thought and action, becomes more nobody-like.

There are relatively simple ways in which we can start practicing being more of a nobody as we live in our daily lives as a somebody. On our way to final liberation, we can increasingly become more like our spiritual heroes and religious archetypes: more Christ-like, more Buddha-like, more *nobody-like*.

Instead of reveling in and glorifying our individuality and uniqueness, we can practice living more as just a regular guy or gal, just an Ordinary Joe.

BE ANONYMOUS—OR AT LEAST UNFABULOUS

We've seen that the "nobody self" is nameless and unnamable. By becoming more *anonymous*—a word that derives from the Greek phrase "no name"—we mirror and imitate our true nature.

My birth name is "Brian Smith." The "Brian" part is the name my parents gave me, but the surname is a total invention. I might just as well be called "Brian X" or "Brian Doe."

Here's the story: My paternal grandfather (the professional wrestling fan) was left as an infant on the doorstep of some orphanage in late-nineteenth-century England. His parentage was unknown—there was no note or anything pinned on the swaddling clothes. And so the staff gave him the most generic last name possible for that time and place: Smith.

I know that there are some people who can trace their family lineage back to the *Mayflower* or whatever, but I personally am only a couple of generations removed from complete obscurity when it comes to my genetic origins. My bloodline disappears into namelessness and anonymity pretty quickly.

And truth be told, no matter how far back your family genealogy can be traced, eventually we all discover that we end up as . . . well, no one in particular. We all, if we look into the matter, are of indeterminate origin. Despite the different names that distinguish us, at bottom we are really all just generic human beings.

Practicing being more anonymous, and posing less as the amazing, special somebody we all think we are, is an acknowledgment of our basic commonality. It's not only our true nature, the "nobody self," that we share with all others. Even as individual somebodies, we're all really "just folks," and embracing our generic ordinariness leads to a closer affinity with our fellow human beings (themselves all "just folks" too).

Little acts done incognito teach us to be less and less identified with our sense of particularity, our ego, our "somebody self." Acting as anonymous agents of good in the world, we train ourselves to be more of a hybrid, more of somebody who is practicing to be more nobody-like.

There are many, many ways in which we can think and act more anonymously in our lives. Here are just a few tips to get you started in your new career as Secret Agent 000:

* If you live in a city that still has them, plug someone else's depleted parking meter and save them a ticket! And don't stand around waiting for the owner to come back so you can be thanked. (Putting money into someone else's parking meter is, by the way, illegal in many municipalities, so, by doing this little act of civil disobedience, you can also get in touch with your inner Che Guevara.)

* Take a "first-person-pronoun-free day" where you avoid using the terms "I," "me," or "mine" for twenty-four hours. Trying to keep up this practice over an extended period of time will make you more aware of how often we think of (and talk about!) ourselves, and only ourselves.

* Give presents to people without them knowing it was you who was the donor. You might want to stick on one of those little tags, filling out the "To" part but leaving the "From" line blank.

* Do somebody else's job for them—a task at work that your office mate is responsible for, or a chore at home that your partner usually takes care of—and do it secretly and transparently.

* Slip some money into the purse or wallet of someone that you know is having financial challenges. This reverse pick-pocketing will require the same sort of cleverness and stealth that criminals employ. And you will experience the same thrill that the successful

thief enjoys, while simultaneously doing something nice for someone else!

* It used to be a tradition on May Day to place a basket of food, flowers, or presents on a neighbor's doorstep, ring the doorbell, and then run away. Becoming Secret Agent 000 could singlehandedly revive this tradition, and not just on May 1.

* Next time you're at a restaurant, pay for some stranger's dinner. Just randomly select someone, call the waiter or waitress over, and secretly pick up that person's tab. You can sneak a peek at the person's reaction when they are told that an anonymous benefactor has paid their bill, and surreptitiously share in the little unexpected spike of happiness you brought to someone else's life.

* There's a similar practice that's currently gaining traction in some cities. Next time you go to Starbucks for your grande soy decaf nonfat sugar-free latte, lean in and quietly whisper to the barista that you will be paying for two coffees—one for you and one for the next person in line. And be sure to tell the server not to mention who paid it forward.

• • •

If you can't be anonymous, at least work at being *unfabulous*. The individual self strives to be remarkable, cool, clever, important, and distinctive. Somebody who is trying to be more like nobody reverses this impulse and endeavors to be ordinary, common, simple, nondescript, and undistinguished.

In this day and age of reality television, of Facebook and Twitter self-promotion, of the endless quest to be *more of a real somebody*, it's really fighting the power to be content with being average and unfabulous.

One simple way to do this is to reduce one's preferences in life—what one prefers to wear and to eat, which people we prefer to be around—and learn to be more *equanimous*. Our preferences help to define us as unique individuals, and so being a little more *non-preferential* and *impartial* is another way to train somebody to be more nobody-like.

I had a habit for several years of never buying new clothes. When I needed something to wear, instead of going to Macy's, I went to the Salvation Army. There's nice stuff at Sal's, especially at outlets located in affluent neighborhoods—a dirty little secret for minimizing the austerity of this practice!—and I saved a lot of money by shopping exclusively at such places.

But all the clothing at secondhand stores is, of course, used; it has been previously selected, bought, worn, and then discarded by someone you don't know. And there's something about wearing other people's clothes that makes an impression on one's psyche. You usually feel a little less fabulous, and a lot more like an Ordinary Joe, when you pull on a five-dollar secondhand shirt that you are aware used to belong to some stranger.

Looking totally unfabulous was, of course, the original intent behind the robes worn by monks, nuns, priests, imams, and other clergy. These are *uniforms*, designed to make every individual look alike. Nowadays such a presentation often conveys the exact opposite impression—"Here's somebody dressed differently who must be *special!*"—and when I was wearing the robes it made me very uncomfortable to imagine people thinking this. The real purpose of such a uniform was to iron out particularities (and to make one's sartorial choices every morning much easier), not to confer some exceptional status.

Even while I was still an ordained monk, I eventually made the decision to appear in public as an ordinary layman. Dropping the unusual veneer provided by the flowing red robes took down a barrier between me and the people around me. It was hard at first—the costume does provide a kind of protective shield—but the advantages of appearing "normal" outweighed the vulnerability that accompanied looking like an ordinary Clark Kent instead of giving the impression of being some kind of spiritual Superman.

There's a great virtue in appearing as an Ordinary Joe. Instead of setting ourselves apart by what we wear, we can send a different message when we don clothing more typical and common to whatever context we find ourselves in. For some this will mean an off-the-rack business suit rather than a tailored Brooks Brothers ensemble, while for others it will entail unbranded and inexpensive jeans and T-shirts rather than whatever new and cool garb is currently in fashion.

Another way to feel less distinctive is to minimize one's food preferences. I know there are plenty of people who really like those fungi known as mushrooms, and there are others who enjoy that fruit with the suitably unappetizing name "eggplant." But I don't particularly care for either—*I am somebody*, defined in part as a person who doesn't prefer such supposed edibles.

And I avoid them if possible. But when someone has gone to the trouble of cooking a meal that includes such items, I eat them. It's not a big deal, but this act, in its small way, diminishes the ego's need to be a special somebody, distinguished by what one will and will not eat.

This practice may be a lot more challenging for self-defined vegans or vegetarians. But there's an ancient instruction for monks and nuns—those who are professionally committed to humility and self-effacement—to uncomplainingly accept and eat whatever is put before them, without making a fuss about "being" one thing or another when it comes to food.

It is a time-honored religious practice to be less picky and just eat what has been offered. One of my students spent several years

living as a Buddhist nun in England, where they maintained this tradition. Every day, she told me, the monastics would go to the local
village, begging bowls in hand, and stand and wait for edible dona-
tions. The villagers would come along and put whatever they could
give into the bowls—and in whatever order: carrots on top of ice
cream, cheeseburgers piled onto lentils. And that was dinner; that's
what the ordained would eat.

One need not go to such extremes to benefit from a practice
of not being so particular about what one consumes. While there
are undoubtedly many benefits to a vegetarian or vegan diet, being
overly attached to what one prefers to eat strengthens rather than
weakens the individual's sense of distinctiveness.

Being less preferential about what one wears and eats is just
the tip of the iceberg when it comes to being *unfabulous*. There are
countless ways in which we can train ourselves to be less demanding and more accepting, less exclusive and more inclusive, less of a
special somebody and more of an Ordinary Joe.

It's like this now—now there's only this one shirt that fits me on
the rack; now there are mushrooms on my plate; now someone has
prepared and served me a cheeseburger.

And now I find myself with this kind of person. We all have preferences when it comes to the people we choose to be with. And we all
tend to hang out with pretty much the same kinds of people—people
who are more or less like ourselves. Getting along with others who
are not in our social clique is yet another way to be more nobody-
like in our daily lives.

• • •

In the 1983 mockumentary *Zelig*, Woody Allen portrays a character who so badly wants to fit into his social surroundings that he

literally takes on the physical characteristics of those around him. This "human chameleon" transforms into a rich patrician when around the *Great Gatsby* set, and then into a plain-speaking regular guy when he's with the servants. He becomes a Native American, an African American, and a Hasidic Jew when around such kinds of people.

This spoof displays, by means of an extreme caricature, the perils of conformity. But read in a different way, it also can be viewed as a comic version of the serious spiritual practice of living like an Ordinary Joe.

As we've argued in this book, the need to be unique and special is itself unexceptional and general to us all. It is not a sign of our distinctiveness to want to be distinctive. The deeper conformity we are all susceptible to is our common and quite ordinary desire to be extraordinary and set apart—to be a *real somebody*.

When with others, somebody who is trying to be more nobody-like tries to fit into the situation and to make others feel more at ease. Instead of clinging to our uniqueness and specialness, when we're with other people, especially those who appear different from ourselves, we remember the more fundamental ways in which we are all alike. The "somebody self" who is working at being more nobody-like feels more affinity to the others who come within his or her purview.

We are all human, and nothing human can be completely foreign to any of us. So when you encounter the checkout girl at the supermarket or the driver of your taxi or the fellow behind the counter at the dry cleaners, just ask about their day, tell a little joke, and treat them with respect. It doesn't take much to make another person's life a little better, but it does require acknowledging them as human beings fundamentally no different from oneself.

When you're with people who are different from you—whether they're a plumber from New York or a cowboy from Tucson—take an interest in what that kind of life must be like, learn a little bit about what's entailed in doing that for a living. When you're around rich people, stop with the class struggle already and recall that they're essentially as ordinary as you are. When you're with people of different ethnic or racial backgrounds, remember that they're basically just like you—burdened with the same kinds of problems, harboring the same desires for happiness, and endowed with the same fundamental true nature.

It was in part out of such considerations that, in October of 2013, I made the difficult decision to give back my monk's vows after living for eight years as an ordained monastic. While I have only admiration and respect for those who commit to this kind of life, for me personally being a monk in the Tibetan Buddhist tradition no longer seemed to accord with my developing nondenominational spiritual orientation, nor with the desideratum to try to live more as a nobody instead of a special somebody. The very terms "monk" and "monastic" are derived from the Greek word for "alone" (*monos*), and can be interpreted to refer to someone who has set themselves apart from others.

As the scripture says, "Give up such distinctions as, 'I am so-and-so, but not such-and-such.'"[31] Working to be more of an Ordinary Joe in our interactions with others helps us to recognize the real bonds that we share with every other person.

This is not a matter of being inauthentic or pretending to be someone you're not—you don't have to turn into Zelig, the "human chameleon." But we can authentically think and act less like the special somebody we might believe we are, because we are all authentically and really nobody.

And when we're in between being nobody, we're all authentically just "everyday people," trying our best to get through life. So if you need some help as you interact as Ordinary Joe with others who

seem quite different from yourself, you can hum the old Sly and the
Family Stone song and remember the refrain:

> I'm everyday people, yeah yeah . . .
> Oh sha sha—we got to live together.[32]

NOBODY IS EVERYBODY (AND VICE VERSA)

Yes (oh sha sha), we really do have to live together. None of us is an
island; our human archipelago is actually one big land mass under
the surface. As Zen teacher Thich Nhat Hanh has declared, the
whole purpose of our lives is to overcome our sense that we are isolated, discrete individuals: "We are here to awaken from our illusion
of separateness."[33]

Grasping onto our individuality and uniqueness—to the "somebody self" we've talked about so much in this book—is premised upon
and further propagates this "illusion of separateness." Some of our
strongest inborn instincts—this is the "devil" part of us—encourage
the selfishness that detaches us from others. And our modern culture
of narcissism and self-promotion ratifies and exacerbates our innate
egoism.

But all this self-centeredness is based on illusion, not reality, and
the inner "angel" who suspects this needs to have her voice ampli-
fied. The self we are so centered on—independent, disconnected,
and alone—doesn't really exist at all, and the idea that we pursue our
own happiness by feeding this phantom is wholly misguided.

Our spiritual traditions have for millennia been telling us that
our selfishness and egoism must be put aside if we are ever to find
true happiness. And our scientists are now joining their voices in
the chorus, pointing out that there is no findable "pearl self" at
all; that what we call the self is just a bundle of functions wrapped

together by our self-conception; and that the age-old religious virtues revolving around selflessness—altruism, empathy, compassion, gratitude, and forgiveness—will inevitably bring more happiness to one's life.

And at least some of our scientists now agree with the long-standing spiritual claim that our sense of separation from others and the world around us is a misconception. "A human being," observed Albert Einstein, "is part of the whole, called by us 'Universe.'"

> He experiences himself, his thoughts and feelings as something separated from the rest—a kind of optical delusion of his consciousness. This delusion is a kind of prison for us, restricting us to our personal desires and to affection for a few persons nearest to us. Our task must be to free ourselves from this prison by widening our circle of compassion to embrace all living creatures and the whole of nature in its beauty.[34]

· · ·

So we end by restating the million-dollar question, adding a million-dollar adverb:

Who da hell am I . . . really?

Really, beneath all our differences and distinctions, we are all equally nobody. And being really nobody is the condition of possibility for becoming a better somebody—somebody who increasingly realizes that he or she is part of a much larger whole.

We'll always be somebody, so when we're in between being nobody we can live happier, more fulfilling lives by being more nobody-like, more of an Ordinary Joe and less of a special, distinctive little snowflake, set apart from others. Since we're all *really* nobody, everybody is *really* just like everybody else.

Remembering that we all live in "interbeing," we can think and act more in accordance with the interdependence that defines our existence in the world. Dispelling the illusion of our separateness, we can find solace in the reality of our interconnectedness, in being everybody.

Detaching from the monopolizing claims of the atomistic "somebody self," we can integrate more with the world around us and identify more with the fount of our very being, the ultimate reality that is our true self.

This is the path to real happiness, for happiness can only be founded in truth, not in illusion.

Remember, they say nobody's perfect.

So why not *be nobody*?

Action Plan: Secret Agent 000

Your mission, should you choose to accept it, is to commit to one act of kindness for someone else every day—*anonymously*. Spend a few moments at the beginning of the day making a plan for how you will pull this off. And keep your eye out during the course of the day to see if unexpected opportunities arise to help others incognito. Practice being Secret Agent 000 in all the little ways you can.

Knock,
And He'll open the door.
Vanish,
And He'll make you shine like the sun.
Fall,
And He'll raise you to the heavens.
Become nothing,
And He'll turn you into everything.

—Rumi

Acknowledgments

I am inexpressibly grateful to the phenomenal mother-daughter team Wendy and Cindy Lee for the time they took to read the earliest drafts of each chapter and for their invaluable advice and perspectives.

David B. Fishman painstakingly went through the manuscript word by word and vastly improved the quality of my prose. It is a great mitzvah to have a full-fledged genius take the time to carefully review what an ordinary man has written.

I have also been blessed to have superb editors at Beyond Words. Many thanks to Emily Han and Henry Covey for their help in making a much better book out of the original manuscript, as well as to my literary agent, Joelle Delbourgo, for her unflagging advocacy and support.

I am very grateful to those who assisted me in my research—Chantal Carleton, June Maker, Darin McFadyn, Claire Thompson, the Rev. Anne Deneen, Karl Whiting, and my daughter, Sophia

Fleming-Benite—and to the many volunteers who have transcribed oral teachings under the efficient management of Catherine Eaton.

To all whose generosity and hospitality make my life on the road so trouble-free, I cannot begin to thank you enough. And to my benefactors and patrons, I remain in your debt. I hope this book will be of some benefit to others and thus justify, at least to some extent, your support.

There is no way to repay what I owe to my teachers—my spiritual mentors, academic guides, close friends, fellow travelers on the path, and those who pose as my students.

Finally, although it may sound stupid, I'm really grateful to my computer and all it makes possible. I simply could not have written this book without the magic that has become available to us. We live in amazing times.

Appendix:
Dropping into Your
True Nature

O ur true nature is always with us. It has never been born and so
can never die; it is eternally unchanging and ever-present; it is
the "nobody self" that lies behind and beneath all iterations of every
"somebody self."

And so it is always accessible. It is perpetually there whenever
we quiet the ego's chattering, mute the ongoing inner narrative, and
relax into the silence, spaciousness, and serenity of *being nobody*.

In what follows below, you'll find a set of simple meditative
exercises, correlating to each of the seven chapters in this book, for
dropping into that supreme state of bliss anytime you wish. They can
be used as full-fledged meditations or merely as ways to catch a few
moments of peace at any time during your day.

The exercises are drawn from 112 such meditations, or *dha-
ranas*, that comprise the bulk of an ancient Sanskrit text from the
Hindu tradition of northern India called the Vijnana Bhairava Tantra (VBT).* The VBT purports to be a conversation between two

deities, Shiva (aka Bhairava, representing ultimate reality) and his beloved and inseparable partner Shakti (symbolizing the world of appearances and form). When Shakti asks Shiva to teach her how to discover the highest nature of things, the latter replies, "Shakti is the very face of Shiva." That is to say, the deepest aspect of reality is found nowhere other than within the day-to-day world we live in.

The extraordinary is discoverable within the ordinary; the ultimate within the relative; the transcendent within the immanent. This same truth is summarized within the classical Buddhist scripture the Heart Sutra: "Emptiness is not different from that which takes form, and that which takes form is not different from emptiness." The void and the plentitude are two sides of the same coin.

In the VBT, Shiva proceeds to teach Shakti an array of straightforward techniques for recognizing her true nature in the midst of everyday life. The methods are simple—deceptively so. They aren't hard to do, but they do require paying close attention to what's happening to your consciousness when you're engaged in them. They are, after all, meditations.

I hope you'll give these exercises a try. If you do, you'll find them to be relatively easy ways to get a little taste of what it feels like to *be nobody*. You'll be able to drop into your true nature whenever you want.

MEDITATION FOR CHAPTER 1

Look at the clear blue sky with an unwavering gaze, keeping the body still. Immediately you will reach your true essence. . . . When one places the mind on outer space—which is unchanging, without support, empty, all-pervasive, and free from limitation— one enters the realm of spacelessness.†

Remember how nice it was, when you were a kid, to just lie down on the grass and look up at the sky? Here's a quick, easy, and enjoyable way to break out of your limitations and get out of your own head, anytime during the day or night. Just take a moment to stop and go outside (or at least look through the window) and lose yourself in the unlimited expanse of the atmosphere or in the inconceivable vastness of outer space.

The mind takes the form of what it perceives. If what you perceive is the limitless, well, you've just dropped into your true nature.

MEDITATION FOR CHAPTER 2

> Because of placing the mind at the meeting place of the two breaths, either inside (i.e., where the inhalation ends and the exhalation begins) or at the outer limit (i.e., where the exhalation ends and the inhalation begins), the yogi attains equanimity and becomes a proper vessel for knowledge.[‡]

Ever heard the expression "Just take a deep breath?" We're breathing all day, every day, so here's a way to gain a little peace whenever you need it. Take a deep breath, but do so mindfully. Notice that at the end of each inhalation and exhalation there is a gap, a pause, before the next exhalation or inhalation, respectively. Gently, without holding the breath or interrupting the natural respiratory flow, place your mind fully on that pause and rest in the respite between breathing in or out.

Fall into the gap! And when done without self-consciousness of being in the gap, you've just found your true nature. There's no need to go to church or temple to find the sacred; it's there with every breath we take.

MEDITATION FOR CHAPTER 3

One who meditates nonconceptually on the emptiness of the body, even for just a moment, loses all conceptions and comes to possess the self-nature of what is beyond conceptual thought. . . . One should concentrate on just the skin encasing the body like a wall [while thinking], "There is nothing inside." Meditating on that, one becomes joined with the imponderable. . . . [Then] meditate on the self taking the form of empty space, stretching out endlessly in all directions . . . [and] being freed from any resting place, then one sees his own true nature. §

We're all pretty attached to the idea that we *are* our physical bodies, and so this brief meditation helps us to break out of our identification with our corporality at the same time it puts the mind on the infinite.

First, imagine that inside the body there is nothing but empty space, like clear blue sky. Mentally empty out all the guts and bones until it is completely void, right up to the ends of the fingers and toes, encased only by the thinnest layer of skin.

Then erase even the outline of the body and open up into the infinite empty space outside. Nothing to the left as far as you can imagine, or to the right, or up, or down, or in front, or in back.

Relax and reside in complete spaciousness, and enjoy your true nature.

MEDITATION FOR CHAPTER 4

When one experiences desire, anger, greed, delusion, intoxication, or jealousy, one should place the mind on it unwaveringly until only the bare essence of it remains.‖

When you're on the verge of losing the Big Smackdown with an incipient mental affliction, stop and do this meditation. Close your eyes and go deep within. Locate the feeling you're struggling with and then analyze it. Is it really one, complete, seamless, full-blown "feeling"?

Or is it, upon investigation, separable into moments? Before it's designated "anger" or "jealousy," isn't it just a series of momentary instances of consciousness over which the mind superimposes a label?

If you can get this far, then have a look at what makes up each of these little moments. Doesn't each instant of what we call "anger" or "jealousy" have its own beginning, middle, and end? And what about the beginning of each momentary fragment of what we name "a feeling?" Mustn't it also have its own beginning, middle, and end?

And down you go. There are no partless parts, no moments of the so-called mental affliction that aren't further divisible. When you get tired of analyzing your feeling into parts of the parts of the parts of the parts, ad infinitum, you'll get to its "bare essence," as the text says—its emptiness, its true nature—which is the same as yours!

MEDITATION FOR CHAPTER 5

When one experiences great bliss, or when one sees a long-lost relative, one should meditate on the arising of the bliss and thoroughly dissolve the mind in it. . . . One should let the mind rest on things remembered or places one has seen. One's body will lose its support (i.e., one will forget one is embodied) and the Lord will arise.#

We all spend at least some time every day daydreaming, so this little meditation should be easy. Take a moment to immerse yourself in a pleasant memory. Lose yourself completely in the reverie; stop thinking you're stuck inside your physical body. Fully relive being in some beautiful place, or the wonderful times you've had with a loved one, or any other memory of when you were perfectly happy. Focus on the feeling of bliss that arises, and completely merge your consciousness with it.

This simple exercise also has the potential to evoke a sense of gratitude in us for the good times we've had and the great people we've known in our lives. And gratitude, as it happens, is another very potent antidote and cure for depression and low self-esteem.

MEDITATION FOR CHAPTER 6

One should meditate on the pleasure that arises from eating and drinking—the bliss of that tasty flavor—and then the state of plenitude and great bliss arise. Through the unequalled joy of becoming absorbed completely in the sound of beautiful music and such, the yogi's mind is elevated and becomes one with that."

Our true nature is accessible in even the most commonplace of activities, like eating and drinking. But we need that *mindful unself-consciousness* in order to be fully absorbed in what we're doing when we taste the food or beverage. Try it. Use your daily meals and morning coffee or tea as a chance to encounter the "nobody self."

And the text gives us another method for relaxing into our true nature. Turn on one of your favorite pieces of instrumental music (no distracting lyrics). And then really get into it! Don't focus on individual notes or even the musical phrases, but lose yourself in the melody as a whole. When you're not there listening—that is, when you've been wholly engrossed in the music—there it is again! You've dropped back into your true nature.

MEDITATION FOR CHAPTER 7

One should realize that the consciousness in others' bodies is the same as in one's own. Having abandoned concern for one's own body, one soon becomes all-pervasive.[††]

We believe that we are *really* separate from others, not only because we have separate physical bodies but also because we have our own peculiar thoughts (some more peculiar than others!). And other beings have their own separate bodies and, we presume, their own particular thoughts too.

This meditation requires us to concentrate neither on the thinker inside the body nor on the particular thoughts the thinker thinks, but rather on the field of consciousness itself. What is the sphere or arena in which all thinking, in any body, occurs? The focus here is on what makes awareness of anything possible; it is on *pure* consciousness, not self-consciousness or any other consciousness *of something*.

This ability to be conscious—regardless of what specific thoughts are being thought by which individual thinker—is exactly the same in all living beings. Focus on that and the mind becomes "all-pervasive," and we are drawn into the universal true nature we all share.

Notes:

* For those interested in reading the full text, my complete translation is online at http://lamamarut.org/wp-content/uploads/2012/01/VijnaBhairavaTantraHandout.pdf.

† VBT, verses 84 (with minor changes from the original) and 120.

‡ VBT, verse 64.

§ VBT, verses 23, 48, and 92.

|| VBT, verse 101.

\# VBT, verses 71 and 119.

** VBT, verses 72 and 73.

†† VBT, verse 93.

Endnotes

Preface

1. Pew Research Center's Religion and Public Life Project, "Religious Landscape Survey, Report 1: Religious Affiliation," http://religions.pewforum.org/reports.

2. Jason Palmer, "Religion May Become Extinct in Nine Nations, Study Says," *BBC News*, March 22, 2011, http://www.bbc.co.uk/news/science-environment-12811197.

3. John McManus, "Two-Thirds of Britons Not Religious, Suggests Survey," *BBC News*, March 20, 2011, http://www.bbc.co.uk/news/uk-12799801.

4. Dan Merica, "Survey: One in Five Americans Has No Religion," *CNN Belief Blog*, October 9, 2012, http://religion.blogs.cnn.com/2012/10/09/survey-one-in-five-americans-is-religiously-unaffiliated/?hpt=hp_c2.

5. Ibid.

6. Kathryn Blaze Carlson, "Organized Religion on the Decline? Growing Number of Canadians 'Spiritual but Not Religious,'" *National Post*, December 21, 2012, http://life.nationalpost.com/2012/12/21/organized-religion-on-the-decline-growing-number-of-canadians-spiritual-but-not-religious/.

7. Dominique Mosbergen, "Dalai Lama Tells His Facebook Friends That 'Religion Is No Longer Adequate,'" *Huffington Post Religion*, September 13, 2012, http://www

.huffingtonpost.com/2012/09/13/dalai-lama-facebook-religion-is-no-longer-adequate
-science_n_1880805.html.

8. His Holiness the Dalai Lama, *Beyond Religion: Ethics for a Whole World* (Toronto: Signal Books, 2011), xii, xiv.

9. Cited in Acharya Peter Wilberg, *Tantric Wisdom for Today's World: The New Yoga of Awareness* (CreateSpace Independent Publishing Platform, 2009), 112.

10. Galatians 3:28. All Biblical citations in this book are from the New Revised Standard Version, found online at the Oremus Bible Browser, http://bible.oremus.org.

Introduction

1. Tom Wolfe, "The 'Me' Decade and the Third Great Awakening," *New York* magazine, August 23, 1976, http://nymag.com/news/features/45938/.

2. Christopher Lasch, *The Culture of Narcissism: American Life in an Age of Diminishing Expectations* (New York: W. W. Norton, 1979). Some of Lasch's observations were foreshadowed not only by Tom Wolfe but also in Peter Marin's "The New Narcissism," *Harper's*, October 1975. The "world view emerging among us," wrote Marin, centers "solely on the self" and has "individual survival as its sole good."

3. Lasch, ibid., 34.

4. Ibid., 50. Narcissism is elsewhere described as the "distinctive personality type suited to the requirements of [our] culture," 238.

5. The continuing relevance of Lasch's portrait of our society is readily apparent. "The personality of his time, it seems, is even more the personality of ours," writes Lee Siegel in his *New York Times* essay, "The Book of Self-Love," February 5, 2010, http://www.nytimes .com/2010/02/07/books/review/Siegel-t.html?pagewanted=all&_r=0.

6. Justin Bieber, of course, became a superstar on the basis of a YouTube video posted by his mom, and later paid it forward by promoting on YouTube what would become, thanks to Bieber's home movie, an international hit song by Carly Rae Jepsen, "Call Me Maybe." A YouTube-engendered star gives birth, via YouTube, to another instant celebrity.

7. There were 3.14 billion email accounts worldwide in 2011, according to Royal Pingdom, http://royal.pingdom.com/2012/01/17/internet-2011-in-numbers/. An estimated 6 billion mobile phone subscriptions, from which 200,000 text messages are sent every second, according to World Mobile Media, http://worldmobilemedia.com/sponsor/. Twitter reaches half a billion accounts in 2012, according to a Semiocast study, http://semiocast

.com/en/publications/2012_07_30_Twitter_reaches_half_a_billion_accounts_140m_in_the_US.

8. Emil Protalinski, "Facebook Passes 1.11 Billion Monthly Active Users," *The Next Web*, May 1, 2013, http://thenextweb.com/facebook/2013/05/01/facebook-passes-1-11-billion-monthly-active-users-751-million-mobile-users-and-665-million-daily-users/.

9. In fact, the addiction to Facebook seems to be having the opposite effect. Check out Stephen Marche, "Is Facebook Making Us Lonely?" *The Atlantic*, May 2012, http://www.theatlantic.com/magazine/archive/2012/05/is-facebook-making-us-lonely/308930/. Marche not only links the addiction to Facebook to an increase in feelings of loneliness among some of its users but also cites research that has found "a significant correlation between Facebook use and narcissism." "In fact, it could be argued that Facebook specifically gratifies the narcissistic individual's need to engage in self-promoting and superficial behavior." Cf. Geoffrey Mohan's "Facebook Is a Bummer, Study Says," *Los Angeles Times*, August 14, 2013, http://articles.latimes.com/2013/aug/14/science/la-sci-sn-facebook-bummer-20130814.

10. C. S. Lewis, *Mere Christianity* (New York: HarperSanFrancisco, 1952), 6. See also Timothy Keller's observation in *The Freedom of Self-Forgetfulness: The Path to True Christian Joy* (Chorley, England: 10Publishing, 2012): "Up until the twentieth century, traditional cultures (and this is still true of most cultures in the world) always believed that too high a view of yourself was the root cause of all the evil in the world. . . . Traditionally, that was the reason given for why people misbehave. But, in our modern western culture, we have developed an utterly opposite cultural consensus. Our belief today—and it is deeply rooted in everything—is that people misbehave for lack of self-esteem and because they have too low a view of themselves."

11. Patrice Lescoe, "How Much Have Depression Rates Increased?" *eHow*, http://www.ehow.com/way_5627919_much-depression-rates-increased_.html#ixzz2Le3SK2UA.

12. Maia Szalavitz, "What Does a 400% Increase in Antidepressant Use Really Mean?" *Time*, October 20, 2011, http://healthland.time.com/2011/10/20/what-does-a-400-increase-in-antidepressant-prescribing-really-mean/#ixx2LS6bouMr.

13. See *Mental Health: A Call for Action by World Health Ministers* (Geneva: World Health Organization, 2001), http://www.who.int/mental_health/advocacy/en/Call_for_Action_MoH_Intro.pdf.

14. This according to an article entitled "In Defense of Self-Esteem," written by Senator John Vasconcellos, Robert Reasoner, Michele Borba, Len Duhl, and Jack Canfield: http://www.self-esteem-nase.org/amember/newsarticles/InDefenseofSelf-Esteem.pdf. The article was published in response to a critique of the self-esteem movement written by Lauren Slater,

"The Trouble with Self-Esteem," *New York Times Magazine*, February 3, 2002, http://www
.nytimes.com/2002/02/03/magazine/03ESTEEM.html?...all.

15. Lewis, *Mere Christianity*, 197.

Chapter 1

1. Cited in John Broomfield, *Other Ways of Knowing: Recharting Our Future with Ageless
   Wisdom* (Rochester, VT: Inner Traditions, 1997), 73.

2. Alan Watts, *The Book: On the Taboo against Knowing Who You Are* (New York: Vintage
   Books, 1989), 55. For a more weighty enunciation of the same problem, here's eighteenth-
   century philosopher David Hume's frustrated *cri de coeur*: "For my part, when I enter most
   intimately into what I call *myself*, I always stumble on some particular perception or other,
   of heat or cold, light or shade, love or hatred, pain or pleasure, colour or sound, etc. I never
   catch *myself*, distinct from such perceptions." David Hume, *Treatise of Human Nature*, ed.
   by L. A. Selby-Bigge (New York: Oxford University Press, 1978), book 1, part 4, section 6.

3. William Shakespeare, *As You Like It*, act 2, scene 7.

4. Jane Wagner and Lily Tomlin, *The Search for Signs of Intelligent Life in the Universe*.

5. Miles Orvell, *The Real Thing: Imitation and Authenticity in American Culture, 1880–1940*
   (Chapel Hill: University of North Carolina Press, 1989), xxiii.

6. Fred Rogers, "You Are Special," 1967. The complete lyrics to the song can be found online
   at http://pbskids.org/rogers/songLyricsYouAreSpecial.html.

7. For a rendition of the speech the Reverend Jackson did with a multicultural audience
   of small children on the television show *Sesame Street*, see http://www.youtube.com
   /watch?v=iTB1h18bHlY.

8. The Bhagavad Gita 6.5. All translations from Sanskrit and Pali texts cited in this book are
   my own unless otherwise noted.

9. Ashtavakra Gita 8.4.

10. *Guide to the Bodhisattva's Way of Life* 8.134–135.

11. Quoted in John Michael Talbot and Steve Rabey, *The Lessons of Saint Francis: How to Bring
    Simplicity and Spirituality into Your Daily Life* (New York: Plume, 1998), 49.

12. Quoted in Robert Wingate, *Pocket Wisdom: Inspirational Quotations from East and West
    for Daily Living* (CreateSpace Independent Publishing Platform, 2011), 65.

13. Thomas Merton, *New Seeds of Contemplation* (New York: New Directions, 1961), 8.

14. Quoted in Heinrich Robert Zimmer, *Philosophies of India* (Princeton, NJ: Princeton University Press, 1969), 462.

15. Quoted in Kathlin Austin, *Wise People Quotes* (CreateSpace Independent Publishing Platform, 2013), 15.

16. Lynn Hirschberg, "The Misfit," *Vanity Fair*, April 1991. Reprinted in *All about Madonna*, http://allaboutmadonna.com/madonna-interviews-articles/vanity-fair-april-1991.

17. For one indication of the negative effects of the cultural emphasis on being "special," see "Why Generation Y Yuppies Are Unhappy," *Huffington Post*, September 15, 2013, http://www.huffingtonpost.com/wait-but-why/generation-y-unhappy_b_3930620.html.

18. Dalai Lama, *Beyond Religion*, 28, 29.

19. Mihaly Csikszentmihalyi, *Flow: The Psychology of Optimal Experience* (New York: Harper & Row, 1990), 1.

20. Qur'an 2:213. From the online translation found at http://quod.lib.umich.edu/k/koran/.

21. See *Guide to the Bodhisattva's Way of Life* 7.2, where "depression" (*vishada*) and "low self-esteem" (*atmavamanya*) are listed among the obstacles to the cultivation of "joyful effort," the enthusiastic energy needed to overcome unhappiness and suffering.

22. *Guide to the Bodhisattva's Way of Life* 7.17–18.

23. Katha Upanishad 1.2.18.

24. Ashtavakra Gita 18.9.

25. Shvetashvatara Upanishad 4.6–7.

Chapter 2

1. Lewis, *Mere Christianity*, 122.

2. Johnny Cash, "No Earthly Good," *The Rambler* (Columbia Records, 1977). The complete lyrics can be found at www.lyricsondemand.com/j/johnnycashlyrics/noearthlygoodlyrics.html.

3. William Paul Young, *The Shack* (Los Angeles: Windblown Media, reissue edition, 2011), 159.

4. Eckhart Tolle, *A New Earth: Awakening to Your Life's Purpose* (New York: Penguin Books, 2005), 67.

5. Quoted in Lama Surya Das, *The Big Questions: How to Find Your Own Answers to Life's Essential Mysteries* (Emmaus, PA: Rodale Books, 2007), 215.

6. Matthew 7:2–3.

7. Matthew 7:4–5.

8. Lewis, *Mere Christianity*, 121–22.

9. Professor Roy Baumeister, interview by Neal Conan, *Talk of the Nation*, National Public Radio, February 4, 2002, http://donpugh.dyndns.org/Psych%20Interests/Self-esteem /Questioning%20the%20conventional%20wisdom%20of%20self-esteem.htm. Baumeister also makes reference to a study that found that 90 percent of us think we're above average drivers. Another research project discovered that *none* of the high school students surveyed thought they were below average in the ability to get along with others. Like Garrison Keillor's fabled "Lake Wobegon," where "all the women are strong, all the men are good looking, and all the children are above average," we often seem reluctant to say we're just average, even when we are. See http://prairiehome.publicradio.org/about/podcast/.

10. *Guide to the Bodhisattva's Way of Life* 7.57–58.

11. Cf. ibid., 8.127: "Because of my wish to be elevated in importance, I will find myself in unpleasant realms, ugly, and stupid."

12. Jack D. Maser, "About Anxiety and Depression," *Freedom from Fear*, accessed November 29, 2013, http://www.freedomfromfear.org/AboutAnxietyandDepression.en.html.

13. Lewis, *Mere Christianity*, 121.

14. Tolle, *A New Earth*, 44.

15. Ibid., 51.

Chapter 3

1. Anup Shaw, "Poverty Facts and Stats," *Global Issues*, January 7, 2013, http://www.global issues.org/article/26/poverty-facts-and-stats.

2. Yoga Sutra 2.4; 2.13.

3. Yoga Sutra 2.5.

4. Maha Satipatthana Suttanta, verse 5. From *Dialogues of the Buddha*, trans. T. W. Rhys Davids and C. A. F. Rhys Davids (1910; repr., Delhi: Motilal Banarsidass, 2000), and cited in Edwin F. Bryant's *The Yoga Sutras of Patanjali* (New York: North Point Press, 2009), 180.

5. Jone Johnson Lewis, "Gloria Steinem Quotes," *About.com*, "Women's History," http://womens history.about.com/cs/quotes/a/qu_g_steinem.htm.

6. Ashtavakra Gita 1.11 (emphasis added).

Chapter 4

1. Julian Baggini, *The Ego Trick: What Does It Mean to You?* (London: Granta Books, 2011), 40.

2. Bhagavad Gita 2.40.

3. Yoga Sutra 2.4.

4. Matthew 7:16–18.

5. The Tolstoy quote is cited in a recent edition of Ralph Waldo Emerson's *Self Reliance* (The Domino Project, 2011), 50.

6. *Guide to the Bodhisattva's Way of Life* 5.14 (emphasis added).

7. Cited in Csikszentmihalyi, *Flow*, 121. Modern films like *Memento* and *Total Recall* (for the latter, see chapter 7) turn on the question of what becomes of self-identity when memory is erased.

8. Csikszentmihalyi, *Flow*, 133.

9. *Guide to the Bodhisattva's Way of Life* 4.37–38.

10. *Guide to the Bodhisattva's Way of Life* 4.44.

11. *Guide to the Bodhisattva's Way of Life* 4.29, 43.

12. See also the *Guide to the Bodhisattva's Way of Life* 6.41, where Shantideva says that it is better to get angry at anger itself than at a person who provokes anger in you.

13. *Guide to the Bodhisattva's Way of Life* 7.55–56: "Everything should be conquered by me; I should be defeated by nothing! I should carry myself with pride, for I am the child of the Conquering Lions. Those pitiable beings who are defeated by pride are not those who possess pride. Those possessed of pride never become slaves of the enemy which is pride; others have turned into slaves." Compare this to French author Georges Bernanos's dictum:

"It's a fine thing to rise above pride, but you must have pride to do so." *The Diary of a Country Priest: A Novel* (Cambridge, MA: Da Capo Press, 2002), 224.

14. Quoted in Daniel Akst, *We Have Met the Enemy: Self-Control in an Age of Excess* (New York: Penguin Press, 2011), 2.

15. *Guide to the Bodhisattva's Way of Life* 7.72.

16. Csikszentmihalyi, *Flow*, 9.

17. Josie Billington, *Eliot's Middlemarch*, Reader's Guide (New York: Continuum, 2008), 89.

Chapter 5

1. Quoted in John Cook, comp., and Steve Deger and Leslie Ann Gibson, eds., *The Book of Positive Quotations* (Minneapolis: Fairview Press, 2007), 27.

2. Thich Nhat Hanh, *Interbeing: Fourteen Guidelines for Engaged Buddhism*, ed. Fred Eppsteiner, 3rd ed. (Berkeley, CA: Parallax Press, 1988).

3. Desmond Tutu, *No Future without Forgiveness* (Colorado Springs, CO: Image, 2000), 31.

4. Ursula K. Le Guin, *The Left Hand of Darkness* (New York: Ace Trade, 2000), 151.

5. Dean Martin, "You're Nobody 'til Somebody Loves You," *The Door Is Still Open to My Heart* (Capitol Records, 1960). The complete lyrics can be found at www.metrolyrics.com/youre-nobody-till-somebody-loves-you-lyrics-dean-martin.html.

6. Ibid.

7. Bhagwan Shree Rajneesh, *Tantra: The Supreme Understanding* (Poona, India: Rajneesh Foundation, 1975), 17.

8. Quoted in Alain de Botton, *The Consolations of Philosophy* (New York: Vintage, 2001), 146.

9. *Guide to the Bodhisattva's Way of Life* 7.31.

10. Bhagavad Gita 18.64–65.

11. Bhagavad Gita 15.15.

Chapter 6

1. Csikszentmihalyi, *Flow*, 4.

2. Ibid., 71.

3. Jiddu Krishnamurti, *Think on These Things* (Ojai, CA: Krishnamurti Foundation of America, 1964), 65.

4. Abraham Maslow, *Religions, Values, and Peak-Experiences* (New York: Penguin, 1970), 62.

5. John Stuart Mill, *Autobiography*, in Harvard Classics, vol. 25, ed. Charles W. Eliot (New York: P. F. Collier & Son, 1909), 94. Or as Csikszentmihalyi puts it, "It is by being fully involved with every detail of our lives, whether good or bad, that we find happiness, not by trying to look for it directly" (*Flow*, 2).

6. Tyler Kingkade, "Millennials Are More Stressed Out than Older Generations," *Huffington Post*, February 8, 2013, http://www.huffingtonpost.com/2013/02/08/millennials-stress_n_2646947.html.

7. Ed Smith, "What Some People Call Idleness Is Sometimes the Best Investment," *New Statesman*, July 19, 2012, http://www.newstatesman.com/business/business/2012/07/what-some-people-call-idleness-often-best-investment.

8. For one analysis of how we are keeping ourselves constantly available for work even when we're supposedly on vacation, see Bob Sullivan's "How the Smartphone Killed the Three-Day Weekend," *CNBC*, May 24, 2013, http://www.cnbc.com/id/100765600.

9. Rajneesh, *Tantra*, 73.

10. Ashtavakra Gita 18.57.

11. Matthew 6:25–34.

12. Quoted in Joe Tichio, *Greatest Inspirational Quotes: 365 Days to More Happiness, Success, and Motivation* (CreateSpace Independent Publishing Platform, 2013), 46.

13. Bhagavad Gita 6.1.

14. Bhagavad Gita 6.2.

15. Quoted in Suhail Murtaza, *Reflections: A Collection of Essays on Life, Happiness, Roots, and Responsibility* (New York: Perseus Press, 2007), 79.

16. Johan Huizinga, *Homo Ludens: A Study of the Play-Element in Culture* (1938; repr., London: Routledge, 2008), 3.

17. Ibid., 9.

18. William Sax, ed., *The Gods at Play: Lila in South Asia* (New York: Oxford University Press, 1995), 4.

19. Bhagavad Gita 3.22, 25.

20. Quoted in *Packers: Green, Gold and Glory* (New York: Sports Illustrated, 2013), 53.

21. Lao-Tzu, *Tao Te Ching*, trans. Steven Mitchell (New York: Harper Perennial, 2009), chapter 68, http://acc6.its.brooklyn.cuny.edu/~phalsall/texts/taote-v3.html#75.

22. Matthew 18:1–4.

23. Ashtavakra Gita 18.49.

24. Ibid., 18.64.

25. Quoted in Wayne W. Dyer, *Wisdom of the Ages: 60 Days to Enlightenment* (1998; repr., New York: William Morrow, 2002), 29.

26. Norvin Hein, "Lila," in *The Gods at Play: Lila in South Asia*, ed. William Sax (New York: Oxford University Press, 1995), 15.

27. Quoted in Neal Ranzoni, *The Book on "Art Quotes"* (CreateSpace Independent Publishing Platform, 2012), 45.

28. Quoted in Cay Lang, *Taking the Leap: Building a Career as a Visual Artist*, 2nd ed. (San Francisco: Chronicle Books, 2006), x.

29. Quoted in Ellen J. Langer, *Mindfulness* (1989; repr., Cambridge, MA: Da Capo Press, 1990), 117.

30. Cited in Csikszentmihalyi, *Flow*, 59.

31. This quote, which circulates around the internet, is attributed to one Hans Bos, who apparently lives in Terre Haute, Indiana, and is neither a professional dancer nor writer. See http://www.bdancer.com/HansBos.html.

32. Quoted in Joseph Campbell, *The Inner Reaches of Outer Space: Metaphor as Myth and as Religion,* 2nd ed. (Novato, CA: New World Library, 2002), 92.

33. Bhagavad Gita 5.8.

34. Quoted in Meredith Gould, *Deliberate Acts of Kindness: Service as a Spiritual Practice* (Colorado Springs, CO: Image, 2002), 70.

35. Bhagavad Gita 4.20.

Chapter 7

1. Baggini, *The Ego Trick*, 7. A little later in his book, Baggini says, "The most important finding, which seems to be universally accepted by all researchers into the self and the brain, is that brain research has given up on the search for the pearl of the self" (28).

2. Ibid., 69.

3. Dhammapada 3.42–43. The translation is Thomas Byrom's *The Dhammapada: The Sayings of the Buddha* (New York: Random House, 2010).

4. Quoted in James R. Miller, *Voices from Earth: A Book of Gentle Wisdom* (Victoria, BC: Trafford Publishing, 2006), 22.

5. Ashtavakra Gita 18.35.

6. Katha Upanishad 1.2.18.

7. Tao Te Ching, chapter 1, trans. Mitchell.

8. Vijnana Bhairava Tantra, verses 14–15.

9. Mandukya Upanishad 7.

10. Uttara Tantra 1.79–80.

11. Lawrence Kushner, *The River of Light: Jewish Mystical Awareness* (1981; repr., Woodstock, VT: Jewish Lights Publishing, 1991), 122.

12. For a comprehensive survey of ancient and modern "apophatic discourses" in the West, see William Franke, ed., *On What Cannot Be Said: Apophatic Discourses in Philosophy, Religion, Literature, and the Arts* (Notre Dame, IN: University of Notre Dame Press, 2007).

13. Rajneesh, *Tantra*, 12.

14. Ibid, 5.

15. Vijnana Bhairava Tantra, verse 124.

16. Ibid., verse 61.

17. Ibid., verse 62.

18. Roy J. Matthew, "Psychoactive Agents and the Self," in *The Lost Self: Pathologies of Brain and Identity*, eds. Todd E. Feinberg and Julian Paul Keenan (Oxford: Oxford University Press, 2005).

19. Quoted in Baggini, *The Ego Trick*, 202–203.

20. Ashtavakra Gita 18.18.

21. Chögyam Trungpa, *The Myth of Freedom: and the Way of Meditation* (Boston: Shambhala, 2002), 6.

22. Ibid., 104–105 (emphasis added).

23. Ashtavakra Gita 18.65, 60.

24. Ashtavakra Gita 18.59.

25. Shvetashvatara Upanishad 4.6–7.

26. Uttara Tantra 1.149.

27. Uttara Tantra 1.154.

28. Philippians 4:7.

29. Philippians 2:2–4.

30. Philippians 2:5–8.

31. Ashtavakra Gita 15.15.

32. Sly and the Family Stone, "Everyday People," *Stand!* (Epic, 1968). The complete lyrics can be found at www.lyricsmode.com/lyrics/s/sly_and_the_family_stone/everyday_people.html.

33. Quoted in Eleanor "Ndidi" Hooks, *Finding Joy—Finding Yourself* (CreateSpace Independent Publishing Platform, 2013), 57.

34. Quoted in Jon Kabat-Zinn, *Full Catastrophe Living: Using the Wisdom of Your Body and Mind to Face Stress, Pain, and Illness* (New York: Delta, 1990), 165.

Selected Bibliography

Baggini, Julian. *The Ego Trick: What Does It Mean to Be You?* London: Granta Books, 2011.

Byrom, Thomas. *The Dhammapada: The Sayings of the Buddha.* New York: Random House, 2010.

Csikszentmihalyi, Mihaly. *Flow: The Psychology of Optimal Experience.* New York: Harper & Row, 1990.

Dalai Lama, H. H. *Beyond Religion: Ethics for a Whole World.* Toronto: Signal Books, 2011.

Doniger, Wendy. *The Woman Who Pretended to Be Who She Was: Myths of Self-Imitation.* New York: Oxford University Press, 2004.

Hanh, Thich Nhat. *Interbeing: Fourteen Guidelines for Engaged Buddhism.* Edited by Fred Eppsteiner. 3rd ed. Berkeley, CA: Parallax Press, 1988.

Huizinga, Johan. *Homo Ludens: A Study of the Play-Element in Culture.* 1938. Reprint, London: Routledge, 2008.

Keller, Timothy. *The Freedom of Self-Forgetfulness: The Path to True Christian Joy.* Chorley, England: 10Publishing, 2012.

Krishnamurti, Jiddu. *Think on These Things.* Ojai, CA: Krishnamurti Foundation of America, 1964.

Lao-Tzu. Tao te Ching. Translated by Stephen Mitchell. New York: Harper Perennial, 2009.

Lasch, Christopher. *The Culture of Narcissism: American Life in an Age of Diminishing Expectations.* New York: W. W. Norton, 1979.

Lewis, C. S. *Mere Christianity.* New York: HarperSanFrancisco, 1952.

Maslow, Abraham. *Religions, Values, and Peak-Experiences.* New York: Penguin, 1970.

Merton, Thomas. *New Seeds of Contemplation.* New York: New Directions, 1961.

New Revised Standard Bible. New York: Oxford University Press, 1989.

O'Flaherty, Wendy Doniger. *Origins of Evil in Hindu Mythology.* Berkeley, CA: University of California Press, 1980.

Rhys Davids, T. W., and C. A. F. Rhys Davids, trans. *Dialogues of the Buddha.* 1910. Reprint, Delhi, India: Motilal Banarsidass, 2000.

Satchidananda, Swami. *Beyond Words.* Yogaville, CA: Integral Yoga Publications, 1977.

Tolle, Eckhart. *A New Earth: Awakening to Your Life's Purpose.* New York: Penguin Books, 2005.

Rajneesh, Bhagwan Shree. *Tantra: The Supreme Understanding*. Poona, India: Rajneesh Foundation, 1975.

Tutu, Desmond. *No Future without Forgiveness*. Colorado Springs, CO: Image, 2000.

Watts, Alan. *The Book: On the Taboo against Knowing Who You Are* (New York: Vintage Books, 1989), 55.

Wolfe, Tom. "The 'Me' Decade and the Third Great Awakening." *New York*, August 23, 1976.

Zimmer, Heinrich Robert. *Philosophies of India*. Princeton, NJ: Princeton University Press, 1969.

• • •

All translations from Sanskrit and Pali texts cited in this book are my own unless otherwise noted:

Ashtavakra Gita

Badarayana's Vedantasutras

Bhagavad Gita

Bodhicaryavatara (*Guide to the Bodhisattva's Way of Life*)

Katha Upanishad

Maha Satipatthana Suttanta

Mandukya Upanishad

Nagarjuna's Mulamadhyamaka Karika (*Root Verses on the Middle Way*)

Shvetashvatara Upanishad

Vajracchedika Sutra (*Diamond Cutter Sutra*)

Vijnana Bhairava Tantra

Yoga Sutra